1990

Ethics for the Media

Ethics for the Media

William L. Rivers
Cleve Mathews

PRENTICE HALL
Englewood Cliffs, New Jersey 07632

Library of Congress Cataloging-in-Publication Data

Rivers, William L.
    Ethics for the media.

    Includes index.
    I. Journalistic ethics—United States. I. Mathews,
Cleve. II. Title.
PN4888.E8R5 1988   174'.9097   87-7363
ISBN 0-13-290560-4

Editorial/production supervision
    and interior design: Evalyn Schoppet
Cover design: Ben Santora
Manufacturing buyer: Edward O'Dougherty

©1988 by Prentice-Hall, Inc.
A Division of Simon & Schuster
Englewood Cliffs, New Jersey 07632

Printed in the United States of America

10 9 8 7 6 5 4 3 2 1

ISBN 0-13-290560-4

Prentice-Hall International (UK) Limited, *London*
Prentice-Hall of Australia Pty. Limited, *Sydney*
Prentice-Hall of Canada Inc., *Toronto*
Prentice-Hall Hispanoamericana, S. A., *Mexico*
Prentice-Hall of India Private Limited, *New Delhi*
Prentice-Hall of Japan, Inc., *Tokyo*
Simon & Schuster Asia Pte. Ltd., *Singapore*
Editora Prentice-Hall do Brasil, Ltda., *Rio de Janeiro*

TO MARION

Contents

Preface

This book springs from the authors' convictions that an overview of ethics—substantive and practical—should be presented in a single volume. This is not to say that *Ethics for the Media* is definitive; *the* complete book on the many subjects covered here can exist only in imagination. But there are so many similarities among the major instruments of the mass media—as well as public relations and advertising—that a single-volume treatment is logical. Certainly, the easy movement of highly competent journalists from one medium to another, from and to public relations and advertising, suggests that the similarities are more important than the differences.

Perhaps some will say that this is a critical book. In a sense, we hope it is. Surely we have not tried to gloss over the shortcomings of the media as we see them. It was not criticism in the sense of fault-finding that was uppermost in our minds as we wrote. Rather, we have tried conscientiously to make this book critical in the sense that it is an analysis of both the strengths and weaknesses of the media and their adjuncts as they play their roles in society.

In writing this volume, we have benefitted from the ideas of a number of friends, academic colleagues, and perceptive reviewers of our manuscript. It is impractical to name all the persons to whom we are indebted, but a few deserve special recognition. As students, Jennifer Koch, who wrote six profiles in this volume, and Tim Grieve, who now works for the *Sacramento Bee*, were valuable workers. As colleagues: Elie Abel, who advised us about the National Press Council; Robert Beyers, one of the best public relations workers anywhere; Samuel V. Kennedy III, an understanding department chairman; Edward C. Stephens, a supportive and appreciative dean; Lyle Nelson, a now-retired professor; and Wilbur Schramm, also retired and living in Hawaii, were, as usual, irreplaceable advisors.

William L. Rivers
Cleve Mathews

WORDS ABOUT DEMOCRACY

Democracy is that form of society, no matter what its political classification, in which every man has a chance and knows that he has it.

—James Russell Lowell

A democratic society might be defined as one in which the majority is always prepared to put down a revolutionary minority.

—Walter Lippmann

Democracy is finding proximate solutions to insoluble problems.

—Reinhold Niebuhr

The idea that you can merchandise candidates for high office like breakfast cereal is the ultimate indignity to the democratic process.

—Adlai Stevenson

Democracy is the recurrent suspicion that more than half of the people are right more than half the time.

—E. B. White

If one man offers you democracy and another offers you a bag of grain, at what stage of starvation will you prefer the grain to the vote?

—Bertrand Russell

INTRODUCTION

Democracy and Ethics

Democracy is a device that insures we shall be governed no better than we deserve.

—George Bernard Shaw

The *Wall Street Journal* asserted in an editorial (July 15, 1983), "We are going to have to kill ethics before ethics kills us." That newspaper, which frequently comments on ethics in its editorial pages and covers ethical problems in its news columns, expressed a feeling common to many people. Misbehavior attracts news coverage; society pays heed to the news; politicians respond by writing laws; soon everyone seems to get snared by the laws, and the public is submerged in Watergate, Abscam, Briefingate, Ethicsgate, Billingsgate.

In an editorial on May 30, 1984, the *Journal* stated the problem as this:

> We have formalized into explicit law areas of public and political life that are more effectively controlled by informal politics or less constricting legislation (than the Ethics in Government Act). It's not obvious that the informal procedures produced a healthier political climate.

The *Journal*'s point is worth remembering—Ethics can easily become rigid and ritualistic. The code on the wall is more a fossil than a facilitator of good behavior. The "knee-jerk" approach to ethics leads to the kind of reactions that the *Journal* in a subsequent editorial (May 24, 1984) described as having "little to do with high ethical standards" and "everything to do with the politics of character assassination."

Journalists are as likely as anyone else to adopt rigid behaviors. In their case, the rigidities can be imposed on the work they do and can spread their stereotyped views to their publics. This may distort the messages they disseminate—which is contrary to their ethical principle of telling the truth.

Rigid journalistic thinking causes further wrong by putting stories into compartments, which encourages different kinds of treatment. For example, "Life style" sections in newspapers still carry "soft" news. The very word "hard" indicates something of the rigid nature of news concepts. Black news is too often covered in the split-run "Neighbors" section. The bias, unconscious as it may be, goes beyond the content of the paper or program. How many women journalists get less pay for equivalent work done by male journalists with the same qualifications? How many Blacks can one find in the newsrooms of the nation?

The category of "politician" is another one subjected to damaging stereotypes. Most journalists appear to see political figures as unprincipled, ambitious demagogues and portray them as such. How does this affect readers—and democracy itself? Reporters covering government meet many upright and devoted public servants. They report their activities, yet not in ways that stamp the public mind with their positive images.

Why are journalists so unfriendly to politicians? It is one of the central ironies of democratic life that the politician and the journalist have so much in common. They both are generalists who must comprehend overarching issues in an age of specialization. They both are committed to serving the people. They both make their mistakes in public. Above all, they depend upon each other. Yet, why are they so often at swords' points?

Former Secretary of Labor Willard Wirtz once offered an answer to this question in a speech on March 21, 1964:

> A considerable part of what the public reads and sees and hears about the conduct of its public affairs is such a diluted and artificially colored version of fact and truth that if it were a mouthwash the Federal Trade Commission would divide three to two on whether to let it on the market. Perhaps that is the answer—a Pure Speech and Press Law recognizing the consumer's equal need for protection against what gets into his stomach through his mouth and what gets into his head through his eyes and ears.
>
> . . . There would be a box at the head of a story of a speech: "Written by Jones, who wasn't present, from ticker tape item filed by Smith, who wasn't there either. All quotes from speech taken out of context. Reported crowd reactions, including pickets, dubbed in. Headline written by Shrdlu, who can count but cannot read English. Dangerous if taken seriously or without a large grain of salt.

Few public officials are so eloquent in their denunciations, but many share Wirtz's suspicion that the news media emphasize trouble simply because it pays so well. Still, it is not enough to say that the news media are subverted by the dollar. Many journalists and publications and broadcast programs are quite obviously devoted more to public affairs than they are to profits. Moreover, the accusation bypasses the press's watchdog function. Officialdom must be challenged by outside agencies, and Wirtz himself is a case in point. Immediately before the 1962 congressional elections, when it was to the advantage of the Kennedy administration to make it appear that all was well with the economy, Labor Secretary Wirtz announced that unemployment had reached a three-year low and that the number of unemployed had declined by two million since Kennedy had taken over. Only after the election returns were in did Wirtz admit that his statement had been marred by certain "invalid" statistical comparisons.

THE OTHER SIDES

> *What is good is what I feel good after, and what's bad is what*
> *I feel bad after.*
>
> —Ernest Hemingway

In response to Wirtz and many other critics of the press, we might cite all U.S. administrations that have been lanced and deeply wounded by the media; however, the most glaringly evident scandal occurred during the second Reagan administration. In November 1986, while millions of American citizens fed and cherished their hatred of Iran, a Lebanese magazine, *Al Shiraa*, was the unlikely source that reiterated how much the media are massive opponents of secrecy in government. The magazine revealed that months earlier our White House had secretly sent five government officials to Iran bearing gifts. Moreover, there was even a promise to leading Iranian officials that they would receive Colt automatic pistols. Finally, as weeks and months passed, the Congress and the media showed that high officials were involved from the beginning in this sordid affair with so many different countries and with so many gifts, that the American people could only be described as watching dirty magic.

Emphasizing his distaste and distrust of the media, President Reagan appeared on television shortly after *Al Shiraa* published its findings and described the magazine as a "rag."

Long before the Iran situation, the *Wall Street Journal* expressed concern about "the ethical circus" that toppled or threatened such top members of Ronald Reagan's government as Richard Allen, Anne Burford, and Edwin Meese as well as Democratic vice presidential candidate Geraldine Ferraro. "The dilemma of investigative reporting is to find a way to discharge the duty of informing readers without appropriating the role of prosecutor. The one-new-charge-a-day campaign . . . cripples the official without much helping the reader."

Again, before the Iran scandal, Charles Krauthammer, essayist for *Time* magazine, criticized journalists for shooting first and asking questions later (*Time*, July 15, 1985). Journalism, he wrote, "is a medium of display and demonstration" and is not equipped to handle the problem of evil. The result, he said, is that in cases like the TWA hijacking in 1985, when terror needed "a partner in crime to give the event life," the media obliged. "Like pornography," he went on, "terrorist television, the graphic unfolding of evil on camera, sells."

Even though some forays are patently unnecessary, investigation is always necessary for the media. Nonetheless, how can the media cope with their many problems? Some have suggested that they must learn from other professions. The medical profession, for example, is also wracked with ethical pains. Malpractice suits, bitter debates over what to do about comatose patients, spillover burns from the heated wrangles over abortion—these are some of the issues. Medical schools have started courses on ethics and have put distinguished thinkers on their faculties. The profession has supported the work of the Hastings Center, a think tank on ethics. But, like other professions, medicine has not taken licenses away from very many practitioners.

How about law, which, in 1983 revised its code of ethics? Bar associations in some influential states, like New York and California, resisted the changes. The National Bar Association also refused to adopt a proposed change calling for lawyers to disclose continuing fraudulent activity by their clients.

Social workers, who face many of the same questions as journalists, are just as caught up in ethical debates. Frederic G. Reamer, associate professor of social work at the Rhode Island College School of Social Work, recently deplored the increased "ethical mischief in our profession" (*New York Times*, Dec. 9, 1984). He noted that social workers were caught between the pressures of the institution or agency they work for and the interests of the client. "The primary obligation is to the client," he observed, but "we all have an interest in keeping our jobs."

Ethics is a hotter topic in business than it is in the media, though Wall Street's insider scandals show business has little to teach the media about good behavior. A regular unfolding of such cases as E. F. Hutton's 2,000 felony counts for fraud and General Electric's 108 false claims for payment from the Air Force have helped to give the issue salience. One response, for example, is Sanford McDonnell, head of McDonnell Douglas aircraft, who has sponsored seminars on ethics for his company and others. Chairman Reuben F. Mettler of TRW also has strengthed his company's ethical credo.

Journalism's basic text is the First Amendment, from which it draws its creed and to which it offers obeisance, and that is why it cannot agree to the kind of licensing that distinguishes other professions. Even if journalism is considered a profession, it is different from other professions. Medicine and law serve individual clients, journalism serves publics, which is why it chooses to publish information in the public interest even though it may not be in the subject's private interest. While other professions tend to control the information that is the base of their power, the journalist's *raison d'être* is to spread information to the lay public.

The conclusion, then, seems to be that the media are on their own in charting a way through the ethical frontier. Just inside that frontier are shifting sands on which many have tried to erect a landmark called responsibility. A profession must confront this task, for ethical behavior is responsible behavior. Responsibility must be clearly defined and understood. The First Amendment bars any outside authority from imposing responsibility on the media, so the authority must come from within. However, none of the various codes adopted by media institutions indicates any willingness to impose responsibility. So "within the profession" really means "within the individuals practicing the profession."

This does not necessarily mean abandoning expectations of responsible behavior. Journalists are already expert at responding to the expectations of their publics. Responding to those expectations is central not only to economic survival, but to achieving some purposes—such as gaining money, power, promotion, and prestige. The weakest of these motives may seem to be prestige, yet, in the long run, it may be the most important to the individual. After all, money is the least important facet about a Pulitzer Prize. If the profession were to honor outstanding examples of responsible media performance, it might help to nourish the ethical sensitivity of media professionals. The two sides of the First Amendment are freedom and responsibility. In honoring responsibility, the profession would pay homage to freedom.

Expecting responsibility to come from within individuals—when so many individuals make up the media—is not as unrealistic as it may sound at first. What is democratic government but the widespread expectation that individuals are willing to abide by majority decisions? Democracy is a risky form of government which holds that the means are more important than the ends. An authoritarian government puts the emphasis on the ends. To many Americans, Soviet Communism seems to put the end—that far-off perfect society—above the means—the unruly give and take of the here and now.

Democracy relies on an informed public, and informing the public is the media's function. Lyndon B. Johnson had a prescription for the press as it fulfills this function. Although his advice comes from "musings" he wrote for the *Encyclopaedia Britannica Book of the Year* (1969) after he left the White House, and although his aim was to criticize both himself and the media, he had the same advice for both: "Try harder."

TWO APPROACHES TO ETHICS

There is only one ultimate and invariable duty, and its formula is "Thou shall love thy neighbor as thyself." How to do it is another question. . . .

—William Temple

When *Situation Ethics* by Joseph Fletcher was published in 1965 by Westminster Press, it excited at least a few religious journalists, some nonreligious journalists, and at least a sprinkling of professors. On page 18, Fletcher begins by stating that "one enters into every decision-making situation encumbered with a whole apparatus of prefabricated rules and regulations." After taking his readers through many failing methods in ethics, Fletcher ends this discussion with these words: "The heart of this explanation of ethics lies in its six propositions." At the beginning of each additional chapter, he lists one proposition. They run this way:

1. Only one thing is intrinsically good; namely, love: nothing else at all.
2. The ruling norm of Christian decision is love: nothing else.
3. Love and justice are the same, for justice is love distributed, nothing else.
4. Love wills the neighbor's good whether we like him or not.
5. Only the end justifies the means; nothing else.

6. Love's decisions are made situationally, not prescriptively.

Love dominates this list. Many who have read Fletcher's propositions laughed, thinking much like psychiatrist Joost Meerls, who once dismissed thoughts of love with these words:

> Sometimes it means: *I desire you* or *I want you sexually.* It may mean: *I hope you love me* or *I hope that I will be able to love you.* Often it means: *It may be that a love relationship can develop between us* or even *I hate you.* Often it is a wish for emotional exchange: *I want your admiration in exchange for mine* or. . . .

The reason for paying attention to Fletcher is that his ethical system comes closest to the one that prevails in most mass media situations. He urges people to draw on society's ethical heritage for guidance in making decisions, but to be willing to compromise if mankind is better served thereby. His guideline for making that judgment is to follow the dictates of loving concern for mankind.

In 1972, Ralph Potter wrote "The Logic of Moral Argument,"* in which he created the valuable Potter Box. The Potter Box has four parts: Definition, Values, Principles, and Loyalties.

Here are the four parts of a Potter Box:

Definition is an ethical problem that anyone can face.

Values are what a person, a group, an organization considers worthy of esteem.

Principles are the proper rules of conduct.

Loyalties call for faithfulness to persons, government, ideals, or causes.

Potter found these four parts excellent because they enabled him to work with finesse through many moral arguments. To journalists, though, the Potter Box is cumbersome when confronting ethical decisions.

In the first chapter, we present our system for ethical decision making. However, we must bow to Potter, whose work both stimulated and suggested our system.

---

*In *Toward a Discipline of Social Ethics*, Paul Deats, ed. (Boston University Press, 1972), pp. 93–114.

ETHICS, MORALITY, AND POLITICS

Those who would treat politics and morality apart will never understand the one or the other.

—John Morley

Morality is simply the attitude we adopt toward people whom we personally dislike.

—Oscar Wilde

When a man deliberates whether he should do a thing or not do it, he does nothing else but consider whether it be better for himself to do it or not to do it.

—Thomas Hobbes

Morality is the custom of one's country and the current feeling of one's peers. Cannibalism is moral in a cannibal country.

—Samuel Butler

The justification of majority rule in politics is not to be found in its ethical superiority.

—Walter Lippmann

In law, a man is guilty when he violates the right of others. In ethics, he is guilty if he thinks of doing so.

—Immanuel Kant

Moral indignation is jealousy with a halo.

—H. G. Wells

CHAPTER 1

Making Final Decisions

The health of a community is an almost unfailing index of its morals.

—James Martineau

In September 1981, President Ronald Reagan singled out Dr. Joseph Giordono of the George Washington University Hospital for special praise. Giordono had attended the president after the attempt to assassinate him in 1981. As Reagan was wheeled into the operating room, he said with a grin: "Please assure me that all of you are Republicans." Reagan credited Giordono with saving his life. Reagan viewed Giordono's rise to prominence as a classic American success story: The son of an Italian immigrant who became a milkman and worked hard, struggled, and sacrificed to put his son through college and medical school.

Was Dr. Giordono a Republican?

Moreover, as the son of a struggling milkman, did Giordono give credit for his success in life to federal social programs of the kind President Reagan criticized: low-interest government loans to students and Federal funding for biomedical research?

Ethical issues arose when Giordono had to choose among saying nothing, telling the truth, or lying. The problem, then, for Giordono, is to choose among A, B, and C. In other cases as well, there are many options—especially for the media. Journalists always face options, option, options. Which is right?

Before discussing Giordono's decision, let us adapt the idea of Ralph Potter's box so that it fits the journalistic situation better. Journalists are unlikely to bother with language and concepts that seem remote from the everyday world they report.

Instead of "Definition"—Potter's term—we have substituted "Problem," a term journalists use for ethical and other difficulties.

We merge "Values" and "Principles" into a single idea we call "Beliefs," which covers one's ethics—one's views of right and wrong that have come from experience and education.

Our third element encompasses Potter's "Loyalty" but combines it with the effect of an ethical decision on those to whom one is loyal. We use the word "Result" for this step.

Our final step is the decision, but it is made by weighing its likely impact against one's beliefs about right and wrong. We term this the "Justified Final Decision." Justification of questionable behavior is what ethics is all about.

Apply this to Giordono's decision about lying, telling the truth, or saying nothing. His problem was which choice to make. His beliefs involved his view about the importance of telling the truth and about whether there are occasions when it is all right to tell a little fib. The result for him would mean the impact of his reply on the president's state of mind or on federal programs important to Giordono in case the president is irritated by his reply. In weighing the possible result against his beliefs, he would take into consideration whether the president was serious or joking in asking the question.

On the actual occasion, Giordono said nothing to the president as they moved toward the operating room. But later, he said, "Yes," to reporters who asked him if he was a Democrat and if he was grateful for federal programs. His decision in one situation differed from his decision in another, but he did not violate his belief in the importance of truth.

Is it important to adopt this method, or the Potter Box, or an entirely different system? Yes. Otherwise many students, instructors, and professionals will continue to confess that they are always groping in ethics.

In some ethical cases, no system is necessary because the cases are so simple. In other cases, it is not possible to learn enough about an ethical case to apply a system effectively. From this point on, when it fits a case, we will refer to it as the Final Decision.

DIFFERENT CASES

The foundation of morality is to have done, once and for all, with lying.

—T. H. Huxley

Case No. 1 The tax assessor of Midcity retires unexpectedly at the age of 58 after the mayor learns he has been taking bribes to enable the city's largest employer to evade taxes. The mayor has a fine record and is a leading prospect for governor. The assessor is his lifelong friend. The mayor's public information officer is directed to say the assessor retired for "reasons of health." A physician friend of the mayor attests to the assessor's poor health and says he advised him to retire to the Sun Belt.

Case No. 2 The Midcity *Record* learns from a reliable source that the city attorney is about to seek an indictment in a rape case. The *Record*'s policy is not to identify rape victims "unless the situation demands it." A reporter finds out that the victim is a 22-year-old woman described as "slightly retarded but not enough to prevent her from working effectively for a house-cleaning agency." The source says that the suspect in the rape is a local minister whose home is cleaned weekly by the agency. The reporter tells his editor that he saw an aggressive reporter for a local television station talking with the same source and later heard the television reporter asking a telephone operator for the minister's number.

Case No. 3   The new owners of the Midcity *Light* are reshaping the image of the former afternoon daily into an all-day, lively package of entertainment, pictures, and crusading journalism. They are competing strongly with the long-dominant *Record.* The *Light* has won readers by running stories about cheats among auto repair and appliance repair shops. The editors are considering buying a commercial property they know is drastically underassessed for taxes. Thy suspect bribery and plan to operate the business under cover in order to trap city tax officials seeking payoffs.

These cases exemplify three major kinds of ethical questions that confront mass-media professionals. Should the mayor's PR aide fabricate a story? Should the *Record* publish details about the rape case? Should the *Light* run a "sting" operation to expose wrongdoers and bolster circulation? The three categories involve (1) truth—the integrity of the information, (2) justice—the use or abuse of media power, and (3) craft morality—the treatment of sources, colleagues, and the communications process itself. As a beginning, refer to John Stuart Mill's prophetic words on the facing page.

THE ROOTS OF MORALITY

The health of a community is an almost unfailing index of its morals.

—James Martineau

Six men said and wrote so many true things—especially about ethics—that they have planted roots that still flower. These men are Confucius, Socrates, Plato, Aristotle, Immanuel Kant, and Walter Lippmann. We will present them in historical order.

Confucius

Confucius (551–479 B.C.) was the greatest sage of ancient China, and his impact on modern China and modern America is almost limitless. His father died when Confucius was three years old and the boy was brought up by his mother. While a child, he loved ceremonials, which are an expression of religious and cultural tradition. Confucius said late in life:

At 15, I set my heart on learning. At 30, I was firmly established. At 40, I had no more doubts. At 50, I knew the will of Heaven. At 60, I was ready to listen to it. At 70, I could follow my heart's desire without transgressing what was right.

JOHN STUART MILL

If all mankind minus one were of one opinion, and only one person were of the contrary opinion, mankind would be no more justified in silencing that one person, than he, if he had the power, would be justified in silencing mankind.

These are the words of John Stuart Mill, who lived in England from 1806 until 1873. Shortly after the middle of the nineteenth century, Mill justified free expression with his book *On Liberty.* All human action, he wrote, should aim at creating the greatest happiness for the greatest number of persons. This happy state will come about if the individual is free to think and act as he or she pleases. The individual needs freedom to bring his or her capabilities to their fullest flower, Mill argued. As each individual flourishes, society as a whole benefits.

Liberty is the right of mature individuals to think and act as they like, as long as they harm no one else by doing so. Harm to others is the only reason for restraint, Mill wrote. For its own protection, society may try to advise, instruct, and persuade individuals, but it may not coerce them for their or its own good.

Mill emphasized that government, the traditional enemy of liberty, was not the only threat to individual freedom. He warned not about the tyranny of government but about the tyranny of the majority, which, through its intolerance of minority opinion, might stifle innovation, insight, and, indeed, truth. George Sabine, a student of political theory, has observed "what Mill recognized, and what the older liberalism had never seen, was that behind a liberal government there must be a liberal society."

Those who fight for liberty think of government as their chief enemy, Mill said, and think that they have won the battle when they have thrown off the yoke of government. Still, the majority can tyrannize just as surely as government by imposing its collective opinion on the individual:

There needs protection also against the tyranny of prevailing opinion and feeling; against the tendency of society to impose, by means other than civil penalties, its own ideas and practices as rules of conduct on those dissent from them; to fetter the development, and, if possible, prevent the formation, of any individuality not in harmony with its ways, and compel all characters to fashion themselves upon the model of its own.

Such arguments underlie Mill's case for free expression. Liberty is not just a way to the individual's happiness; it is instead, a basic part of all happiness.

> Only through liberty can the individual grow to his or her potential. If the majority silences a minority of one, it may be silencing the truth. Even a wrong opinion may contain a grain of truth necessary for finding the whole truth. Mill wrote that even if the accepted opinion is the whole truth, people will hold it not on rational grounds, but as a prejudice unless they are forced to defend it. Unless opinions are contested, they lose their vitality and their effect on character and conduct.
>
> John Stuart Mill lived more than a hundred years ago, but his opinions still hold true. Mill is one of the men who are still quoted by eminent philosophers—and perhaps by you.

To Confucius, knowledge meant wisdom, especially the kind of wisdom that would contribute to a better life for the individual and society. Confucius was foremost a reformer of men and government.

A key element of Confucian ethical thought was propriety. Whether a practice is considered virtuous depends on whether it is done with propriety. An often-cited teaching of Confucius is reciprocity, his version of the Golden Rule. "What you do not want done to yourself," he taught, "do not do to others."

A bit more specific was the Confucian list of three universally binding values. These are knowledge, magnanimity, and energy, which some translate as wisdom, compassion, and courage. It is interesting how closely these match the virtues advocated a century later by Plato—wisdom, temperance, and courage.

When Confucius was asked what he would do first if it were left to him to administer a country, he replied, "it would certainly be to correct language."

The man who asked the question was puzzled. "Why?" he asked.

"If language is not correct," Confucius answered, "then what is said is not what is meant; if what is said is not meant, then what ought to be done remains undone; if this remains undone, then morals and arts deteriorate; if morals and arts deteriorate, justice will go astray; if justice goes astray, the people will stand about in helpless confusion. Hence, there must be no arbitrariness in what is said. This matters above everything."

Socrates, Plato, Aristotle

The glory of Greek philosophy is reflected in the three consecutive teacher-pupil generations—Socrates (470-399 B.C.), Plato (428-348 B.C.), and Aristotle (384-322 B.C.).

Edith Hamilton wrote that one of the great legacies of the Greeks is "the idea that only the man who holds himself within self-chosen limits can be free." In today's discourse, that legacy is expressed as responsibility, the limits within which freedom is exercised and preserved.

A comment attributed to Socrates amounts to an eloquent statement of the journalistic ethic:

I say again that daily to discourse about virtue, and of those other things about which you hear me examining myself and others, is the greatest good of man, and that the unexamined life is not worth living.

Plato, in *The Republic*, argued that the overarching virtue of justice is achieved by harmonizing three other elements: wisdom, temperance, and courage.

As imperatives to journalists, wisdom can be seen as gaining understanding of the world, temperance as guiding the way to good judgments, and courage as living up to those judgments.

Although he was committed to ideals, Plato did not let any system of thought lead him to unwelcome conclusions. One such conclusion is whether you should lie to save someone from a murderer. "Yes," said Plato, "when dealing with enemies or when a friend in a fit of madness is going to do harm." But then he went on, "In the tales of mythology . . . because we do not know the truth about ancient times, we can make falsehood as much like truth as we can, and so turn it to account." Plato was wise, but his advice could lead to fictionalizing history, and that raises ethical questions for us today.

Aristotle was for 20 years a student of Plato's, but he differed in some important ways from Plato. Aristotle was more accepting of the world as he found it. He joined in the general agreement among people that the good is happiness, although he noted that people differed over what constituted happiness. To Aristotle, happiness was the exercise of reason in accordance with virtue.

Aristotle said that the doing of just acts involves making choices. In making a choice, a person faces a range of possibilities. The right choice—the virtuous one—lies between the vice of excess and that of defect. Virtue is a kind of mean not unlike the "steadfast mean" taught by Confucius. In the teachings of both men, there is a blurring of two meanings of the word "mean"—the median and the method. Ethical questions are about means. We often agree on the ends; it's how you reach them that causes problems. Those problems arise from letting desirable ends become the justification for unethical means. One way that democracy can be differentiated from dictatorship is that democracy puts priority on the means whereas dictatorship puts it on the ends. To bring the issue down to journalistic specifics, unethical reporting (a mean) is often justified by claiming that it serves the good of the community (an end). Aristotle was clear about it when he said that "the exercise of the virtues is concerned with means." The end does not justify the mean.

In comparison with earlier and contemporary civilizations, the Greeks of Plato's time were free. Slaves did the ignominious work, but citizens, even if poor, could exercise a wide range of choices about how they lived. The freedom to make choices causes people to consider what is proper to choose. No wonder, then, that so many ethical questions still pertinent today were dealt with by the early Greek thinkers.

The mystical, Neoplatonic vision of Augustine shaped the western European church and culture through the Middle Ages. The awakening that followed came with a slow transition to a mentality more like Aristotle's—an objective view focused on the factual world.

Immanuel Kant

Immanuel Kant (1724–1804), a German philosopher, was born in East Prussia. In any presentation of ethics, he occupies something near center stage. He is not there for his charisma or for the attractiveness of his writings, but is there for the substance of what he said. He didn't take to philosophy until he was in his late 50s; his earlier work had been devoted to science. He was struck by how David Hume had undercut causality and he turned his thought to this problem. He acknowledged that he was in a hurry to cover a great deal, and, hence, did not take the time to give his writings "a popular form." Like journalists, he knew that clarity takes time. Kant dealt with the uncertainty of Hume's succession of perceptions by asserting the existence of inherent forms of thought, which he called "categories" and which are independent of experience. Causation arises from necessity, because we cannot understand experience without it.

Kant then applied his critique to the practical reasoning underlying morality. We each have a moral consciousness, which is not the product of experience but which responds to a categorical imperative to do right for its own sake—a conscience. This imperative directs us to follow that maxim which we would willingly accept as a universal law, and, further, to treat everyone as an end, not merely as a means.

The "everyone" Kant had in mind includes the journalists' audience, sources, subjects, and peers.

Walter Lippmann

Walter Lippmann (1889–1974), the only American discussed here, was a journalist and political philosopher. Despite brief adventures in socialism and progressivism, Lippmann was a classic conservative. He endorsed the principle of aristocratic government where the people are not sovereign. Lippmann claimed that there is a law higher than the will of the people—the law of reason.

Rivalry, conflict, and power are in the arena of politics. Statesmanship makes certain that no one people deal with another people arbitrarily. Statesmanship is achieved in a system where powers are restrained through checks and balances.

In his work, *Public Opinion*, published in 1922, Lippmann painted an excellent portrait of the pseudo-environment. The objective world that man deals with, Lippmann said, is "out of reach, out of sight, out of mind." In his head, man makes for himself a more or less trustworthy picture of the world outside. Thus men behave not on the basis of direct and certain knowledge of the real world, but on pictures they have made or derived from others. What a man does depends on those pictures in his head.

Public Opinion begins with the peculiar matter-of-fact power that informs all of Lippmann's writing:

> There is an island in the ocean where in 1914 a few Englishmen, Frenchmen, and Germans lived. No cable reaches the island, and the British mail steamer comes but once in sixty days. In September it had not yet come, and the

islanders were still talking about the latest newspaper which told about the approaching trial of Madame Caillaux for the shooting of Gaston Calmette. It was, therefore, with more than usual eagerness that the whole colony assembled on the quay in mid-September to hear from the captain what the verdict had been. They learned that for over six weeks now those of them who were English and those of them who were French had been fighting in behalf of the sanctity of treaties against those of them who were Germans. For six strange weeks they had acted as if they were friends, when in fact they were enemies.

Lippmann goes on to show how little the world as it really is conforms to the picture of the world that we carry in our heads. He defines our stereotypes:

For the most part we do not see first, then define; we define first and then see. In the great blooming, buzzing confusion of the outer world we pick out what our culture has already defined for us, and we tend to perceive that which we have picked out in the form stereotyped. . . . That is why accounts of returning travellers are often an interesting tale of what the traveller carried abroad with him on his trip. If he carried chiefly his appetite, a zeal for tiled bathrooms, a conviction that the Pullman car is the acme of human comfort, and a belief that it is proper to tip waiters, taxicab drivers, and barbers, but under no circumstances station agents and ushers, then his Odyssey will be replete with good meals and bad meals, bathing adventures, compartment-train escapades, and voracious demands for money.

This internal picture-making process inevitably colors the messages that man gets from the world outside. Man uses stored-up images, preconceptions, prejudices, motivations, and interests to interpret the messages, fill them out, and, in turn, direct the play of attention and the vision itself. These interpretations and expansions become patterns, or stereotypes. And these stereotypes, Lippmann thinks, determine human action. Originally, a stereotype was the plate made by taking a mold of a printing surface and casting type metal from it. According to Lippmann, the minds of men are also poured into molds—their pictures of the world outside. The minds then reproduce ideas and react to stimuli according to the patterns of the molds.

Lippmann was writing only of the relationship between public opinion and newspapers. However, his concept can profitably be extended to all mass media. As a chief source of knowledge, the media provide people with messages from the outside world. People use these messages to form mental pictures of the world of public affairs.

The mass media can also be viewed as creating a kind of pseudo-environment between man and the objective, "real" world. This view has important implications for the role of the media in society. For one thing, the media have brought speed, ubiquity, and pervasiveness to the traditional role of communications. Therefore, the media are sometimes seen as enveloping modern man in a kind of artificial reality. For another thing, as a means by which the dominant institutions exercise social control, the media are widely regarded as so imbuing the public with the prevailing values and beliefs of their culture, that society is in danger of becoming stagnant. The fear is that because the commonly accepted pattern goes unchallenged, people will behave toward one another in almost ritualistic fashion and their lives and institutions will become fossilized.

Ironically, in his 1928 book, *A Preface to Morals*, Lippmann's words seem to be a capstone to his career:

> The evidence converges upon a theory that what the sages have prophesied as high religion, what psychologists delineate as matured personality, and the disinterestedness which the Great Society requires for its fulfillment, are all of a piece, and are the basic elements of a modern morality.

EXERCISES

Remember, the Final Decision runs: Problem, Beliefs, Result, and the Final Decision. Attempt to apply the Final Decision in these cases. Go through each fully before the Final Decision.

1. As a reporter for a newspaper, you learn that a female cashier in a store thwarts a robbery, but the robbers escape.
   a) The store manager asks that you not identify the woman. Would you identify the woman?
   b) The store manager tells you that if you identify the woman, she might suffer reprisals. What would you do?
   c) Would you use her name, but no address in your story?
   d) Would you omit the name and describe her only as a cashier?

2. During a city council meeting, a city official launches a savage attack on a local paving contractor, saying that neither the contractor nor his employees know how to pave streets properly. As an editor, your reporter cannot get the contractor's side of the story because the contractor is off on an elk hunt. Do you publish the attack or wait for the return of the contractor? When the contractor returns, you interview him for his side of the story, and, in doing so, learn that he was on an elk hunt with a state official who controls some of the funds that go into local paving contracts. Do you include this information in the story?

   Before reaching your decision, go through the various parts of the Final Decision.

MASS MEDIA AND ETHICS

We do not what we ought;
What we ought not, we do;
And lean upon the thought
That chance will bring us through.

—Matthew Arnold

If you sat down all the political reporters in a room, and told them only
those who had never given advice to a politician should stand up, hardly
a soul would dare rise.

—Mary McGrory

As journalists, our responsibility is to our readers. Anything we learn,
or think, belongs first to those readers. Not to a politician who happens
to be a friend.

—David Broder

Because 16 million people hear you on television every time you open
your mouth, don't think that makes you any smarter than you were
when your voice reached only the other end of this bar.

—Charles Kuralt

The saddest words of tongue or pen
Are those you didn't think of then.

—Betty Billipp

CHAPTER 2

Two Standards in Conflict

*The more we do our job of questioning accepted norms,
the more we can be expected to be questioned.*

—David Halberstam

The young reporter was visibly upset. She waved her hand, half-rose from her chair, and gasped to attract the speaker's attention. At his nod, she unloosed a torrent of words and sputters.

> What do you mean, we were unethical? We were telling what happened. Who do you think you are, telling us we should be boosters of the community? Our job is to tell what's going on, what happened, what *really* happened, not sugar-coat the news or ignore it because it might make somebody unhappy. If we did that, soon we would not be reporting anything actual.

The speaker replied that he had not called anyone unethical. He had been trying to show that journalists should consider the readers' feelings, especially in a small community where the media are expected to be boosters of the community.

This encounter took place in the office of the *Finger Lakes Times*, a daily newspaper with a circulation of almost 20,000 in Geneva, New York.

The editor, Donald Hadley, had invited the speaker, a professor of journalism with 25 years of experience as a reporter and editor, to lead a discussion of ethics.

The paper had received protests and angry letters about its reports of an automobile accident in which a young man had died. The victim, the 26-year-old son of a Geneva, New York, businessman, had been killed when the car he was driving struck a telephone pole shortly after 3:00 A.M. on a Thursday. The Thursday paper ran the story with a graphic four-column picture of the demolished car.

But the protests centered on the Friday follow-up story, which reported that the young man had been drinking although the coroner would not say whether he was legally intoxicated. The story included details on the injuries that caused the man's death. Protesters said that the Friday story was unnecessary, sensational, and grossly overdone. Editor Hadley was especially prepared to listen because of a

DAVID HALBERSTAM

A half-smiling, overly aggressive David Halberstam will not stop interviewing a person. He will interview someone once, then, never satisfied, Halberstam will return again and again, always looking, not only for the crux of what the interviewee knows, but everything surrounding it, including facts that only Halberstam wants to know. Literally hundreds of people will go through this routine with Halberstam. Three years later, Halberstam will confront mound after mound of notes, books, magazines, newspapers, and anything else that bears any relation to his subject. After several years, he will have produced a huge, unwieldy manuscript that an editor of a publishing house will sigh over; become glum about; and then cut page after page for nearly forever, fuse the many remaining pages into a wonderful manuscript, and have it published. Almost inevitably, Halberstam's book will approach the top of the The *New York Times* best-seller list, and his book will linger here and there on the list for at least fifteen weeks.

The above story is true, but there is much more to Halberstam, who, at first, was a failure. Born in 1934 in New York City, he seemed to have great promise. While a student at Harvard, he wanted to quit school, but remained a student. After graduating, he became a reporter at one of the smallest newspapers anywhere, the *West Point Daily Times Leader* in West Point, Mississippi. He worked there for two years, then became a satisfied reporter at the *Nashville Tennesseean*, where he stayed for five years. But his journeys had just begun.

James Reston, then the Washington bureau chief of The *New York Times*, lured Halberstam to Washington, and Halberstam flopped. Reston said to him, "Dave, maybe you need a hotter climate and darker people." Halberstam asked to go to the Congo. There he wrote eyewitness accounts of fighting, suffered a minor wound when a jet strafed the Elizabethville airport, and won a Page One Award.

The *Times* transferred him to Saigon, where he probed so relentlessly into official intrigue and covered the fighting so well that the struggle for Vietnam became known as "Halberstam's War." Many of his reports contradicted the optimistic reports of U.S. officials. Later, when it became clear that Halberstam had been right all along, he shared a Pulitzer Prize.

Meanwhile, Halberstam—judged by his later successes—was a failure with books. Beginning in 1961, he wrote four books, none of which can now be remembered. With publication of *The Best and the Brightest* (Fawcett, 1973), a Book of the Month Club alternate selection, Halberstam was on his money-strewn way.

After seven years of Halberstam's research and writing, Alfred A. Knopf publishers brought out his *The Powers That Be* in 1979. Here are a few of the many reviews:

Richard Rovere, The *New York Times Book Review* on April 22, 1979: "*The Powers That Be* is a prodigy of research and of tendentious but sharply focused narrative and analysis. . . . Halberstam, essentially a newspaperman, has a surer feel for the daily publication than for the weeklies or broadcasting. In any event, *The Powers That Be* will remain stirring history."

Paul Gray, *Time* magazine: "Halberstam's constant switching back and forth among different organizations lead[s] to a dizzying repetition . . . and his obsession with details sometimes takes him far down the road to trivia. . . . But the excesses of the book are, in part, the excesses of journalism itself. Better, perhaps, to have too much rather than too little."

Walter Clemons, *Newsweek: "The Powers That Be* will certainly be this summer's most read book."

While Halberstam read the above reviews, he was probably smiling in thanks to Charles Elliott, who, as Halberstam said in his "Acknowledgments," "took an immense and complicated manuscript and helped fuse it together."

recent article in the American Newspaper Publishers Association publication *press-time* about how vivid writing compounded the tragedy for the family of an auto victim. The issue became the topic of the next staff meeting.

The case serves well to illustrate the difficulties of ethical decisions. The stories did not involve inaccuracy, distortion, or deception. They were accurate. The Final Decision was, of course, Yes. Why, then, was there a controversy?

It arose because of a conflict of standards. The journalists' standards come from the lore of their craft. They seek to find out and honestly report what happens. They argue that any infringement upon them, whether imposed from outside or by themselves, will cause more harm to the community in the long run than easing the hurt of a few people today. Their concern with public acceptance rests more on maintaining their credibility than with responding to public sensitivity about the impact of what they report.

The public's standards put more emphasis on the impact of the stories. Members of the public want to know what is going on, but the context in which they want information is a web of community interactions—interactions that are more potent than their interactions with the media. When people are aware of the communities to which they belong, as is the case in small towns, they are inclined to believe that the media should support the community in the same way that other community leaders support it. As researchers Phillip J. Tichenor, Clarice N. Olien, and George A. Donohue have shown in their studies at the University of Minnesota, this may mean withholding information about situations unhealthy to a community in which everyone knows everyone else. The community leaders can then cure the malady privately. In big cities, where most people are strangers to one another, journalists serve community purposes by revealing problems so that they can be solved through political or social action.

Conflicts like those in Geneva, New York, may arise because journalists and members of the public each adhere to their own standards automatically and force-fully. The discussion in Geneva illustrates that journalists feel just as strongly about such matters as members of the public. No wonder that emotions make it hard to find common ground. Moreover, journalists accustomed to manipulation by political and business leaders may extend their adversarial stance to private individuals. Members of the public may extend their insistence for support of community interests to support for private interests.

The *Toronto Star* in its issue of November 11, 1985, asked its readers whether they would consider running the following story: The newspaper had evidence that a man regarded as a leader of the community had stolen $50,000 from a charity drive. The *Star* alone had the story and no charges had been laid. The man, con-tacted by the newspaper, promised to make a full restitution and urged the *Star* not to print the story because his wife was in the hospital with a serious illness. He was fearful that public disclosure of what he had done could kill her.

The *Star* asked:

a) Would you run the story?
b) Would you wait until you've talked to the doctors and know the woman is out of danger before printing the story?
c) Would you give the man a chance to make restitution, and, if he does, write nothing?

After the *Star* published this question, it received 589 responses from readers. The *Star* had 21 editors answer this question. Here are the percentages of readers and editors who said "Yes" to each question:

	Readers	Editors
a)	22	62
b)	45	33
c)	30	0

The *Star* also asked its readers to judge this story: The 19-year-old son of a well-known politician who has taken a hard line against drugs was arrested for possession of a small amount of marijuana.

Here are the percentages of readers and editors who said "Yes" to each ques-tion:

	Readers	Editors
a)	54	71
b)	78	90
c)	67	81

In both cases, the Final Decisions are "Yes."

THE PUBLIC INTEREST AND THE MEDIA

If you want to understand democracy, spend less time in the library with Plato, and more time in the buses with people.

—Simeon Strunsky

Considering "the public" one great mass is a common folly. The world, a nation, a city, a small town—each by the fact of its existence represents a single community of attention, but each also embraces an overwhelming multitude of varying interests and concerns. The smallest township is actually a patchwork of groups with different political allegiances, religious loyalties, and so on. What concerns one public may be trivia to another.

Moreover, the definition of each public is never static; it changes as the issues change. For example, when Florida is voting for a governor, a Gainesville college student is a member of a large and diverse public that includes a Miami dockworker and excludes a college professor at the University of Maine. But when higher education in the United States is at issue, the college student is a member of a public that includes the professor and excludes the dockworker—except that the dockworker's partner may have a daughter who attends the University of Idaho—and so on, into bewildering variety.

It will not do to take this concept of the many publics too far, to chop and dice and refine to the point of absurdity. As A. Lawrence Lowell pointed out in *Public Opinion and Popular Government* (Longmans, Green, 1914), "If two highwaymen meet a belated traveler on a dark road and propose to relieve him of his watch and wallet, it would clearly be an abuse of terms to say that in the assemblage on that lonely spot there was a public opinion in favor of redistribution of property."

Yet, there *are* many publics, and much of the criticism of the mass media occurs because it is impossible to please them all. Moreover, the mass media attempt not only to inform, but to guide and entertain as well. How does one inform, guide, and entertain simultaneously a bank president and the janitor who keeps the bank clean; a Pulitzer Prize winner and his or her cousin, who was content with a tenth-grade education; a novelist and a city sanitation worker; a wealthy member of the Junior League and a poverty-stricken mother of five; a rabid Republican and a Democrat; a Catholic and a Baptist? The answer, of course, is that the media inevitably fail.

ALIENATION AND FREEDOM

Depend not on fortune, but on conduct.

—Publilius Syrus

Although a mass communications enterprise cannot reach everyone, its success hinges on acceptance by its public. When the audience is well established, the communications fare may seem an academic question. But, with daily circulation in decline and with the merry confusion of today's television options, it is unwise to alienate *any* mass communication audience.

Ethical behavior can be important in maintaining an audience. Media codes stress behaviors that promote credibility. Reporters carefully maintain the appearance of objectivity. Most journalists do discuss ethical problems, fairness, balance. and objectivity, as Philip Meyer found in a 1983 study done for the American Society of Newspaper Editors.* However, public feeling is more likely to be aroused over hurt inflicted by the media on innocent individuals or on society. If people think the press is slinging mud at their leaders or institutions or "getting the story at any price," they may accept abridgements of press freedom. If people in the news think that the reports are usually distorted, they may support external controls over reporting.

The situation can easily put editors in a double bind, no matter how noble their intentions. In *The Quill* of May 1981, professors at Washington and Lee University described the ethical dilemma a newspaper faced in considering a rape case:

> Twenty-nine-year-old Gaspar Farquardt is dead. He was beaten to death because he had raped a 16-year-old girl. He was killed by the rape victim's father.
>
> There is no mystery here. The father told the police all details of how Farquardt broke into the house, held the girl and her youthful companions hostage for several hours, and raped the girl. He told how he arrived home, and, in a rage, beat Farquardt to death with a poker.
>
> The police have reluctantly charged the father with murder.
>
> It's a "good" story. But what should the story contain?
>
> Is this the time we break the rule about never publishing the name of a rape victim? How can we print the whole story, giving sufficient background to explain the motive for the killing, without revealing the girl's name? Even printing the name of the father—as we would the name of anyone else accused of murder—would reveal the girl's identity. If we do not suggest the motive for the killing, this probably justifiable homicide would be presented as a brutal beating death. . . .

In asking four editors about this case, almost nothing could be learned, according to the editors. "Sometimes," one of the editors said, "you must decide about what to do—and you will always be *wrong*." Another editor said that if you decide to publish everything known, you will be attacked by some people. There is *no* generally accepted solution to this case.

To maintain the respect of the public affects much more than newspaper readership, however. It influences the very existence of a free press.

In the United States, the press is considered a defender of personal freedom. Read what the late Justice William O. Douglas of the Supreme Court wrote in *The Rights of the People* (Doubleday, 1958):

*Philip Meyer, *Editors, Publishers, and Newspaper Ethics* (American Society of Newspaper Editors, 1983).

134,927

Man's right to knowledge and the free use thereof is the very essence of the American political creed. . . .

The concept of our Bill of Rights is the concept of a politically mature people. It is the concept which makes the American way of life the ideal for every people. For its essence is tolerance for all shades of opinion, persecution for none. Under our way of life a man should never go to jail for what he thinks or espouses. He can be punished only for his acts, never for his thoughts, or beliefs, or creed.

It is important, I think, to adhere to first principles. We must adhere to them if we are to have the capacity to cope with the tremendous problems of the age.

One cannot assume press freedom today merely because we wrote a guarantee of press freedom into the First Amendment in the eighteenth century. Today, more countries lack a free press than have one, even if it is described as free. An observer said at a symposium:

Man can seem to be free in any society, no matter how authoritarian, as long as he accepts the postulates of the society, but can only *be* free in a society that is willing to allow its basic postulates to be questioned.

American political philosophy requires us to keep the basic postulates of our society open to question, though some influential groups are opposed to argument. These are challenges to the right to knowledge. Now, the free press, having been freed in the eighteenth century, must two centuries later find how to keep itself free.

The best defense for freedom today, on the part of the press, is responsibility. But the relationship between freedom and responsibility is a difficult one.

FREEDOM AND FREEDOM OF THE PRESS

The theory of a free press is that truth will emerge from free reporting, not that it will be presented perfectly and instantly in any one account.

—Walter Lippmann

It is essential to look at the old realities of the press to understand the contrast over the years.

In the fading years of the nineteenth century, a handsome, dashing newspaperman named Richard Harding Davis took the world for his beat. In clothes of the most fashionable English cut, he covered his assignments and found news where other reporters did not. He disguised himself as a burglar and hung out in shady dives to expose a robber band and get the full story of its operations for his paper. The best magazines bid for his manuscripts. He posed for Charles Dana Gibson's illustrations for the leading magazines of his day. At parties, he traded conversation with such celebrities as Oscar Wilde, Mark Twain, Sarah Bernhardt, and Ellen Terry, and in the quiet elegance of Delmonico's, where dining was a ritual, he ordered dinners and wines with the discrimination of a continental gourmet. Leaving such comforts from time to time, Davis dashed off to cover the little wars that broke the tedium of the later Victorian age. When love came to him, he met the young lady's rebuffs with a characteristic flourish, handing to the messenger at his club in London a note for Miss Cecil Clark, Prairie Avenue, Chicago. The imperturbable Jaggers carried the message across the Atlantic, and, in time, in the best storybook tradition, Miss Clark became Mrs. Richard Harding Davis.

In the years when Denver was growing from a raw mining town into the metropolis of the Rockies, its daily *Post* was owned by two flamboyant publishers, Harry Tammen, a former peripatetic bartender, and Frederick Bonfils, a one-time lottery operator. A story's sales value, not its significance, was their guide in judging news, and no cause was too minor for their newspaper to champion. When two children complained that a vendor had sold them a nickel's worth of rancid peanuts, Bonfils turned loose three reporters to expose "the peanut situation." The publishers got their readers into the proper spirit for Christmas by having a National Guard plane fly over the community with a huge neon-tube cross affixed to its underside. Tammen once hired a sports writer named Otto Floto because he had "the most beautiful name in the world"; and when Bonfils and Tammen became owners of a circus, they worked in the writer's name—Sells-Floto Circus—even though he owned no part of it. Using a composite of their own names, they named an elephant Tambon; and, when Tambon died, Tammen sorrowfully had it stuffed and mounted in a large glass case outside of his office.

For almost a quarter of a century, until a day in 1918 when his own newspaper carried a headline saying that he was wanted for murder, Charles Chapin drove the staff of the New York *World* in his fanatic worship of "that inky-nosed, nine-eyed, clay-footed god called News." More heartless than any city editor in fiction, he fired reporters who missed getting a story by as little as a minute or two. "That," he once told the assembled city-room staff, "is the hundred and eighth man I've fired." One reporter, whom Chapin had warned not to return without his story, plunged into the icy East River to get an interview with a woman ambulance driver at Bellevue Hospital. After he was dragged from the river unconscious and taken to the hospital, someone thoughtfully telephoned Chapin to let him know that the reporter would survive. "Tell him that he's fired," Chapin replied. And then one night Chapin quietly murdered his wife, hung a "Do Not Disturb" sign on the door of the hotel suite in which the body lay, wandered through the city for hours, and finally turned himself in. His life thereafter was spent cultivating beautiful gardens on the prison grounds at Sing Sing, where he served out his sentence until his death in 1930.

Such people, and scores of others just as colorful, really lived. They live on today in books of reminiscences; in novels, movies, and comic strips depicting newspaper work; and in television dramas in which the reporter exposes corruption in city hall, solves a mysterious murder, and wins the pretty girl. It is unfortunate they bear so little relationship to reality today.

TODAY'S PROBLEMS

*Today's reporter is forced to become an educator more concerned
with explaining the news than with being first on the scene.*

—Fred Friendly

In journalism, the standards of more than fifty years ago are in conflict with
modern standards. Today's editors and reporters cannot be as confident as were
the old editors and reporters. The ensuing century brought new responsibilities,
a more demanding public, and a growing sense of professionalism mirrored by
codes, professional training, and professional organizations, such as the American
Society of Newspaper Editors. The problems of responsibility have clearly become
more central and urgent than before, because only responsibility by the press will
protect freedom of the press. Here is how the late Zechariah Chafee described it:

> In the last hundred years, little news sheets issued by obscure printers have
> turned into enormous plants, in each of which a handful of men can inform
> and influence millions of citizens. Other business enterprises which have
> grown from small beginnings to great power in the same period, like Standard
> Oil Company, the New York Stock Exchange, chain stores and chain banks,
> have eventually aroused public alarm and been put under substantial govern-
> ment control to restrain public abuses. They can no longer run loose. Yet it
> is the first principle of our Bill of Rights that the government must let all the
> powerful enterprises in the press run loose.*

Chafee saw it as a moral responsibility "to prevent abuses of power and to
make sure that the press increasingly performs the services which the American
people need." A newspaper, he said, is something like combining in one organization a college and a business enterprise—the one devoted to educating the public,
the other to making money for its owner. This awkward combination constitutes
one of the awesome strengths of a communication system free from government.

Journalists admit that press freedoms bring obligations—one of which is to
preserve the freedom of the press for the next generation. Freedom survives by
being used; irresponsible use erodes support for freedom. Media ethics, then,
embraces more than fairness; it protects and preserves freedom itself.

MASS MEDIA ARE ONE-WAY STREETS

*The press is like the beam of a search-light that moves restlessly about,
bringing one episode and then another out of darkness and into vision.*

—Walter Lippmann

*Zechariah Chafee, "An Outsider Looks at the Press," *Nieman Reports*, Vol. 7 (January
1955), p. 3.

One of the most important distinguishing characteristics of mass communication is that it is mostly a one-way situation. Seldom is there a quick or easy way for the reader, viewer, or listener to talk back, to ask questions, or to get clarification if it is needed.

Second, it involves a good deal of selection. The medium, for instance, chooses the audience it wishes to reach. The *New Yorker* is aimed at a sophisiticated, urban readership. *Successful Farming* is aimed at farmers in the richly agricultural Midwest. The *New York Times* and *New York Daily News* each seeks different types of readers. Those on the receiving end, on the other hand, select among the media. They decide whether they will switch on the television set or pick up a book or newspaper. They choose what they want from the available content. They may listen to a television news program, but switch to another channel when a comedy program comes on. They choose the times that they will use the media.

Third, because the media are capable of reaching vast, widespread audiences, there is actually a need for fewer media than there used to be. To transmit a message throughout the entire United States by the human voice alone, one needs the assistance of many, many speakers. But a single broadcasting network can reach millions of people at the same time. This has its parallel in the whole economic and social system. Under the American system of mass production, for instance, a relatively small number of manufacturers can turn out an astronomically large number of standardized products.

Fourth, to attract as large an audience as possible, the media are addressed to some mythical modal point at which the largest number of people cluster. It is seldom the lowest common denominator, but, for many instruments of mass communication, it is not quite up to middle range. City editors used to tell their cub reporters to write for "the people who move their lips when they read." These people were the lowest common denominator of the newspaper audience. If the uneducated could understand the newspaper's stories, so could the better educated. According to readability studies, three-fourths of the American people—those with average education—can be expected to understand writing at the level of that in the slick-paper and digest magazines. Because the media are addressed to a mythical reader, listener, or viewer, they lose the intimacy of communications addressed to a single individual. A newspaper account of an event is vastly more impersonal than a letter from a friend telling about it.

Fifth, in mass communications, the communicating is done by a social institution that is responsive to the environment in which it operates. As this book will indicate, there is an interaction between the media and society. The media not only influence the social, economic, and political order in which they perform, but they are influenced by it. To understand the media properly, therefore, one must understand the society in which they exist; to understand society, one must examine its setting, its major assumptions, and its basic beliefs.

THE LEADING MEDIA

> *A lot of caution must be used. Nowadays, we are victims of mass media and publicity.*
>
> —Vatican Spokesman

A brief overview of the condition of each medium today may be helpful, especially because the coming of television has altered the shape of mass communication.

Newspapers. Only a few years ago, it was widely assumed that newspapers were dying. If they survived the competition with television, it was said, they would be weak and ineffectual—a minor medium. Such prophecies seemed safe and metropolitan newspaper after metropolitan newspaper died, often suddenly. As the 1980s began, however, it became clear that the newspaper world had only been going through a realignment, though a severe one. While many of the giant papers were dying, others were surviving because they had developed strong ideals of service; in addition, the suburban dailies were growing much stronger.

Magazines. Like newspapers, magazines have had to adjust to new conditions. As with newspapers, the giants have done much of the suffering. But, as most of the big general weeklies and some of the general monthlies disappear, magazines that cater to special interests have become much stronger. Significantly, some of the greatest successes in publishing during the last twenty years are special-interest magazines: *Sunset, Yachting, Sports Illustrated, TV Guide,* and *Scientific American*, to name only a few. In the magazine world, it is no longer the era of *Collier's* and the *Saturday Evening Post*, two old household words which died. However, the era of specialization is yielding healthy magazines.

Broadcasting. Radio has had to move over for its more glamorous sister, television. It has done so by going local through a more decisive readjustment than was forced on either newspapers or magazines, and it may have been saved by the transistor. Network radio, which dominated many a household in the 1930s and 1940s, is almost dead. Radio stations not only are distinctively local, but they reach for a share of the audience rather than for the total audience. Many also are making the kind of special-interest appeal with which we associate. Many radio stations are profitable, but, in the large metropolitan areas where competition is fierce, station after station is hard put to hang on.

Television is still growing, even though it already dominates much of the world of mass communication. There are soft spots; some advertisers have decided that television commercials are priced far beyond budget and reason. The great uncertainty in television is the future impact of technological change. What will be the ultimate effect of pay TV and of cable television?

Films. It is a curious fact that films, which are the object of so much of the fervor of youth in a country whose population is rapidly growing younger, are in deep trouble. *Daily Variety*, the trade paper of the entertainment industries, summed up the gloom: "Never before has Hollywood seen such a crisis." Part of the reason for the Hollywood decline, of course, was that films were being made elsewhere—not only overseas, but in cities across the United States as well.

Books. The contrast of films with books could not be sharper. Book publishing was for years a sedate business, as Paul Reynolds has pointed out in a speech on November 1, 1960:

> In the book world's halcyon days in the 1920s, trade book publishing was said to be a gentleman's occupation. A publisher sat at his desk, authors submitted manuscripts, the publisher selected what seemed to him the best, and contracted for them at modest dollar guarantees against conventional royalty rates. He published the books in a routine fashion, advertised them in a staid manner, sold them to book stores, and pocketed a reasonably certain profit. Rarely was the profit exorbitant. On the few occasions when he made a sale of subsidiary rights, the money involved was small and had little effect on his balance sheets.

All this began to change with the coming of paperbacks, especially as they became widely popular and paperback reprint rights reached great heights.

American book publishers have become increasingly business-oriented, not only because of the enormous profits to be made from best sellers, but also because increased emphasis on education has made nearly all publishing—perhaps especially the publishing of textbooks—seem a blue chip. Many a publishing house has been swallowed up in conglomerates, and the old gentleman's occupation is now fiercely competitive—and profitable.

AUDIENCES FOR THE VARIOUS MEDIA

> *The day of the printed word is far from over. Swift as is the delivery*
> *of the radio bulletin, graphic as is television's eyewitness picture, the*
> *task of adding meaning and clarity is urgent. People cannot and need*
> *not absorb meaning at the speed of light.*
>
> —Erwin Canham

Figures showing the sizes of the various media audiences are dramatic and impressive, but they can also be misleading. They can easily give the impression that each newspaper, each magazine, each book, and each broadcast program tries to reach all the people. But newspapers are restricted by geography. With rare exception, they concentrate their circulation within the trade area served by the community in which they are published. The audiences of individual radio and television stations are also restricted, their boundaries being limited by the station's wavelength. In addition, all the media are restricted by the tastes, interests, and motivations of the public.

Therefore, mass communication does not mean communication for everyone. On the contrary, mass communication involves a selection of *classes*—groups or special publics, which might be quite large numerically—within the *masses*. The media and their audiences come together through a process of mutual selection. The media tend to select their audiences primarily by means of content. The audiences also tend to select among and within the media primarily on the basis of content. As noted above, geography is also important; some media are simply not available where prospective users live. Of course, other factors help to determine selection, including literacy, habit, age, and costs. Researchers are now trying to fathom the influence of personality traits.

The audience attracted to one medium may be quite different from that attracted to another, although obviously there will be a great deal of overlapping. Television counts among its fans many who would never leaf through a book, let alone own one. Newspapers have readers who rarely attend a movie. Even within a single medium, the audience may differ widely in composition from one unit to another. The typical magazine, for example, is aimed at some homogeneous body of readers within the total population—readers sharing a common profession, common interests, common tastes.

Newspapers

Reaching all but the very young, newspapers attract a highly heterogeneous audience. About 98 percent of all readers read something on the front page; about 58 percent, some item on any other given page. But after the front page, subject matter is more important than the page number in determining what is read, for different readers seek out different things.

Age, education, sex, and socioeconomic status are all factors in determining what will be read. In general, young people are likely to use the paper for entertainment, older readers for information and views of public affairs. Adults do more news reading than young people, who seem to be introduced to the paper by its pictorial content and then branch out to crime and disaster news. The more educated a person is, the more likely he is to use the paper for information; the less educated, the more he is apt to use it for entertainment.

The amount of newspaper reading also tends to increase with education. Men tend to read newspapers at greater length and with greater intensity than women, and they are more likely to use papers for information rather than for entertainment. Higher economic status is generally accompanied by an increase in the reading of public affairs news, and by an increase in the reading of sports and society news. Higher economic status, however, does not bring with it decreased attention to pictures and cartoons.

Broadcasting

Before the advent of television, radio ranked with the newspapers as the most universal of the media. The most distinctive characteristic of its audience was that it had no distinctive characteristic; radio appealed to all types, although tastes in programs and extent of listening varied. About 95 percent of all American adults listened at least fifteen minutes a day, with the heaviest listening after 6 P.M. Now television has become a medium as universal as radio was in its heyday. Like radio, it has so broad an appeal that it reaches all segments of the population—although, of course, with different programs.

The great popularity of television has been largely at the expense of radio. Radio listening has dropped off sharply since the television set became a fixture in the American living room. In 1949, the typical American family played its radio an average of about four-and-one-half hours a day; the average is now approximately two hours a day. In that same period—when the television set was becoming a fixture—the family's television viewing time increased from almost nothing to more than four hours a day—a figure that increased to about six hours.

Since television came along, the circumstances under which people listen to radio and their purpose in listening to it seem to have changed. Out-of-home radio listening apparently has increased, to judge from the sales of automobile and portable sets. Unlike television, which requires fairly close attention, radio can be heard with a so-called third ear. There is some evidence that people now use radio as a personal companion while driving to work or doing the housework or reading, whereas they usually watch television as a member of a family group. Having lost to television its pre-eminence as an entertainment medium, radio has become somewhat more selective in seeking its audience. It now beams its programs at little publics within the population, as with disc-jockey shows aimed at teenagers.

Motion Pictures

Television has hit motion pictures only a slightly lighter blow than it has dealt radio. Since television made the living room a private theater, movie attendance has dropped precipitously. Despite higher ticket prices, movie admissions also represent a declining percentage of total U.S. amusement expenditures.

Today, as has been the case almost from the beginning, movies depend largely upon youth for their support. The emphasis on youth is much stronger today, however, in part because movie-makers see that they have a youthful audience and lure even more young people by catering to those they have. According to a study made by the Opinion Research Corporation, the great majority of moviegoers are under thirty, more than half are under twenty, and almost a third are under fifteen. Adults of fifty or older seldom attend at all. Whatever their age, the unmarried attend movies more regularly than married people.

Even aside from content, it is not difficult to explain why movies are chiefly a medium for the young. The mere act of going to the movies, which is a social activity, may be as important to them as what is on the screen. Then, too, the young are barred from some types of recreation—night-clubbing, for example—and have not become involved in activities like lodge meetings, bridge clubs, and PTA meetings, which eat into the time of settled adults. In many communities, there are few places that a young couple on a date can go besides the movies. The lure of the movies for the unmarried can be explained by the fact that many of them find the social experience of moviegoing preferable to the solitary use of other media.

Books

Books attract people who are above average not only in education, but also in their heavy use of the serious content of the other media. Books are more likely to attract young adults rather than older ones, people living in urban communities rather than rural ones, and people of high rather than low income. Readers of books are more likely than people who do not read books to be critical of other media.

Studies have shown consistently that book reading and education go hand in hand. As the level of formal education declines, so does the extent of book reading. Some of the other characteristics of the book audience can be explained partly by this one factor of education. For instance, while young adults read more books than old ones, age may not be the governing consideration, since the older the population group, the less formal education it has had. Similarly, the great amount of reading by urban dwellers may be explained by the higher level of education in urban areas. However, it seems obvious that more than education is involved. The resident of a rural area has less access to books than a city dweller, and the person with a low income cannot easily spare money for books.

In summary, then, what can we say about the influence of the mass media? Wilbur Schramm said in a speech at Stanford University on March 17, 1977:

> Any given communication that comes to an adult enters into a situation where millions of communications have come before, where group norms are already ingrained, and where the mind is already made up and the knowledge structured on most subjects of importance. The new communication is therefore usually not an earthshaking event, but merely another drop in the long slow process that forms the stalactites of our personalities.

EXERCISES

Go through the various parts of the Final Decision.

1. In the case of the *Finger Lakes Times*, assume that you are the brother or sister of the young man who died in the automobile accident. Write a paper of at least 200 words in which you state why you protested the *Times* story.

2. In the case of the *Finger Lakes Times*, assume that you are a resident of Finger Lakes who does *not* know the young man who died in the automobile accident. Write a paper of at least 200 words in which you explain why you protested or did not.

3. Read again in this chapter about the lives of Richard Harding Davis, Harry Tammen, Frederick Bonfils, and Charles Chapin. Write a paper of at least 300 words in which you state whether you are happy or unhappy with working today rather than in the time of Davis, Tammen, Bonfils, and Chapin.

4. Imagine the existence of one newspaper, one magazine, one radio program, one television program, one book, and one film that *you* consider perfect. Name each of these media.

WORDS ABOUT ETHICS

It is the mark of the cultured man that he is aware of the fact that equality is an ethical and not a biological principle.

—Ashley Montagu

Morality is a private and costly luxury.

—Henry Adams

The world has achieved brilliance without conscience. Ours is a world of nuclear giants and ethical infants.

—General Omar Bradley

Science presented us first with normative ethics, then with relativistic ethics, and last with no ethics at all.

—George Faludy

I have never believed there was one code of morality for a public, and another for a private man.

—Thomas Jefferson

It would be strange to demand of a moralist that he teach no other virtue than those he himself possesses.

—Arthur Schopenhauer

I shall endeavor to enliven morality with wit, and to temper wit with morality.

—Joseph Addison

CHAPTER 3

The Journalistic Virtues

One today is worth two tomorrows.

—Francis Quarles

Perhaps the best advice about becoming virtuous was expressed by Dianne Feinstein, mayor of San Francisco, who was answering a question from a reporter. Summing up the lessons of recent years, she was quoted in the *San Francisco Chronicle* of November 8, 1984 with these words:

> I basically believe we're here for an instant in eternity. The only thing that matters is how well you use that instant, because when we're gone, it doesn't matter. No matter what you look like, your race, none of that really matters. It's what you're able to do with that instant.

POPULAR INTEREST, POPULAR VIRTUES

Virtue is its own reward.

—John Dryden

Popular interest in media ethics has generated books, articles, movies and television programs, seminars and conventions, television discussions, and editorial gray hair. However, the hard part remains—applying discussions during the rush to cover the news.

The best journalists can do is to strive to fulfill the journalistic mission of conveying timely information, accurately and effectively, so that the picture of the world in the heads of the members of the public becomes more accurate after exposure to the journalists' messages.

There is no simple way to achieve this "best." Frank McCulloch, executive editor of the McClatchy Newspapers, put it plainly. In a column for *Editor and Publisher* (Feb. 6, 1982), he said he enjoyed going to conferences on ethics, but "other than trying harder," he didn't know what to do with all the suggestions.

The essence of communications standards is to spread truth. For the mass media and those working for them, this means accuracy and more: It means presenting to readers a full and accurate picture of the world. Any behavior that conflicts with this goal is suspect.

Truth?

Still, reporters learn early that truth is elusive and objectivity can be illusion. Reporters and editors distill the facts from various sources and produce a blend; or, alternatively, they indicate where the information came from so readers or watchers can size it up for themselves.

Such is the idealized mission of journalism. In the real world, of course, reporters may not understand the story they are covering; they go to the wrong sources, ask poor questions, make bad judgments, emphasize the wrong points, write the story imprecisely, and fail to double-check. Editors, who may not understand the story either, process the story and try to make it simple and attractive. They may misjudge its news value, its bias, or the background knowledge of its audience. In turn, each member of the public perceives the story uniquely. Where does accurate knowledge of the world emerge in such a series of transactions?

Surprisingly, a good deal of information does make its way into the head of the interested consumer—but that fact should bring encouragement rather than complacency. The most profound changes in media performance are apt to be through improving the education of future communications practitioners. Still, performance in the field can be improved now if reporters and editors communicate better. "Any clear-cut line of communications between management and staff avoids problems 90 percent of the time," according to Ray Timson, managing editor of the *Toronto Star*. He was taking part in a session on ethics held in 1983 by the Canadian Daily Newspaper Publishers' Association. Talking it out is one way of developing guidelines and achieving an understanding of them.

THE GOLDEN RULE OF JOURNALISM

> *The formula for Utopia on earth remains always the same:*
> *to make a necessity of virtue.*
>
> —Clifton Fadiman

Starting with the realization that journalistic ethics are based on striving to present accurate knowledge about the world, one can identify a range of journalistic virtues and sins. At the most virtuous end of the range is honesty. The public also considers honesty important. The *Des Moines Register and Tribune* found in a poll, reported in the *New York Times* (Aug. 15, 1983) that Iowans thought lying more sinful than smoking marijuana or engaging in premarital sex. Yet, as Theologian Walter Kaufmann says in *The Faith of a Heretic* (Anchor Books, 1963), thorough honesty is the rarest and most difficult of all the virtues.

Sissela Bok has examined lying and its justifications and effects in her book, *Lying: Moral Choice in Public and Private Life* (Pantheon, 1978). She does not flatly condemn all lying. Rather, she strongly urges the prospective liar to adhere to a principle of veracity that dictates, first, seeking nondeceptive alternatives, and, second, putting yourself in place of the person you are lying to and asking how you would feel about it. Even then, she would limit such lying to a situation like a bazaar where both buyer and seller are aware of the deceptions of trying to outwit each other. Reporters find dealing with some sources much like haggling at a bazaar.

Dangers lurk in Bok's recommendations, however. Reporters can misunderstand or misuse the information from a source. The source may want to remain off-the-record or be unidentified. Reporters may suspect that competitors have obtained the story elsewhere and be tempted to publish the off-the-record information. Situations that start with being open and nondeceptive seldom raise such problems.

Some critics are firm about not lying. In an interview on with the *Syracuse Post-Standard* (March 7, 1983), Charles Seib, who was ombudsman at the *Washington Post* after being editor of the *Washington Star*, commented on the *Chicago Sun-Times* running a tavern to catch city inspectors engaged in shakedowns. Seib said that he thought the sting amounted to lying and that reporters were never justified in lying.

Honesty, however, is often not enough. Reporters are human. Even the Supreme Court accepts honest mistakes made under deadline and protects journalists from libel verdicts because of them. The assumption is that if the reporters had more time they would catch the errors; a further assumption, generally supported by the press, is that corrections will be published later. Still, the reporter is expected to be accurate the first time. A trickier problem occurs when a report is inaccurate because information is omitted or because a report is biased. Bias is not intentional: biased observers reach conclusions without being aware of the logic taking them there. All of us, reporters included, live in a web of presumptions and prejudices, but it is reasonable to ask reporters to consider their biases and try and keep them out of their stories.

Expectations may also mold a reader's mind. Once, a journalist was looking for comments about Justice Oliver Wendell Holmes. Holmes was eighty-eight years old and at the time nicknamed "The Great Dissenter" for his independence of judgment. The journalist stopped a few people in the street and asked if they had heard of Holmes. Replied one man, "Oh, sure! He's the young judge on the Supreme Court that's always disagreeing with the old guys."

THE ETHICS OF CRAFTSMANSHIP

The analogy of morals is rather with art than with geometry.

                                                                    —J. A. Froude

So far, we have discussed failings rather than sins. Since the failings undercut accuracy, they are targets for constant efforts at correction. But, there is a shadowy

SISSELA BOK

(Interview with Roc, age seven): "I'm going to tell you two stories. There were two kiddies and they broke a cup each. The first one says it wasn't him. His mother believes him and doesn't punish him. The second one also says it wasn't him. But his mother doesn't believe him and punishes him. Are both lies they told equally naughty?—No.—Which is the naughtiest?—The one who was punished."

—Jean Piaget, *The Moral Judgment of the Child*

This story appears as the introduction to a chapter entitled "Excuses" in Sissela Bok's book, *Lying: Moral Choice in Public and Private Life.* A professor at Brandeis University, Bok has written several books and articles on ethics and truthfulness in both personal and professional situations. She has come a long way professionally since she was born in Sweden in 1934. Bok traveled to the United States at age twenty-one. She received her B.A. and M.A. degrees in psychology from George Washington University, and obtained a Ph.D. in philosophy from Harvard in 1970. A former lecturer of decision making in medicine in the Health Sciences and Technology division of Harvard University, Bok also taught courses in the core curriculum there for the past several years.

In reference to *Lying*, J. M. Cameron said in the *New York Review of Books* (June 1, 1973); "We need Dr. Bok's book because a great many people who would be ashamed openly to justify killing the innocent or torturing prisoners think lying is no great harm. . . . Physicians, in particular, as Dr. Bok is able to show, in general treat truth roughly and have good consciences about the deceptions they practice."

Lying covers a wide range of moral issues, including examining the nature of lying and how it affects human choice, the consequences of lies, and the approaches to white lies, and providing an analysis of what circumstances help to excuse lies. The book also discusses the kinds of lies that are commonly considered justifiable, such as lies told in wartime, lies told to conduct research, and those told to children or to the sick and dying.

In the introduction to *Lying*, Bok raises questions of morality in situations such as a doctor lying to a patient, a professor exaggerating the performance of a student on a recommendation, and parents concealing from their children the knowledge that they were adopted. She also discusses issues of social scientists lying to their subjects, government lawyers lying to congressmen for "the good of the people," and journalists lying to their sources in an effort to expose corruption.

"Lines seem difficult to draw, and a consistent policy out of reach," Bok says in her introduction. ". . . In law and in journalism, in government and the social sciences, deception is taken for granted when it is felt to be excusable by those who tell the lies and who tend also to make the rules."

Appearing at the beginning of a chapter called "Never to Lie?" is a quotation by John Wesley, from *Sermon.* It reads: ". . . [T]here is no absurdity, however strange it may sound, in that saying of the ancient Father, 'I would not tell a willful lie to save the souls of the whole world.'" Also included is a statement by Immanual Kant, from the *Doctrine of Virtue:* "By a lie, a man throws away and, as it were, annihilates his dignity as a man."

An intriguing ethical question is presented by Francis Hutcheson in *A System of Moral Philosophy* (1755). This dilemma is reprinted at the beginning of Bok's chapter on "Lies In a Crisis," and is followed by a discussion of threats to survival and the danger of expanding deceptive practices:

> May not a singular necessity supersede the common rule of veracity, too? Suppose a Ghengis Khan, or any such Eastern Monster, resolved on the massacre of a whole city if he finds they have given any protection to his enemy, and asking a citizen in whom he confides about this fact, whether his enemy had ever been sheltered by the citizens; and that by deceiving the monster, he can preserve the lives of hundreds of thousands, and of their innocent babes; whereas to tell him the truth shall occasion the most horrible slaughter; could a wise man's heart reproach him justly for breaking through the common law of veracity, and conquering the natural impulse toward it, upon such strong motives of humanity?

In a particularly thought-provoking chapter, entitled "Deceptive Social Science Research," Bok presents the paradox of lying in an effort to achieve positive societal gains. She quotes Robert Rosenthal: "The behavioral researcher whose study might reduce violence or racism or sexism, but who refuses to do the study because it involves deception, has not solved an ethical problem, but only traded it in for another." Bok then discusses the "game" of deception played by increasingly manipulative scientists.

Walter Clemons of *Newsweek* calls *Lying* "a provocative, highly intelligent book," and Hans Bynagle of the *Library Journal* labels it as an "excellent and eminently readable book," which ". . .narrows the limits within which deceit might appear defensible."

Perhaps Bok's concern with both private and professional ethics is best summarized by a statement concerning the feelings of those who must face the consequences of deception. In the introduction to *Lying*, she says: "The fact is that reasons to lie occur to most people quite often. . . . [T]o be given false information about important choices [in life] is to be rendered powerless."

—Jennifer Koch

region of journalism that leads to distortion, but is not considered unethical: The effects of time and space limitations.

A journalistic message is highly condensed, especially in broadcast journalism. Less-newsworthy stories may literally be trimmed to nothing. The shorter the story, the less fully accurate it is. At best, trimming eliminates some secondary information, always at the discretion of a fallible, human editor. The result may be distortion.

Since condensing is a matter of craftsmanship, why mention it when discussing ethics? Mainly to call attention to its impact upon accuracy. However, another reason is to link ethical behavior to competence and sensitivity.

Overcondensation is one problem, excessive coverage is another. Some critics charge that the press devotes too much attention to sex, crime, and violence. Drama, scandal, or celebrity may also bring a story more coverage than its content deserves. Attaching the suffix "-gate" to a situation makes it easy to label, but it may mislead. "Herd" news inflates stories and affects the nature of the news itself, for the press becomes part of it. Of more ethical concern, the rights of the people in the story may be abused through prejudical coverage. The question of what may be excessive coverage is debatable, but the need for sensitivity is not.

Hyping a story—making it more sensational—is a more obvious ethical issue. Journalists can easily be tempted to sharpen the facts by dropping a qualifying phrase from a quotation, by focusing on a minor—but juicy—detail, or by fishing for provocative quotations. The objective is not to tell the truth, but to attract attention. Instead, journalists must find in accurate reporting enough interesting facts to attract the public.

INTENTS AND PURPOSES

> *Every case is like every other case, and no two cases are alike.*
>
> —Edmond Cahn

Moving from the shadowy areas into the bright light of more deliberate journalistic practice, we come to the controversial practice of advocacy. The most honest advocates practice outright persuasion: If they include opposing positions, they are presented, at best, as standing alone.

Not all advocacy is that open, however. In newspapers and broadcast news programs, the public expects impartial reporting, unless given some clue to indicate otherwise. Moreover, people who are in the news often are frequently advocates, and the press quotes their opinionated comments—fine, so long as the opinions are attributed and do not mislead. However, selecting opinionated quotations to support one's own position is another matter.

Sometimes, publicity alone is valuable. An English writer once picked up an excellent tip from the novelist Gore Vidal. They were sitting at an international writer's conference, inspecting photos, and Vidal was sitting next to a delegate from India. "I always sit next to a man in a turban," Vidal said. "You get photographed more."

Johnny Weissmuller was on his way to a golf tournament in Cuba when his car was surrounded by a band of guerrillas. Weissmuller stood up and gave his Tarzan yell. The guerrillas said "Tarzan! Tarzan! Welcome to Cuba!" Then the encounter turned into an autograph party.

Journalistic codes frequently call for "independence," not only from partisan politics, but from community involvements and controversies. Independence, like many words in ethical codes, threatens to become a blind guide. Professor Michael J. Kirkhorn, in a wide-ranging critique (*The Quill*, February 1983), argued that insistence on independence keeps the press from collaborating productively with institutions, such as universities, that could enhance reporting.

Occasionally, reporters fabricate facts. Fictional stories about a child in Washington hooked on heroin and a "typical" policeman in Northern Ireland made the news, even though the reporters lost their jobs. But, peccadilloes also may occur when editors honor drama over substance.

Journalists have to be skeptical about their sources' motives and honesty. Skepticism based on an appreciation of the diversity of people and their purposes can be productive, but is destructive. Reporters *can* temper their skepticism. Michael Kirkhorn urges virtuous journalists to draw upon the findings of research centers and historians to understand how the figments of the day are invented.

Like anyone else, journalists know right from wrong. When they do wrong, they often do it because of pressure. Competition among reporters is the stuff of drama in print, film, and television. The dictatorship of the deadline gives the journalist's day a special intensity. Coalescing these into an almost irresistible force is professional pride. "Getting the story at any price" can easily lead to abuses. Reporters learn early that information can be difficult to dig out. To meet the deadline, or what the reporter perceives to be the editor's expectations, a journalist finds it easy to overextend. Pretending to be something other than a reporter can seem like a suitable counter to the resistance shown by a wily, antagonistic source. Even "borrowing" a document without permission long enough to copy it can appear acceptable to a desperate reporter.

To operate properly under such pressure, journalists need an unambiguous voice speaking to them from their professional training, their experience, and their human selves.

Actually, most journalists act ethically, reacting automatically against unethical practices. Philip Meyer found in a study for the American Society of Newspaper Editors* that staff members were stricter about heeding traditional ethical standards than were the editors and publishers. But, he found the automatic quality of their reaction unsettling. He felt that the "knee-jerk response" exhibited to certain ethi-

Editors, Publishers, and Newspaper Ethics, ASNE, 1983.

cal situations often prevented any careful weighing and analyzing of the specific cases at hand.

Kirkhorn also was uncomfortable with the unthinking application of criteria on ethical codes. He said they become "reflexes" and are not applied in authentic and thoroughgoing ways. The wisest answer may not always be the automatic one.

THE VIRTUE OF WISDOM

Common sense in an uncommon degree is what the world calls wisdom.

—Samuel Taylor Coleridge

People tend to think in ways in which they have been trained, or at least have grown accustomed, to think. For example, at an embassy reception, columnist Ann Landers was approached by a rather pompous senator. "So you're Ann Landers," he drawled. "Say something funny." Without hesitation, Landers replied, "Well, you're a politician. Tell me a lie."

Similarly, when people respond automatically to ethical issues, they respond in ways in which they have been indoctrinated. Scholars have shown that journalists are socialized by their colleagues and by the traditions of the newsrooms. They learn to succeed by mastering the social system and earning its rewards. In addition to the handed-down rules of behavior, the newsroom social system serves to satisfy the strong drive to publish regardless of the cost. In the newsroom, each day is a new beginning, an opportunity to correct the mistakes of yesterday and to find out what new things have happened that day. It is no wonder that situation ethics plays a major role in guiding newsroom behavior. This approach assumes that people can call on some universal ethical principles to apply in a particular situation.

The principles called on by journalists are most likely to be those listed in the codes hanging on the newsroom walls. Their application to a specific situation is apt to be automatic, whether or not they are appropriate.

Ethical behavior embraces wisdom, which is the goal of knowledge, fair play, and, perhaps most important of all, courage. To stand up and do what one believes to be right, to assert the truth honestly, to refuse to be bound by a source's demand to go off the record, to resist publishing a hot scoop that hasn't been confirmed— all these take courage.

Most journalistic virtues and sins relate to the major purpose of telling the truth, but woven in is a concern for justice—that is, fair play and compassion. Justice perplexes moral philosophers, so it is no wonder it tests those in public communications as well. To meet the test, journalists must accept the need for recognizing ethical cases.

To avoid becoming entangled during the trek through the ethical thicket in the remainder of this book, one might better follow the philosophy enunciated by Susan Schnur in a column she wrote for the *New York Times*. To her, the ethical thicket consists of "frontsies and backsies," a phenomenon she noticed in kindergarten. "Frontsies meant that you let a kid cut in front of you as you stood in line for a drink," she wrote. "Backsies meant you let a kid cut behind you." This situation is a moral microcosm, Schnur said, that represents the background for ethical hedonists, Machiavellians, Christian ethicists, and others. Schnur's conclusion arose from the comments of a school crossing guard who refused frontsies to one girl. Said the guard, "You should stand where you end up, like the rest of us."

EXERCISES

1. As editor of a newspaper, you learn that a gang of house burglars has moved into your city. Police say they read in your paper obituaries and wedding announcements to select victims among those who will not be at home. Police ask you to discontinue printing these stories for several weeks, saying this will force the gang out of town.
   a. Would you continue publishing obituaries and wedding announcements?
   b. Would you eliminate street addresses?
   c. Would you consent to the police request, then publish a story explaining the purpose of the new policy?
2. A major scandal erupted at a large New York university because of cocaine dealing among students. The news director of the college radio station knew that she should call the Dean of Students for a comment, but she worried that the administration's point of view would certainly weaken the truth of her story. To cover herself, she called the Dean for comment late on a Friday evening when she was sure no one would be there. Was her action right or wrong?

JOURNALISTS ABOUT JOURNALISTS

A news sense is really a sense of what is important, what is vital, what has color and life—what people are interested in. That's journalism.

—Burton Rascoe

And when Franklin D. Roosevelt lectures the press, as he does very often, he ascribes its sins to columnists, editors, and publishers, implying that spot-news reporters are fine fellows.

—Arthur Krock

Moral posturing by the press sounds tinny when the brightest stars in our business behave as cornermen in political debates.

—Sandy Grady

If we do not keep our distance from the arena, are we then journalists or politicians?

—Richard Harwood

The day you write to please everyone you no longer are in journalism. You are in show business.

—Frank Miller, Jr.

The journalist is controlled by that uncontrollable nonsense we call news.

—Reed Whittemore

CHAPTER 4

The Expectant Public

Journalism is literature in a hurry.
—Matthew Arnold

What does the ever-expectant public receive from newspapers and television news? The public thinks it knows what each medium serves, but nearly all people would be surprised by the results of an analysis of the contents of newspapers and television.

A professor read with skepticism a column in the May 27, 1985 issue of *Time* magazine, in which Thomas Griffith wrote:

> Just about the most annoying question a journalist faces is, Why don't you print more good news? This question assumes that reporters get a kick out of reporting the bad, have some political motive for doing so, or know that sensationalism sells papers. Journalism answers testily: Do you want to avert your eyes from reality and live in a dream world?

Griffith's column continues for another 900 words, attempting to justify all the negative news. In Griffith's last paragraph, he wrote, "the American press often seems to be overemphasizing the negative. But do people really want the good news stressed and the bad slighted?"

As if to emphasize Griffith's words, on May 15, 1985, Columnist Leonard Koppett, once a *New York Times* reporter and editor-in-chief of the *Peninsula Times Tribune*, now a highly respected *Times Tribune* columnist, wrote:

> One of the most persistent and heartfelt complaints editors hear is that not enough emphasis is placed on "good" news. Presumably, these readers mean "upbeat" when they say "good," because events themselves can be good or bad according to one's point of view.

After saying that "most papers do carry many upbeat stories every day," Koppett stresses that the Associated Press is the "primary source of world news" that sends newspapers a preponderance of distressing news.

Koppett ends his column with this single-sentence paragraph: "And news is as bad as it is because so much bad happens out there."

No journalist has ever protested Griffith's or Koppett's gloomy views of newspaper negativism. Perhaps all journalists believe that all newspapers feature negative news. With respect for Griffith, Koppett, and most newspaper people, their belief in the negativism of newspapers is, to put it plainly, poppycock. At least one professor believes that positive news is longer and stronger than negative news in newspapers.

In 1970, to write a book entitled *A Region's Press*, this professor read *every page* in three issues of ten newspapers: *Oakland Tribune, San Francisco Chronicle, San Francisco Examiner, San Jose Mercury, San Jose News, Atlanta Constitution, Buffalo News, Los Angeles Times, New York Times,* and *Toronto Globe & Mail.* Although his goal was to judge the various newspapers in another fashion, it dawned on him that all of them were publishing more positive than negative news.

Nonetheless, not until 1984, when he taught "Ethics of the Media," did he have an opportunity to rely on others, rather than himself, to study positive vs. negative news. The professor asked his students whether they believed that most news in newspapers was negative. All but one student said, "Yes"—and that student exploded, "Damned right!"

First, for practice, all students were required to measure a single issue of the *Times Tribune.* When they disagreed, he suggested this pattern:

Positive

Negative

Positive-Negative

Thus, he gave the students the right to assign stories to "positive-negative," because this or that story could not be judged by the student as "positive" or "negative." They were surprised at the results: The *Times Tribune* issue was measured in column inches and was overwhelmingly positive.

Then the students were assigned these newspapers to measure for positive, negative, and positive-negative: *Christian Science Monitor, Los Angeles Times, Oakland Tribune, New York Times, Philadelphia Inquirer, San Jose Mercury-News, San Francisco Chronicle,* and *The Wall Street Journal.* All newspapers were measured by a different student. All measured positive.*

For example, in two issues of the *New York Times,* here are the results in column inches:

	Positive	*Negative*	*Positive-Negative*
March 16, 1984	1,037	833	639
March 17, 1984	1,126	692	335

*Three senior students were appointed as judges of these measurements. When they disagreed, a story would be placed in the positive-negative category. Among the hundreds of stories, they disagreed nine times.

As for two issues of the *Philadelphia Inquirer,* here are the results:

	Positive	*Negative*	*Positive-Negative*
February 3, 1984	1,234	539	1,946
February 6, 1984	1,613	558	1,530

Meredi Haupt, a senior student, commented pointedly:

My analysis of two weekday issues of the *Los Angeles Times* indicates that within the first section, considered to contain more hard news than any other section, there was a markedly greater amount of negative stories than positive. Yet, when the entire newspaper was considered, the positive out-weighs the negative. Although within the other sections, such as View, Metro, Sports, and Business, there are stories of scandal and crime, the space is primarily dedicated to lighter, feature-type stories than hard news. These stories tend to be more positive than negative.

It was not even necessary for me to measure the column space (although I did) in order to arrive at this conclusion. Having been an avid *Times* reader for five or six years, I can support my facts by commenting [that] when I read the front page section, I am overwhelmed with a feeling of gravity con-cerning the serious problems of our world. Yet, the farther I read into the *Times,* the more I am exposed to the better things and lighter side of life.

It is not my intention to sound trite by discussing how the respective sections affect my emotions in differing ways. Instead, I am merely referring to the first student suggestion on distinguishing between positive and nega-tive news:

Negative stories are those which induce depression and cause people to become more pessimistic about the society around them. Because human values vary from individual to individual, there will always be some differ-ences of opinion.

Perhaps the fact that this class is the first group of people to prove that the media largely presents positive news is a result of the trend in presenting news and information in the most entertaining and enlightening manner, to insure a large audience. It seems that, especially in newspapers, because of their struggle to compete with television, a variety of new sections and visually appealing attempts have been initiated. No longer does one simply open up the morning paper to find the top and most current news, but one finds information on food, gardening, special profiles on special people, and similar articles for the betterment of the standard of living.

My findings do not surprise me. I found the *Los Angeles Times* to be both positive and negative, although their presentation of hard news was mostly negative. Although we have conducted a similar assignment, I think it is im-portant that it is verified by a follow-up.

The 1985 Ethics class took Haupt's challenge to follow up in measuring newspapers, and the students were assigned one issue each of these newspapers: *Chicago Tribune, Dallas Morning News, New York Times*, and *Washington Post*. They found much the same for the first three newspapers as did the first students. Here are the measurements for the *Chicago Tribune:*

	Positive	*Negative*	*Positive-Negative*
February 27, 1985	2,896	1,711	738

One student found that the last newspaper, the *Washington Post*, published more negative news than positive news. Here are the results:

	Positive	*Negative*	*Positive-Negative*
March 4, 1985	2,155	2,308	2,341

Even though it carried a greater proportion of negative news than the others, the *Post* came close to a tie between positive and negative.

GRADING TELEVISION

> *The one function that TV news performs very well is that when there is no news we give it to you with the same emphasis as if there were news.*
>
> —David Brinkley

The 1985 students were also assigned television newscasts. Perhaps as no surprise to anyone, ABC, CBS, and NBC in television newscasts have one hue—negative. The students measured half-hour telecasts in minutes and seconds. The results of the ABC news measurements were:

	Positive	*Negative*	*Positive-Negative*
March 6, 1985	6 min. 15 sec.	11 min. 40 sec.	4 min. 30 sec.

As for NBC, the results were:

	Positive	*Negative*	*Positive-Negative*
March 5, 1985	7 min. 43 sec.	8 min. 25 sec.	4 min. 45 sec.

For CBS, the positive and negative measurements were the closest of all the measurements made by many students of the three networks. Here is student Scott Warner's explanation with the numbers:

The Thursday, March 7, 1985, edition of the CBS Evening News was observed and recorded in such a way as to determine how much of the program was devoted to positive, negative, and positive-negative news. The duration of each story was timed to the second, with each story being placed in one of the above categories. A total of sixteen stories were timed with the category totals as follows:

	Positive	Negative	Positive-Negative
March 7, 1984	8 min. 2 sec.	8 min. 43 sec.	4 min. 11 sec.

As can be determined from the above totals, negative news has beaten positive news by 41 seconds. The positive category is only close because it rode on the heels of two relatively long feature stories. If only the total number of stories had been tabulated, negative news would outnumber positive news many times over. Does CBS want its viewers coming away from its evening news depressed? Probably not. CBS probably has the perception of itself as simply reporting news items. But, either consciously or unconsciously, CBS is attempting to keep its viewers from turning away amidst waves of depression.

CBS counteracts the negativity of its news in two ways. The first is that it leads with a positive story and ends with a positive story. "Leave 'em with a smile," the old saying goes. The second counteraction procedure is the volume of time devoted to the positive stories. There is more time devoted to the individual positive stories than to the individual negative ones. This had a leveling effect on the positive and negative categories. The argument could also be made that CBS knows its viewers very well and knows that the national news watcher can stand a little more negativity than the average person. It gives the news a "hard-hitting" look.

WHAT THE PUBLIC EXPECTED

> *If there had been television cameras at Gettysburg,*
> *this would be two countries: the carnage would have*
> *caused the North to let the South go.*
>
> —George Will

When a demonstrator sets himself afire, the community expects a television reporter's first concern to be saving the demonstrator, not taping footage of the story. When reporting on the misfortunes, the press is expected to respect the feelings of the victims. The community expects the media not to allow themselves to be used to corrupt community morals or harm public health. Among recurrent themes sounded by ethical thinkers, those closest to community values and which apply to the media are compassion and temperance, because they serve best to uphold the community.

That the mass media want their messages to be *perceived* as accurate is evident in the attention media professionals give to credibility. Media codes of ethics universally condemn behaviors that raise suspicions among the public.

Inaccuracy heads the list of reader complaints, according to the ombudsman for the *Kansas City Star and Times*, Donald D. Jones. He reported to Thomas Griffith, who writes about the media for *Time* magazine, that "Errors of fact do more to undermine the trust and confidence of readers than any other sin we commit." Herbert Hoover, for one, had accuracy bred in. Once, during a train journey through some farming country, his travelling companion pointed out some sheep that had been sheared. Hoover replied, "Well, on this side, anyway."

Confidential sources also damage credibility. In some circumstances, the public will need to protect the identities of sources, but frequent veiled attribution can weaken the reliability of the reports. A person naturally responds to a surprising assertion with, "Oh yeah? Who says so?" The public has a tendency to discount such statements. If the story is only slightly newsworthy, veiled sources can water the story down too much to justify its use. In addition, a story that doesn't identify sources may be less interesting than one that does. Charles Seib, former ombudsman at the *Washington Post*, says the editor has not done his job when he finds out who the source is. "He has to satisfy himself what the motivation is," Seib told an interviewer in 1983.

The main line of loyalty of reporters trying to convey the truth runs to the public—not to the publisher, not to the source. Getting the story across accurately and effectively is the key to ethical behavior. Other factors may complicate decisions, but the ultimate mission is to portray the world correctly. Survival of the media giving that portrayal depends on the public's acceptance of their messages as worth its attention.

How strongly people feel about their media varies, but those who feel most strongly, whether antagonistic or favorable, have important expectations of the media. They understand that the media are significant to their vision of the world. Those who perceive the media's information as being inaccurate feel betrayed and angry and they call for curbing the press. Many of the public's expectations involve presentation and topics. But the people expect more than that: they expect journalists, who are the source of much of their information about the world, to uphold their view of the world and their values.

ATTACK AND DEFENSE

A story is only as good as the dumbest error in it.

—City Editor

Don Bridge, former general manager of the Rochester (N.Y.) *Times-Union* and *Democrat & Chronicle*, has pinpointed several major criticisms the public makes of

WILBUR SCHRAMM

There is nothing especially esoteric about research. It is the best way to gather information systematically, accurately, and with safeguards that permit one to estimate how reliable the information is. Research is not something that one undertakes without study or training; but neither is there anything magic or mysterious about it.

The above words were spoken at Stanford University on March 17, 1977, by Wilbur Schramm, but no one knows what to quote; Schramm has written so many true, provocative sentences that one must give up from frustration in trying to quote the best sentences he has written. Perhaps the way to understand why Schramm once advised many communication researchers to "Have the courage to write simply," is to quote one of his early articles about research. The following quotation—simply expressed, but loaded with meaning—was published by *Journalism Quarterly* in September 1949:

News exists in the minds of men. It is not an event; it is something perceived *after* the event. It is not identical with the event; it is an attempt to reconstruct the essential framework of the event—*essential* being defined against a frame of reference which is calculated to make the event meaningful to the reader. It is an aspect of communication, and has the familiar characteristics of that process.

I think it is self-evident that a person selects news in expectation of a reward.

This reward may be either of two kinds. One is related to what Freud calls the Pleasure Principle, the other to what he calls the Reality Principle. For want of better names, we shall call these two classes *immediate reward* and *delayed reward*.

In general, the kinds of news which may be expected to furnish immediate reward are news of crime and corruption, accidents and disasters, sports and recreation, social events, and human interest.

Delayed reward may be expected from news of public affairs, economic matters, social problems, science, education, and health.

News of the first kind pays its rewards at once. A reader can enjoy a vicarious experience without any of the dangers or stresses involved. He can shiver luxuriously at an axe-murder, shake his head sympathetically and safely at a tornado, identify himself with the winning team or (herself) with the society lady who wore a well-described gown at the reception for Lady Morganbilt, laugh understandingly (and from superior knowledge) at a warm little story of children or dogs. News of the second kind, however, pays its rewards later. It sometimes requires the reader to endure unpleasantness or annoyance—as, for example, when he reads of the ominous foreign situation, the mounting national debt, rising taxes, falling market, scarce housing, cancer, epidemics, farm blights. It has a kind of "threat value." It is read so that the reader may be informed and prepared. When a reader selects delayed-reward news, he jerks himself into the world of surrounding reality to which he can adapt himself only by hard work. When he selects news of the other kind, he retreats usually from the world of threatening reality toward the dream world.

Almost anyone will understand whatever Schramm is writing. Many journalists and researchers read his articles and books, no doubt shaking their heads at how Schramm can make everything clear to anyone. Charlene and Trevor Brown, both students of Schramm, who are now at Indiana University, wrote of Schramm's ability at thinking and writing:

> We have long admired the grace and clarity of his writing and his unmatched ability to synthesize findings relevant to communication from a half-dozen or more disciplines. We are indebted to him for his contribution as scholar, colleague, and teacher to the intellectual lives of all of us.*

So many other successful students have left Schramm's teaching and writing with regret that at least some of them have wondered how he mastered so many disciplines. It is not possible to trace such a career and fix on *the* answer, but it is instructive to know where he began and was educated. Schramm was born in Marietta, Ohio, in 1907 and went to Marietta College—graduating *summa cum laude.* Much the same occurred at Harvard University, where he earned his M.A. in English: again, *summa.* The same thing happened with Schramm's Ph.D. in English from the University of Iowa: highest honors.

Since receiving his Ph.D., Schramm has written so many articles and papers (120) and books (30, 25 of which were translated into other languages), and won so many honors that many who admire his work probably do not know that long ago he won the O. Henry Prize for fiction. In the 1940s, Schramm decided to leave English and focus on journalism.

Schramm—still vigorous, still handsome—has a book list so long that it is not possible to name them all here, but one must mention the latest, *From Painted Cave to Microchip: The Story of Human Communication* (in press). It was written in his late 70s, and no doubt many people who understand what Schramm has accomplished with *Four Theories of the Press* (University of Illinois Press, 1963) with Frederick Siebert and Theodore Peterson, and many other books are waiting eagerly to read it.

As Schramm is now in his early 80s, the many people who appreciate his pioneering thoughts will prophesy that he will go on for a long time, pushing his way through the four continents he has already researched, finding the answer to the massive power of communication.

* *The Media and the People* (New York: Holt, Rinehart & Winston, 1978), p. iii.

the press.* Although these criticisms and Bridge's answers are concerned with newspapers, most apply to the other mass media as well.

1. *Lack of editorial balance.* A few newspapers in the very largest cities can construct their content to appeal to a specific type of audience. This is not so with the vast majority of newspapers. They must appeal to the total literate population of their areas if they are to survive.

2. *Inferior quality of provincial newspapers.* Newspapers with communitywide appeal need not be publications of low quality. Many of them maintain high standards. "Yellow journalism" has largely disappeared.

3. *Overemphasis on crime news.* Newspapers that must serve their complete populations cannot ignore news of the unpleasant facts of life. To do so would distort history. Most newspapers present such news factually and with a minimum of sensationalism.

4. *Obsession with trivia.* More people will read a short story about what happened to someone's lost dog than a long story about what happened in the United Nations. These are reflections of human nature and contemporary life rather than an indication that newspapers are not serving the public properly.

5. *Overplaying and underplaying the news.* Whatever the merits may be in an individual case, the judgments as reflected by publication are those of professional newsmen whose instructions and intentions are to be accurate, fair, and objective.

6. *Slanted headlines.* Complaints about headlines are occasionally justified. Headlines writers are not infallible.

7. *Editorial bias.* The newspaper is wrong in some cases, though the alleged bias may also be in the mind of the reader.

8. *Restrictive monopoly of a one-newspaper community.* The word monopoly in newspaper ownership is used much too loosely. Publishing a good newspaper is expensive and most communities simply cannot support several, particularly in competition with television and radio.

9., 10., 11., *Excessive advertising, objectionable ads, advertiser influence on news policy.* Assembling, manufacturing, and distributing a newspaper produce a tremendously important by-product—advertising space. Without advertising, the cost of good newspapers of general circulation would be prohibitive to most readers.

"As essential as advertising is to the newspaper, the news columns of good newspapers are equally indispensable to business," Bridge said. "Studies indicate that only about 2 percent of all advertisements in all media are seriously objectionable.

"At no time during 45 years of newspaper work, most of it in management

*"Answers to Criticisms," *Editor & Publisher*, Oct. 13, 1962.

positions, have I seen any indication that any advertiser controlled any policy of any newspaper with which I was associated, directly or indirectly."

This is a fairly comprehensive summary of specific criticisms, a fairly typical set of responses—and neither gets to the heart of the real dispute. The criticisms and the defenses are accurate with regard to some newspapers. But, do the critics who denounce the mass media as "sensational" really mean to include in their indictment the *New York Times*, the *Los Angles Times*, the *Christian Science Monitor, Commentary*, and "CBS Reports"? And does Bridge really mean that no newspaper ever prints anything to sell more papers?

PUBLIC ALIENATION

The people—that great beast!

—Alexander Hamilton

Surveys indicate that the public has become increasingly alienated from the media. The Harris organization, for example, found in its assessment of attitudes toward institutions, such as medicine and government, that the print and broadcast media rank near the bottom of the list.

Journalists frequently respond that the mass media are suffering from the general decline of confidence in all social institutions. They attempt to explain away public disaffection by arguing that in troubled times the messengers are blamed for the unpleasant messages they bring. Just as the herald of old suffered for bringing the message that the Romans would sack the city unless it surrendered, a stigma attaches to the media because they bring so much bad news. But attacking these modern messengers is not always rational, for they do not bring *all* the news, and they are not passive channels. Still, they select among thousands of items every day, and, in gathering and reporting the news, they cut it, splice it, condense it, and shape it, usually with laudable expertise, but sometimes erroneously.

Still, the avenues for redress for those injured by the media is forbidding. They can protest—but seldom with any real hope that their complaints will be heeded. Reporters and editors may become cynical and brusque through frequent encounters with the self-serving. They are usually right in being skeptical of those who speak in their own cause. But, when they are wrong, the citizen in the news feels powerless and resentful.

Perhaps the most important alienating factor is the distance between the media and the public. In the early years of this country, newspapers and magazines served many publics. Although each publication had a relatively small circulation, the journalists spoke to the central interests of their readers and could usually count on their loyalty. The journalists' views might be opposed and their plants might be attacked (the plants of some abolitionist papers were destroyed), but most readers who opposed the views expressed in one publication could subscribe to others that squared with their own views.

As newspapers and magazines become larger and fewer, and as journalists became obliged to corral mass audiences, separate voices could no longer be raised in the hitherto "free marketplace of ideas." As one astute observer of journalism, Wilbur Schramm, commented in a speech at Stanford University on March 17, 1977:

> The small, numerous media, as we know them in the eighteenth and nineteenth centuries were representative of the people. . . , in fact, they *were* the people. But the larger and more centralized media have, to some extent, withdrawn from the people and become a separate set of institutions, parallel and comparable with other power centers, such as business and government.

This is the main reason so many citizens and citizen groups seek access to the media—to speak for themselves.

The distance, the inaccuracies, and the fears that the media will misuse their power help to cause public alienation. Instead of being grateful to journalists for serving as watchdogs of officialdom, many members of the public view both media and government suspiciously.

SOCIETY'S NEED FOR INFORMATION

Ignorance is the primary source of misery and vice.

—Victor Cousin

What kind of information do the American people need to protect their interests and to function as effective citizens? And what kind of report can communicate such information to the public? People with little education need different kinds of reports than do business executives or professors. Journalists must respond to such diversity. Schramm and his colleagues at the Stanford Institute for Communication Research once addressed the problem of public knowledge by analyzing surveys which were published in the Institute's annual report. Looking not for opinions but for knowledge, they found:

> Only 22 percent of Americans could name their own congressman, and only 35 percent could name one of their two senators.
>
> Although 82 percent of American adults had heard about Medicare, only 10 percent could say correctly who would be covered by the act.
>
> Only 33 percent of the adults could state accurately the meaning of the term "Electoral College," only 48 percent could define "filibuster," and only 33 percent could name five or more of the presidential cabinet positions.

The problem of the journalist is highlighted by the case of a Chicano mother who speaks halting English, lives on welfare in a ghetto, and has four children, one of them with a serious medical problem. To ensure some degree of well being for herself and her children, she needs a wide range of information. She must know about clinics—not just their locations, but also what they can do for her and her children. She must know about nutrition. She must know where to shop. She must be aware of her rights as a tenant. Extending the list is not difficult, but it is already long enough to make clear an ironic fact. The poor, who are least able to inform themselves, may need more information than the affluent do. Yet the poor cannot afford to subscribe to *Consumer Reports*, even if they know of its existence.

Even though the more affluent are better able to protect their own interests, they may not necessarily be informed to the point where they can contribute measurably to society. The uninformed are hidden in every social stratum. Not many citizens in any stratum know how governmental agencies can help and serve them—or even how many offices and agencies are there to help. It is also clear that many citizens at any economic level really don't know how to seek advice on legal, medical, and educational matters.

What this means to the journalist has been summarized aptly by Derick Daniels, former executive editor of the *Detroit Free Press*, in a July 1970 article in *The Quill*. Journalists must recognize the reader's needs and desires, Daniels wrote, and "most of all [know] that he is hungry for information that will help him right now, to do something, or be something, or very simply, that will interest him." He then went on:

> We're going to have to force ourselves to recognize that what's talked about in the kitchen is just as important as what's talked about at the U.N. And I don't mean sitting around and nodding our heads and saying, "Yes, yes, we understand that the poor slob in the kitchen is interested in the price of soap when she *ought* to be interested in the U.N." I mean recognizing squarely, as a matter of intellectual honesty, that the kitchen is really, in fact, just as important. . . .
>
> "Kitchen news," in the broadest sense of that phrase, is being produced throughout the federal bureaus and agencies in terms that are enormous. The amount of knowledge and information collected, studied, and available through the U.S. government is very nearly limitless. A single document—the Yearbook of the Department of Agriculture—contains more usable information in its pages than most newspapers report in a year.
>
> Yet the myth goes on—Capitol Hill is covered five times more than it ought to be and the agencies go under-reported—year after screaming year.

It is clear that the media do not cover "kitchen news" from the federal agencies. Instead, Washington correspondents are lured by the "big stories" involving congressional leaders, the White House, and the State and Defense Departments. Only occasionally does a reporter win a place on the front page or on the evening news with a story from the Federal Trade Commission, meaningful as that story might be. A correspondent who covers the Railroad Retirement Board or the Department of Agriculture, for example, doesn't have the professional standing of correspondents who cover presidential press conferences, Capitol Hill, or the latest

Secretary of State's fact-finding trip to the Middle East. The result is a lack of information on the small, vital facts of government and of American life.

The public expects much more of the journalist, of course. Over many decades these general themes have emerged in the criticism of the press:

They have used their great power to promote the interests of their owners.

They generally have been the tool of big business and big advertisers.

They have resisted social change and perpetuated the status quo.

They generally have been more concerned with the superficial and the sensational rather than with the significant, and have concentrated on entertainment lacking artistic merit.

They have violated the privacy and debased the dignity of individuals, and have deprived those accused of sensational crimes of having fair trials.

They are controlled by members of a single socioeconomic class, and that control is in the hands of a very few people.

They are often inaccurate.

They have socialized people into consumer roles.

They have helped to make their audiences into spectators rather than doers.

They foster immediate success, leading American youth to believe that their desires are instantly attainable and that the long, slow processes of democracy are unnecessary.

They create news by their presence at the scene of news events.

The difficulty in assessing such charges is that examples can be found to support almost any of them—yet, examples alone do not prove general charges. Does anyone who reads the *Christian Science Monitor* or the *New York Times*, for example, really think that these papers are more concerned with the superficial than with the significant? Does the *New Yorker* endanger public morals? The point is that one cannot speak of the media as a monolith, all equally flawed and at fault.

What emerges from all this is the significance of the behavior of all those who take part in public communication. The Washington correspondent working at the highest levels of statecraft, the neighborhood reporter covering the smallest community events, the camera crew at the scene of an accident, the writer of an ad for a deodorant—all have positions of purpose and importance. The work of all influences the attitudes of the public toward mass communication.

THE ETHICS OF INTRUDING ON PRIVACY

Those who would treat politics and morality apart will never understand the one or the other.

—John Morley

An offense to good taste can arouse more emotions in a community than an offense to accuracy. Television producers and photographers are more especially vulnerable to public criticism over poor taste because pictures often have more emotional impact than words. Since taste is highly individual, journalists and advertising writers are largely without clear guidelines. The issue, of course, is privacy. Communicators need to inform themselves about the law of privacy—and to realize that underlying it are some ethical principles.

Members of the public are particularly touchy about stories involving death: pictures of a woman falling to her death stir quick and loud complaints. But stories involving election campaigns, for example, are also tricky. Consider these cases:

Case No. 1—A newspaper found that the mother of a candidate had been involved in a messy lawsuit in a neighboring state.

Case No. 2—A newspaper discovered that a candidate had been tried for manslaughter, but acquitted some years previously.

Should these findings be published?

Both reflect issues of privacy. The first case is relatively easy. It is difficult to believe that a lawsuit involving a candidate's mother in another state would affect the candidate's ability to discharge his duties. To publish these facts would be indulging in gossip, and the newspaper decided not to publish the information.

The second case is more difficult. It would be a fact of importance to the voters if the candidate had been *convicted* of manslaughter. But the candidate was running in a small town, and the editor feared that some of the people in the town would remember the case, that they would tell their friends, and, as so often happens, that the retellings could distort the story—perhaps to the point of reversing the acquittal or changing the charge to murder. The editor decided to head off such rumors by printing the truth.

In both of these cases, the Final Decisions of the editors were correct.

Coverage of prominent figures in the news can also raise questions. An editor reported this case:

Like other papers, we sent reporters and photographers to cover the honeymoon of Mr. and Mrs. X, whose marriage had been exciting news. The honeymooners tried hard to give the press the slip, and were naturally quite irritated at being followed. It seemed to me that famous people have to get used to little privacy, but the idea of following them on their honeymoon bothered me a little.

Is there a limit on the right of the public to know such things, especially when the individuals concerned do not want them known? Of course, the Final Decision agreed with the editor, who had doubts, not with the many reporters and editors.

THE PUBLIC'S RIGHT TO KNOW

There is no greater lie than a truth misunderstood.

—William James

There are cases in which news the public is entitled to know is withheld by the press.

In San Francisco, all local newspapers maintained 60 hours of silence about a kidnapping because they were told by the police that the man's life would be endangered by any publicity. The blackout of information was extended to the news services, the broadcasting stations, and the national networks. A major effort was obviously required to keep the blackout from being lifted somewhere in the country. Not until the man was freed and the kidnappers were taken into custody was the public told about the crime.

Although the public expects to be informed about such a crime, the question is whether reporting it immediately is more important than saving a human life. Most of the San Francisco newspapers expressed reservations, arguing that publicity had helped in solving other kidnapping cases. But the press obeyed the police, who contended that the man's life was truly at stake. Would publicity have contributed to solving the case? There is no way to know. Kidnappers are unpredictable. This case, of course, relies not on Faith, but on Ethics. The Final Decision applauds the editors' decision not to report.

EXERCISES

1. You are the director of the publications office at a university, and have an opening for an internship. You invite students to submit resumes and samples of their writing. To your surprise, two students claim to have had the same job at the same time, when you know there was only one vacancy. On paper, both students are at the top of the application group for your opening. You talk with each one individually, and learn that Student A had knowingly permitted Student B to list A's job on B's resume. Both students confirm these facts.

   What do you do? Reject B? Reject both? Report one or both to the administration?

2. You are the editor of a major college newspaper. When a new president is inaugurated, you publish the text of his address. Three days later, in a plain brown envelope, you receive a marked copy of his address and a speech given earlier by another college president. Six paragraphs are identical.

   You know the president was under much personal pressure when he wrote the speech. His daughter was being married, his wife was in an automobile accident. Presumably, he is embarrassed, but he will make no comment.

   As the editor, what do you do?

3. A young woman, who is 20, is arrested for shoplifting. She calls and pleads with you not to run a story, because "My grandmother is ill and this will kill her." As the editor of a small-town newspaper, what would you do?

NONJOURNALISTS ABOUT JOURNALISTS

Journalism is a profession whose business it is to explain what it personally does not understand.

—Lord Northcliffe

The newspaperman is, more than most men, a double personality; and his person feels best satisfied in its double instincts when writing in one sense and thinking in another.

—Henry Adams

I wonder where Christianity would be today if some of these reporters had been Matthew, Mark, Luke, and John.

—Senator Barry Goldwater

What would you say if a newspaper reporter, because of his fastidiousness or from a wish to give pleasure to his readers, were to describe only honest mayors, high-minded ladies, and virtuous railroad contractors?

—Anton Chekhov

Television is democracy at its ugliest.

—Paddy Chayefsky

Television? The word is half Latin, half Greek. No good can come of it.

—C. P. Scott

We interrupt these commercials to bring you entertainment.

—Ralph A. Brooks

CHAPTER 5

Clearing the Air Over Objectivity

The truth is more important than the facts.

—Frank Lloyd Wright

When a famous British diplomat was arriving in New York, he was warned by a friend about the American reporters. One reporter asked this question of the diplomat: "Do you plan to visit any night clubs while you are in New York, Lord Selwyn?"

Selwyn parried with, "*Are* there any night clubs in New York?"

The following morning, the reporter's newspaper carried a story beginning:

"Are there any night clubs in New York?" That was the first question British diplomat Lord Selwyn asked yesterday as he arrived. . . .

Was this story objective? Of course, the sentence quoted was the first comment Selwyn made to the reporter, as the reporter explained to his editor. By no means, however, could this reporter's explanation pass his editor, who snapped: "This isn't as simple as the law. You're bound by ethics, which is much wider than the entirety of the law."

DEFINING OBJECTIVITY

A definition is the enclosure of a wilderness of ideas within a wall of words.

—Samuel Butler

This chapter was written with the following conviction: No matter how close journalists approach objectivity, objectivity is an illusion.

The late Lester Markel of the *New York Times* attacked the notion of objectivity with these words spoken on September 12, 1968:

The reporter, the most objective reporter, collects fifty facts. Out of the fifty, he selects twelve to include in his story. Thus, he discards thirty-eight. This is Judgment Number One.

The reporter or the editor decides which of the facts shall be in the first paragraph of the story, thus emphasizing one fact above the other eleven. This is Judgment Number Two.

Then the editor decides whether the story shall be placed on Page One or Page Twelve; on Page One, it will command many times the attention it would on Page Twelve. This is Judgment Number Three.

This so-called factual presentation is thus subjected to three judgments, all of them most humanly and most ungodly made.

Also, consider this analysis by Gary Atkins, published in *Mass Media Issues* (Prentice-Hall, 1977):

All interpretation of behavior is not from the participant's standpoint, but from the observer's. The participant is presumed to be biased; the observer, detached and more factual. The result is always an unrecognized and un-criticized subjectivity, which is hidden under the guise of objectivity.

This is a point that almost no one considers—except journalists who have spoken and have been reported.

Atkins also has explored other facets, including this one:

Like a physicist who might study matter first as a wave, then a particle, so the journalist would move from vantage point to vantage point, from outside to inside, from empathy to detachment, realizing all the while that the search for more understanding and recognizing that the method he uses to approach reality will determine the type of truth he obtains. Each angle will provide a type of information and readers will better understand the phenomenon for having seen it from better perspectives.

We use "objectivity" frequently in this chapter, and, like other thoughtful journalists, we do not believe in objectivity. We know only that the better journalists can *approach* objectivity.

TRUTH AND OPINION

> *The true meaning of a term is to be found by observing*
> *what a man does with it, not by what he says about it.*
>
> —P. W. Bridgman

To report the truth is the goal of journalism, but the "true story" is a web of in-accuracies and opinions. Journalists seldom have the time, the resources, or the expert knowledge to find the full truth themselves. Of necessity, journalists gather

GARY ATKINS

Never think that anyone other than Gary Atkins knows what Atkins loves. He is the Chair of the Department of Journalism at Seattle University, but he describes himself this way: "I'm an introspective extrovert with one foot firmly planted in an academic library and the other in a newsroom with a police radio"—the latter because Atkins for six years was an award-winning investigative reporter and feature writer for the *Riverside Press-Enterprise* in Riverside, California. Atkins says:

I've enjoyed best those stories that have let me address both the over-riding social concerns and the impacts of those concerns upon the most "ordinary" people. I'm probably as comfortable keeping company with the homeless residents of a skid row hotel as with the sometimes dis-embodied intellects of a university. [I] consider myself incredibly for-tunate to have had many of my ideas about journalism shaped by experiences with people such as Norman Cherniss, editor; Howard Hays, executive editor; and Gordon Wilson, night managing editor, of the *Riverside Press-Enterprise*—all of whom understood in their very blood the importance of an independent, questioning journalism of high integ-rity, and weren't loathe to demand it of everyone entering their news-room.

Before joining the *Riverside Press-Enterprise*, Atkins wrote his "In Search of Objectivity" while he was studying for his master of arts degree. He began this article with these words:

Seldom has the concept of objectivity been at peace in its journalistic home. Since it became the dominant ideology of newspaper reporting a century ago, the debate about what the word means, and whether it should be an ideal or not, has been almost continuous.

Yet, for all the words written, those persons most concerned with the debate—the journalists themselves—have rarely tried to learn about their own argument, and about the concept of objectivity itself, by studying similar quarrels in other fields. Rather, they have chosen to argue about objectivity as if both they and it exist in a vacuum. They quote each other and rely solely on their own experiences in their argu-ments about old journalism versus new, objectivity versus subjectivity, straight reporting versus interpretation, and they do not raise questions about the origin of their concept of objectivity.

Yet, in that origin, and in the debates in other fields, is a key to understanding what the journalistic disagreement is about and a key to moving journalistic theory beyond the circular, often superficial, quarreling of the past.

Atkins then explored objectivity in what he then thought was at some depth. Compared to most journalists, his thoughts and the kinds of different perspectives certainly were profound, ranging across many outstanding journalists' opinions, thoughts of Johann von Herder, Leopold von Ranke, August Comte, and many other thinkers. For Atkins, then a young journalist, his study of objectivity was a triumph.

Now, though, still weighing and analyzing objectivity in 1987, Atkins wrote these words:

As for further thoughts about objectivity and its influence in shaping American journalism, I think that those using a "sociology of knowledge" approach—such as Michael Schudson, Dan Schiller, and Gaye Tuchman—have added much to our understanding of how the notion of objectivity has arisen in journalism.

In my thinking now, the question, "Does objectivity exist?" is meaningless if what is sought is some description of an "object" or "goal" that can be located within reality. It's a positivistic question that seeks an empirically verifiable state of existence. However, "objectivity" most certainly does exist if we understand it as a particularly potent symbol, a construct of language, that has come to describe and influence a vast number of relationships within American journalism: the relationship between the writer and the words he or she selects for the story; the relationship between the writer's own attitude to his or her subject matter and toward the audience; the relationship between the writer and the source; the type of acceptable style that an audience accepts as demonstrating "truth"; the expectations of the conduct of the journalistic interview; the selected means for empowering, through language, a certain large social and economic class; the types of behavior defined as ethical and unethical within the field of journalism.[*]

While considering many other facets of journalism, Atkins co-authored *Reporting With Understanding*, is co-authoring a book on mass media law, and has engaged in so many pursuits that benefit his students at Seattle University: redesigning and updating the department curriculum, introducing desktop publishing concepts, updating the library collection, and guiding students in preparing the weekly *Spectator*, which won recognition as one of the twenty best collegiate newspapers.

All of Atkins' activities may seem to leave him little time for sleep, but he is especially proud of his 10-year-old son, Nathan, "who keeps me laughing and conducts some of my best interviews."

[*]Personal correspondence, February 18, 1987.

information from those who do. Yet, all too often the experts disagree, and journalists must use their standard technique—attributing the information or opinion to the sources who provided it. The audience can then judge the information by judging the sources.

It would be simple if sources were as objective as journalists try to be. However, journalists and their audiences expect sources to flesh out the facts with judgments and opinions, and journalists have had no qualms about publishing opinions as long as they are clearly opinions. The journalists themselves have always been trained to be mere messengers—to serve as clear channels between the sources and the audience.

Herbert Brucker, the late editor of the *Hartford Courant*, defined one common measure of objectivity—whether a reader can tell the journalist's stand on an issue. If not, the journalist is objective.

What about bias that originates with the source? The journalistic solution to this problem is easy—get opinions from sources on all sides.

For a long time, this kind of objectivity served journalists well. It was comparatively convenient to get second and third opinions, because the reporters could still rely on specialists rather than original research. The journalist specialized in process—on collecting information from qualified sources and splicing it together before deadline. For relatively uncomplicated situations, the system worked.

But, relying on secondary sources in the face of deadlines encouraged journalists to use objectivity as a formula. The first step was to attribute unconfirmed information to a credible source. The source then validated the information. If deadlines prevent second opinions, at least the audience knew where the information and interpretation came from.

The second step was to get the views of the other sources, preferably for the original story. If the alternate views appeared in subsequent stories, it was acceptable, according to the Fairness Doctrine that governs broadcasting.

A third optional step was to recount information given out in the past, so that the audience could compare what the sources were saying now with what they or others had said previously.

For many fast-breaking, controversial stories, the first step was the only step taken—a convention that Senator Joseph McCarthy exploited with great skill. As a United States senator, he was a credible source. However, McCarthy came up with new charges so fast that reporters had difficulty checking his information with other sources—and the other sources themselves were cowed by McCarthy's "Red Hunts."

This narrow conception of objectivity falls short of providing the "essential correspondence between knowledge of a thing and the thing itself," which Donald McDonald has held necessary to produce "a substantially truthful account of contemporary public affairs." McDonald, a former journalism dean writing as editor of *Center Magazine* in the early 1970s, argued that an objective reporter could successfully communicate a complex, unfolding reality through interpretive reporting grounded in the realities of a situation. The reporter's story should make clear,

McDonald explained, the grounds upon which the reporting was based, because this served to establish the reporter's perspective.

An even broader meaning of objectivity gained wider acceptance as a result of encounters and changing expectations in the turbulent 1960s and 1970s. James Boylan, founding editor of the *Columbia Journalism Review*, articulated the change in reviewing Dan Schiller's *Objectivity and the News*. Boylan wrote, "Objectivity has gradually come to be understood not only as an impersonal 'balanced' style of newswriting (which is the commonplace, or newsroom, sense of the word), but also [to be seen as] representing the broader claim of journalism for its position in society—that of an impartial third party, the one that speaks for the general interest." The psychology has switched from seeming to be uninterested to being disinterested.

A more thorough type of reporting has developed in the last 25 years, drawing on careful, detailed research. Today's serious reporter checks out many sources involved in a controversial story, accumulating numerous versions of reality.

The reporter then evaluates the evidence—distilling it, sorting out contradictions, and presenting the opinions in context. Anthony Smith described the process in *Goodbye Gutenberg* (Oxford University Press, 1980). Objectivity, he wrote,

> fostered the collection of information on the basis of a special diction, which restricted the definition of a statement to that which could be assented to by all. . . . It was what was left after the combined scepticisms of the age were stripped away from the reporter's vision of the world.

But, broad or narrow, objectivity remains a means to an end. It is the method used to present a picture of the world that is as honest and accurate as possible within the limits of journalistic practice.

As a means, then, objectivity is a focus of ethical critique. Theodore L. Glasser made this clear when he wrote in November 1984 in *The Quill*, "Objectivity requires only that reporters be accountable for *how* they report, not what they report." The result, he said, is a disregard for "the consequences of their reporting." Objectivity precludes responsibility, he asserted.

Objectivity is supposed to serve the journalistic mission of presenting an accurate picture of the world. Distortion through deliberate misapplication is ethically wrong as well as factually wrong. If the picture is distorted because objectivity is consciously ignored, that is even more clearly wrong. The middle ground of mechanical, unthinking objectivity is the target for most critics.

CRITICISMS

> *No man thoroughly understands a truth until*
> *he has contended against it.*
>
> —Ralph Waldo Emerson

The comments cited above by Donald McDonald were from an article entitled "Is Objectivity Possible?" (*Center Magazine*, November/December 1976). The question is a legitimate one. McDonald concluded that serious journalists could achieve an objectivity that would further their efforts to convey an accurate picture of the world.

Some critics of objectivity, however, shirk constructive criticism by saying it is impossible to be objective in the first place, so why bother. They would find support in the comments of "Gonzo" journalist Hunter Thompson in *Fear and Loathing on the Campaign Trail* (Straight Arrow Books, 1973):

> As for my objectivity, well, my doctor says it swole up and busted about ten years ago. The only thing I ever saw that came close to Objective Journalism was a closed-circuit TV set-up that watched shoplifters in the General Store at Woody Creek, Colorado. I always admired that machine, but I noticed that nobody paid much attention to it until one of those known, heavy, out-front shoplifters came into the place. . . . [W]hen that happened everybody got so excited that the thief had to do something quick, like buy a popsicle or a can of Coors and get out of the place immediately. . . .
>
> So much for Objective Journalism. Don't bother to look for it here—not under any byline of mine; or anyone else I can think of. With the possible exception of things like box scores, race results and stock market tabulations, there is no such thing as Objective Journalism. The phrase itself is a pompous contradiction in terms.

What Thompson overlooked was that his readers neither expected nor wanted objectivity from him. A general circulation newspaper is another story—readers expect straight forward stories, unless the story is actually labeled as opinion.

Richard Strout, longtime Washington correspondent for the *Christian Science Monitor*, gives yet another perspective. On a Public Broadcasting Service program in April 1984, Bill Moyers asked him, "We reporters can never be objective, can we?"

Strout responded, "No, we shouldn't be, but we should keep it under restraint."

Mechanical objectivity can produce simplistic reporting. There are often more than two sides to a situation and the various opinions, with all their qualifications, may overlap. When a reporter must leave out such qualifications—or secondary information and details—to simplify or condense the story, the result can be close to caricature. As Donald McDonald wrote in *Center Magazine* (Nov./Dec. 1976), "Ordinary public affairs do not happen or exist with their explanatory context already built into them. They must be investigated, not simply looked at. And then the materials must be interpreted."

A related criticism is that unthinking objectivity causes incoherent or discontinuous coverage. Stories that rely on expert sources may take on the sources' focus, sometimes at the expense of details that give context. But, giving context means including interpretive, judgmental information that is hard for automatic objectivity to deal with. Over time, ongoing stories are spots in a mosaic without pattern or meaning.

Qualifications and explanation also suffer from space and time limitations because they are considered less newsworthy than breaking events. Thus, a continuing situation is covered sporadically, only when events give it enough interest to exceed the news threshold. The audience can lose the thread of a story, and the journalist must provide context for a story out of the news even for a few days. This criticism, of course, is applicable to the overall news judgment process and not just to objectivity.

Automatic objectivity can lead the story astray if the only available source (say, the White House press office) controls the information. Worse, the source may make the news public shortly before deadline, so that reporters have no time for checking other sources. If the source is the only one qualified to comment, the objective journalist is bound to present the source's version even if the reporter fears it is distorted.

Another criticism of mechanical objectivity is that it treats all opinions as equal. Some opinions come from understanding, some from ignorant reaction; the constraints of tradition do not always allow the reporter to indicate which is valid and which is not.

Some journalists argue that reporters should not give their blessing to any of the opinions given by their sources—that the judgment should be left to the audience.

But can the journalist in conscience dump the task on busy readers and the viewers? The public may not be willing to grapple with the burden of objectivity—and they are just as biased as reporters and editors.

Even the erudite critics must develop a greater awareness that they are sometimes as subject to bias—especially through selective perception—as the most uneducated reader. Thus, a scholarly professor used the discussion period following an address by a free-lance journalist to berate a newspaper that had long been the object of his scorn. The professor had read an Associated Press report of a news conference and found it quite different from the one that appeared in the paper. "They took that Associated Press story, changed the headlines, changed the words, then published the whole biased business," he said. The journalist replied that one part of the change could not be true because the Associated Press does not send headlines with its dispatches. It was enough to cause him to check up on the complaint. He found that the paper had not used the Associated Press report at all, but had printed a story from its own correspondent—and clearly labeled it with a byline. The professor had been schooled in the apprehensions of scholarship, but he had allowed his disdain for the paper to color his perception of its report.

One political analyst says:

Most of the voters I talk with are far more biased in their political views than the newspapers I read. Whatever the newspapers do, most voters will continue to shut their eyes and ears to all except what they agree with.*

But if the thrust of his statement is an indictment of readers, it also indicts the press. "More biased than the . . . press" certainly indicates some measure of press bias. Many thoughtful journalists will admit, even as they defend the mass media, that at least a few newspapers and broadcasts are biased.

Critics of the mass media must begin by recognizing that not all the fault is on one side or the other—that critic and journalist have human failings—or criticism and defense degenerate into a shouting match.

One must recognize further that some journalists are complacent—that they defend their profession by saying that all human enterprises are subject to human failings. As an executive of Time, Inc., said, "All writers slant what they write no matter how hard they try. All readers slant what they read. If not, it's accused of bias." As far as it goes, this is true. But it does not go far enough—especially in considering *Time*. After all, T. S. Matthews, who worked for *Time* for more than twenty years and eventually became its editor, wrote in his autobiography, *Name and Address* (Simon and Schuster, 1960):

> I said that I thought the presidential campaign of 1940 was the last one that *Time* even tried to report fairly. . . . In 1952, when it sniffed victory in the air at last, there was no holding *Time*. The distortions, suppressions, and slanting of its political "news" seemed to me to pass the bounds of politics and to commit an offense against the ethics of journalism.

Although this book is concerned with all the mass media, it is important to consider whether an indictment of one publication says anything about any other. *Time*, for example, does not claim to report the news objectively. Indeed, its founders declared that since absolute, machine-like objectivity is obviously impossible, *Time* would not even attempt to present an objective report. Instead, in judging a controversial issue, the editors would indicate which side "has the greater merit." But newspapers—and many magazines and the electronic media—have an entirely different orientation. They are committed to report as objectively as is humanly possible in their news columns and broadcasts. The extent of the failure of any one to accomplish this aim cannot be judged according to the standards of *Time*, or even by the failings of most other media, but must be judged individually.

Similarly, one must discriminate between entertainment and news. Critics tend to view all the media—newspapers, magazines, radio, and television—as a single entity, and to make scalding judgments about the trivia that seems to pervade the mass media in general. But each medium is different. Radio and television primarily entertain; most newspapers and magazines run information only partly to entertain. One cannot tar all the media with one broad brush.

Mechanical objectivity also feeds cynicism. Reporters may see their sources

*Interview, March 19, 1985.

as tricksters and manipulators. Scholars may take a scoffing stance against both sides. The attitude creeps into the stories. In political coverage, for example, both Democrats and Republicans may be portrayed as low-life politicians. This not only undercuts the trust necessary for a democratic society, but it can alienate un-sophisticated readers and viewers. Reporters sometimes forget that most of their audience is not part of the inner circle in which journalists rotate.

OBJECTIVITY AS PROTECTION

> *Fraud and falsehood only dread examination.*
> *Truth invites it.*
>
> —Thomas Cooper

One school of thought sees objectivity as a technique to protect the journalist. For example, in the January 1972 issue of the *American Journal of Sociology*, Gaye Tuchman described objectivity as a "strategic ritual" that protects journalists from such dangers as libel suits. After spending time in newsrooms observing journalistic behavior, she analyzed the practice of objectivity and found it to consist of four strategies—presenting conflicting possibilities in a situation, presenting evidence to support controversial statements, making judicious use of quotations so that dangerous information is safely attributed to credible sources, and structuring news stories into the inverted pyramid sequence intended to emphasize the newsworthy aspects of the situation. Tuchman held that the decisions behind the strategies were based on news judgment, which she characterized as the sacred knowledge that differentiates journalists from other people. This journalistic creed assumes reporters and editors have the ability to choose "objectively" among competing "facts" in deciding which are newsworthy. When the "facts" are questioned (about the information disseminated by the military in Vietnam, for example), doubts arise about the choice.

Herbert Gans has written a good deal about these matters. He stresses the economics of journalism as well as self-protection in explaining objectivity. In order for the media to produce the required number of news stories for a largely uninterested but potentially hostile audience, he says, journalists need a cost-effective way to operate. The knowledge and time needed to achieve an adequate understanding of all these controversial situations is more than the media can afford. The answer, then, is to get the information from sources who have the knowledge, time, and resources, but to clearly attribute conflicting opinions to these sources.

Barbara Phillips adds to the explanations of Tuchman and Gans her view that objectivity's emphasis on concrete facts at the expense of context interferes with the development of systematic knowledge about a situation on the part of the journalist, and, ultimately, the audience.

Practicing journalists are apt to see objectivity as something more than a protective or cost-cutting device and to feel that it can enable the journalist to put a story into perspective. A. M. Rosenthal, former executive editor and now columnist of the *New York Times*, considers objectivity an essential part of the character of the *Times*.

"It is the character of the paper that has made its readers trust it and therefore made it meaningful and valuable," he wrote in a memorandum for the staff in 1969, when the debate was raging about objectivity. He then listed the beliefs on which that character rests:

> The belief that although total objectivity may be impossible because every story is written by a human being, the duty of every reporter and editor is to strive for as much objectivity as humanly possible.
>
> The belief that no matter how engaged the reporter is emotionally, he tries as best he can to disengage himself when he sits down at the typewriter.
>
> The belief that expression of personal opinion should be excluded from the news columns.
>
> The belief that our own pejorative phrases should be excluded, and so should anonymous charges against people or institutions.
>
> The belief that every accused man or institution should have the immediate right of reply.
>
> The belief that we should not use a typewriter to stick our fingers in people's eyes just because we have the power to do so.
>
> The belief that presenting both sides of an issue is not hedging, but is the essence of responsible journalism.

He then concluded, "The nature of the *Times* rests on what can be demonstrated, . . . reported, dissected, analyzed, rather than on what can simply be labeled or characterized or caricatured."

A few years later, Tom Winship, former editor of the *Boston Globe*, rallied his staff members to serve both sides in a bitter dispute over school busing. "Our news columns must be believed," he asserted, "not just by those who agree with our editorial policy, but by those who disagree."

Objectivity is not some hidden or unconscious strategy, say practicing journalists. Herbert Brucker spoke for them when he wrote in the *Saturday Review* (Sept. 23, 1967):

> Any newsman qualified for his calling and tempered by experience can tell the difference between a slanted story and a fair one. Objective reporting is nothing more than what good reporting has always been: the work of a disciplined professional who has tried his damndest to get the whole story, and then to present it accurately and honestly without letting his own bias creep in.

Often, a strong relationship develops between reporters and sources. Both parties, in a sense, collaborate in constructing the news. As long as the source and reporter share a similar viewpoint, the relationship is usually comfortable. Both parties naturally come to share some perceptions of what is going on. This helps them to understand each other, but it also opens the way for easy abuse of the truth.

Sources and reporters have different loyalties. The sources serve their institutions—the reporters, their audience. Of course, both have secondary loyalties, but professionalism requires that they serve their primary interests first. If the reporters subordinate the audience's interest to that of the sources' institution, the priorities are getting mixed up. In such a case, bias is distorting the truth. Journalists should clearly understand and state, if only to themselves, the justifications for such distortion.

Reporters who cover a complex situation for some time may come to be quite knowledgeable and can interpret the story on their own. Their opinions become credible to members of the public who know they have been covering the story. How can objective journalism allow such reporters to express their opinions?

Traditionally, journalists expressed their opinions through editorials, and some news organizations allow informed reporters to do editorials. Sometimes these are presented as commentary, which identifies the opinions as the reporter's own rather than those of the organization. Television has been more accepting of commentary by its reporters than newspapers have; newspapers more often have reporters write interpretive articles labeled "news analysis." This approach still sharply limits the expression of the reporter's opinions, but it gives the reporter more freedom than news stories.

The tag of news analysis or commentary is a step in a direction being advocated on some fronts today: to include—with or in the article—information that indicates where the journalist stands. The public can then take that into consideration in judging the credibility of the information.

The social scientists confront the implications of objectivity more forthrightly than journalists. The social scientists recognize the influence of the earlier literature in a field, the influence of all aspects of one's culture on how one sees the world, and the forces stemming from one's own personality and experience. These powerful forces have instilled within people valuations, largely hidden from one's belief system, that shape their views. As long as these values operate without people being aware of them, they cannot erase bias by "keeping to the facts" or refining their methods of dealing with information. The late Gunnar Myrdal contends that people must expose such valuations to full light and make them conscious, specific, and explicit. By spelling out such a set of "instrumental value premises," people can see where biases might arise and then compensate for them. Furthermore, scientists or reporters can include information about their value premises in their articles to enable the audience to consider them and judge their impacts on the information being reported.

Journalists could benefit from following Myrdal's advice. If they recognize how they feel about an issue, they can be on guard against letting their feelings affect the way they handle it.

Psychologists and educators have developed various "values clarification" exercises. Here is a modification of one exercise that has proved useful in journalism classes. In a class, it can dramatize the power of mutual values, but, individually, it can illuminate one's own feelings about a controversial topic.

One starts by selecting a topic, preferably a current one. Reporters could choose a topic they may write in the foreseeable future. Some examples are homosexual rights, raising the drinking age, eliminating tax shelters, supplying arms to Central American nations or to the Middle East, or abortion on demand. For this example, select homosexual rights. Most people have pronounced feelings on this subject.

First, one states a forthright proposition about the subject. For example, "Homosexuals of the same sex should be able to marry one another with all the rights enjoyed by heterosexual married couples, including living next door to me and my family, belonging to my church, and having their homosexual friends as guests for a backyard barbecue."

First, one writes a sentence or two or some phrases or clauses that state one's opinion about this proposition. Then, one answers the following questions, marking one point for each "yes":

1. Did you come to your opinion through your own considerations independently?
2. Did you adopt your position after considering other opinions on the issue?
3. Have you made your opinion known to others? (For example, do your acquaintances or members of the public know what your opinion is?)
4. Are you proud of your position on this issue?
5. Have you debated the issue with others, formally or informally?
6. Have you taken overt action to show your opinion—in demonstrations about gay rights, for example?
7. Have you considered the consequences of acting on your belief?

The total score is a measure of how strongly one feels about the proposition. If a reporter's score is closer to seven than to one, the reporter should be on the lookout for bias. Even a low score might reflect an unconscious bias.

The purpose of such an exercise is to bring out feelings, opinions, or assumptions that might otherwise remain below the level of one's awareness—what Wesley Maurer labeled in his journalism classes at the University of Michigan as "inarticulate majors premises." Such depth of feelings is often related to the seriousness with which one takes one's endeavors.

People who take themselves too seriously are so intense about the issue at hand that they fail to see it in its real perspective. One sign of this human quality is that people often don't appreciate humor aimed at their unexamined beliefs. For example, a letter writer, Leland F. Smith, complained to *Editor and Publisher* (Nov. 24, 1979) that the liberal orientation of many editors kept cartoonists and letter writers from caricaturing liberals as heartily as they did conservatives. He said that editors consistently eliminated from his letters any such caricaturistic element as "the cave men who joined their Jane Fondas and picketed against fire had to carry large, flat rocks for their signs." To an extent, Leland Smith's complaint has lost some of its sting in recent years, but his point still deserves to be made. One's biases can affect one's judgment of what is appropriate for publication. By bringing those biases into one's awareness, one can then make better judgments about such matters.

Becoming aware of their biases helps journalists to protect themselves from unconsciously distorting their reporting. But it also brings journalistic ethics more clearly into light, where they cannot be ignored. Could it be that Pandora's Box contained ethical questions rather than the evils themselves? To deal with such questions requires awareness—of the dangers of error, of hurting someone, of betraying a source, of misleading an audience, of losing self-respect. To the sensitive journalist, the advice of Polonius, "To Thine own self be true," takes on a sharp, unforgiving character.

COPING WITH PSEUDO-EVENTS

Prose is architecture, not interior decoration.

—Ernest Hemingway

Recently, a student attended the wedding of a family friend. The reception that followed was stilted and tedious. It was held in a hall that was arranged for dancing, a fact which impressed no one present. Guests sat in chairs along all four walls, staring in the direction of their opposite member on the other side of the room. The family of the bride appeared to be among the bored attendants. The photographer who was covering this event, having already arranged and photographed all possible combinations of relatives, looked to be despairing of his task. Finally, he approached the mother of the bride, who was firmly planted in one of the wall chairs beside her teenage son. The photographer told her that he wanted a picture of mother and son dancing. Without a word passing between them, they rose, adopted the dancing position, feet firmly set on one spot, and looked into the camera. The flashbulb popped, and, still without a word passing, they resumed their seats, staring across the empty dance floor.

Was this actually a pseudo-event? The couple seemed to dance, but they never really danced. What if, at the photographer's suggestion, mother and son had risen and shuffled a bit until the picture was taken? What if they had finished the dance? What if they had tried the next one? What if they had inspired everyone else to join in, until the room was full of dancing guests? Would these have been pseudo-events? Would they have been more or less pseudo? Just what is necessary for a genuine pseudo-event?

Writing in *Current* magazine (June 1962), historian Daniel Boorstin specified four characteristics of a pseudo-event: (1) It is planned, planted, or incited; (2) it is planted primarily for the purpose of being reported or reproduced; (3) its relation to the underlying reality of the situation is ambiguous; and (4) it is usually intended to be a self-fulfilling prophecy. Another characteristic which is implied in Boorstin's description, although not specifically stated, is that it is, more or less, a public event. These qualities do not define, they merely characterize a pseudo-event. Only the first characteristic, the aspect of planning, is both tangible and necessary to the pseudo-event. The other three characteristics serve mainly to describe the trappings these events usually carry. Because planning is the one aspect of the pseudo-event which, as Boorstin describes it, is both necessary and definitive, one can begin to get a better idea of what a pseudo-event entails by considering the planning dimension.

The question of whether or not a train wreck engineered by an individual is a pseudo-event highlights the planning dimension. What are the ways, with regard to planning, that an event may occur? An event may occur as a result of an act of nature, as a result of an unintentional human act, or as the result of an intentional human act. An act of nature is undeniably real. An unintentional human act is also an insufficient basis for a pseudo-event. If a train wreck is caused by a sudden earthquake, it is not a pseudo-event. If it is caused by a careless hobo discarding trash on the track, it is not a pseudo-event. Deliberate planning is essential. But not all planned events are pseudo-events. We confer with our co-workers, we join a jogging club, we gather with our neighbors to pull a boat up on the beach. All are planned, real events. They differ from pseudo-events in that they do not now, and will not in the future, masquerade as spontaneous. Planning a pseudo-event involves the intention to present a false impression or to deceive someone, either at present or in the future, into believing that the event was other than what it was. But is this enough? What about the train wreck that results from someone deliberately throwing a switch? This still fails to qualify as a genuine pseudo-event, because the realities of the situation far outweigh the less essential considerations of cause and motivation. The people involved suffer real injury; the community reacts to real tragedy. The public aspect of this event—the aspect to which the public responds—is real. This can be contrasted to a pseudo-event, in which the whole community responds as if a train wreck has occurred, when, in fact, it hasn't.

Add two specifics to Boorstin's list. The planning should include some intention to deceive, and the unreality of the situation should outweigh its reality. This latter characterization implies the conclusion, that, not only are there real events and pseudo-events, but there is a continuum of somewhat real to somewhat pseudo which lies in between.

Returning to the wedding example, it is marked by the characteristics of intention to deceive and more unreality than reality, along with Boorstin's characteristics of planning and planning primarily for recording. However, the characteristics of ambiguity and planning as a self-fulfilling prophecy are lacking in the event as it actually happened, but present to a greater degree in the hypothesized cases where mother and son graduated from shuffling a few steps to infecting the whole room with the spirit of the dance. Does this mean that the event as it actually happened, was not a pseudo-event at all? That only if the players had tried harder to match reality to the performance would it be a true pseudo-event? A room full of people enjoying themselves as shown in a photograph has a greater claim to the title "pseudo-event" than the sham which occurred.

The answer is that the requirements for ambiguity and for the intention of a self-fulfilling prophecy have nothing to do with how "pseudo" an event is; they relate, rather, to how likely it is that the particular pseudo-event will be successful. The wedding example lies on the far end of the real-pseudo continuum; it is super-pseudo. Because such a false event usually has little chance of being successful, Boorstin does not even consider it. Most people cannot tolerate performing with total disregard of reality; it is, at least, embarrassing. Instead, create an unstructured environment in which unreality is sufficiently sprinkled with reality to allow the deception process to proceed. This adding of reality to the unreality results in the ambiguity and the intention of self-fulfilling prophecy that marks the more usual, and successful, pseudo-event. Few of us could have looked at, or shown, the staged pictures to our friends without being reminded of how deathly dull the event was or of how falsely the pictures represented it. But, to the extent that some people can work this deception on themselves or on others, even ambiguity becomes unnecessary to the pseudo-event.

Thus, revise Boorstin's characterizations of pseudo-events to read: (1) A pseudo-event should be planned, usually for the purposes of being recorded; (2) have a public aspect; (3) include the intention to deceive; and, in some sense, (4) involve more unreality than reality. If such a pseudo-event is to be successful, it should include ambiguity and the intention to become a self-fulfilling prophecy.

EXERCISES

1. You are a professor at your university and tell your students to write a feature story. Surprisingly, two students hand in separate papers, which are almost identical. You remember reading something similar earlier, read back issues of the daily campus newspapers, and find that both have used this newspaper as their source, without any attribution.

    What do you do?

    a) If one of the students were the child of a close faculty colleague, would you do anything different?

    b) If you were not a professor, but simply a student in the class who heard something like this had happened, how would you react?

    c) Should the professor tell the class what happened? If so, should the names of the students be disclosed?

WORDS ABOUT REPORTERS

Journalists write with their feet, not their hands.

—Roy Peter Clark

A political journalist may be a stablemate to a statesman.

—Henry Adams

Some people pay a compliment to a journalist as if they expected a receipt.

—Frank McKinney Hubbard

A political leader is essentially an advocate—a man who is seeking to shape the world toward ends he considers worthy. A newspaperman, on the other hand, is one whose job is to chronicle daily events and to place the facts before the public in some reasonable perspective. Events and facts have a life of their own. They are independent of the dreams and desires of men.

—George Reedy

A journalist is a man who missed his calling.

—Anonymous

CHAPTER 6

The Ethics of Gathering News

What plays the mischief with the truth is that men will insist upon the universal application of a temporary feeling or opinion.

—Herman Melville

When a state held elections a few years ago, a young reporter was assigned to write a profile of the winning candidate for attorney general. He conducted a highly successful interview. The new attorney general was expansive, talking at length about how he had long been an "almost man": almost elected president of the student council in high school, almost elected president of the student body, graduated second in his class in law school. He was overjoyed by the election results: At last, he had finished first. At the end of the interview, he said, "Of course, you'll let me read that story before it's published."

Ignorant of common practice in journalism, the young reporter said, "Of course."

The reporter was proud of the story he showed the attorney general. It was built around a theme, tracing the career of the "almost man" through his many defeats to his eventual triumph. The attorney general admitted that nothing in the story was inaccurate, but he disliked the theme. "If the voters see this kind of emphasis in your story," he said, "they'll think they elected a second-rater." Although the reporter had not agreed to change what he had written, the alternatives were clear. He changed it. The result was a routine story, not nearly as interesting, unified, or true as the first version.

The reporter made two basic errors: First, he should not have agreed to allow the source to read the story before it was published; second, since there was no inaccuracy, he should not have agreed to change it. Why he should not have done either is implicit in the outcome. Most public officials (and many private citizens, especially celebrities) consider total praise not half enough and insist on deleting facts or changing emphases that someone might consider negative. If a story relies on many sources, each is likely to believe that he or she should have been quoted more elaborately—and probably earlier in the story.

This common attitude helps to explain why most journalists yield only with the greatest reluctance to demand by officials or celebrities to check stories. Journalists are almost unanimous in insisting that their stories should never be checked by sources—officials, celebrities, or private citizens—before publication or broadcast.

Unfortunately, the general rule that journalists should not allow sources to check their stories is often observed blindly. Journalists should not be so jealous of their work that they will not call a source and read a passage over the phone to make certain the facts are straight. Those who are that shortsighted contribute heavily to the worst sin of journalism—inaccuracy—and to the widespread and deplorable practice of "writing around" information the reporter does not quite grasp. More reporters should learn from science writers, some of whom are aware that they need to check their work with authorities to make certain that the technicalities and complexities of the subject are reported accurately.

THE NEON'S MISSION

> *To be persuasive, we must be believable,*
> *To be believable, we must be credible,*
> *To be credible, we must be truthful.*
>
> —Edward R. Murrow

Reporters are driven to find out what happened. They have nurtured their sense of curiosity and refined their skills in satisfying it.

A reporter's curiosity may be triggered by almost anyone. Most stories are assignments, which may be handed down from on high, but they often result from discussions between reporters and editors. Something makes them aware of a topic, and their discussions recast the topic into the form of a possible story.

The nature of a story affects both the process of gathering information needed for it and the processes of preparing and presenting it. The requirements of a spot news story are different from those of a trend or feature story. The topic may determine the form of the story, so that the research is simply a matter of getting or confirming the details. Frequently, the topic needs to be presented in a particular form to make it effective or understandable. For example, the placement of the story, the number of photos used, and the space allotted for the story can all have ethical implications, as well as the decision to cover the story at all.

Consider for a moment the many stages involved in producing a newspaper or a broadcast program. Reporters gather news, editors process it, printers and pressmen print it, anchormen and anchorwomen present it, engineers broadcast it, circulation workers deliver it, advertising staffers get the revenues for it. People in one compartment have a hard time communicating with people in another compartment, but the reader or viewer receives the whole as an integrated product and assumes that all those compartments aim to satisfy her or his needs and demands. Ethical questions can arise at virtually any point in the process, but, because of the very complexity of the task, ethical issues may get short shrift. The headline writer may not understand why the story is on page two; the engineer may not understand, for example, why the story must air at 7:00 P.M. instead of at 11:00 P.M. Both decisions affect the impact of a story. Sometimes, the only point of contact between departments is in their shared mission as a media organization.

TRUTH: HONESTY IN ACTION

An intimate truth is also a universal truth.

—John Cournos

The journalists' dominant ethical imperative of truth-telling affects the way they research and write a story. Some information doesn't fit the storytelling task, and they see less need for getting it and testing its accuracy. Awkward facts that don't further the story are likely to be left behind, or even bent. The distinction between usable and unusable information is based not only on craft criteria, but on subjective criteria as well. There is plenty of room for judgments with ethical implications.

From the very outset, journalists ask questions from their understanding of a story's possibilities. A journalistic story describes the significance, impact, or interest of a real event or situation. The facts that a reporter gathers must also convey credibility.

Notice that telling the truth is different from being credible. The journalistic story includes evidence to support its picture of an event or situation, and it adheres to a particular form in the use of such things as language, illustration, organization, attribution.

Because reporters and editors work with a preconceived "plot," if the facts are widely different from what they expected, they are inclined to reject the story as unreal. Furthermore, although reputable journalists are not free and easy with the truth, the journalistic frame of reference gives significance mainly to information that will make the story credible.

So, if these are the criteria, what about the truth? If it is not credible, it will rarely be accepted. Credibility matters even above clarity—and if the information is obviously untrue, it may still be usable if it is attributed to a credible source. If journalists provide all the right clues, the burden of trying to discern the real truth is shifted to the audience.

THE DECEIVING LINE

Tell the truth,
But tell it slant.

—Emily Dickinson

Deceiving the public is a clear breach of traditional journalistic ethics, but deceiving sources has not been as clearly wrong.

Media professionals differ in their assessments of composite characters, fictionalized "true" stories, and books that use novel-writing techniques, such as those of journalists Gay Talese and Tom Wolfe and "journalistic" novels such as those of Truman Capote and Norman Mailer. Few of the "New Journalists" of the 1960s and their successors had the talent of Talese or Capote, but their disregard of traditional objectivity and attribution opened journalism to new possibilities. Those possibilities include a more revealing and entertaining kind of reporting, of course, but they also include practices more revealing of the writer's aims and limitations than of the truth.

Perhaps the two most abused of the techniques of deception have been the use of composite characters and the "re-creation" of events. Examples are rampant: Gail Sheehy's 1969 magazine story in *New York*, "Redpants and Sugarman," was presented as true, although readers were not told that the prostitute and pimp were composite characters. Carl Bernstein and Bob Woodward gave an unattributed depiction of Richard Nixon's private moments in *Final Days* (Simon and Schuster, 1976). Michael Daly of the New York *Daily News* included an unacknowledged, made-up character in his 1981 reports of violence in Northern Ireland. All are examples of what David Shaw, press critic for the *Los Angles Times*, calls "sleight of hand."

"Sleight of hand has no place in journalism," Shaw wrote in the last issue of 1981 in *The Bulletin of the American Society of Newspaper Editors*.

> Do journalism students and young reporters who read and admire Woodward and Bernstein (and Mailer and Talese and Capote and Wolfe) subsequently wonder, when they're writing their own stories: Why can't I reconstruct this conversation as it *probably* took place? And: What difference does it make if someone actually uttered the words I put into his mouth—especially if his name is changed (or withheld)—just so long as the essential truth is there?

The answers to those questions (and others of an ethical nature) come easier when journalists hearken to the expectations of their public. If they present their articles as true, the public expects them to be honest.

The alienation of the public has been a topic of concern among executives of the media, but their focus has too often been on the credibility that comes from "keeping our skirts clean." A potentially more serious cause of alienation lies in blunting the public expectation of media accuracy. In a 1985 speech, Robert MacNeil, one of the most respected of the broadcast journalists, warned that journalists in both broadcasting and print were increasingly competing for public attention with informational and entertainment media forms that do not hold truth as being as important as entertainment. The pressure grows constantly, he said, for journalists to adopt the dramatic values of the theater and the advertiser and let the truth slip. Those values are fine in their place, but not when the public expects the honest truth.

DAVID SHAW

Except for a few brief years—say, between the ages of seven and ten, when I was absolutely certain that I was destined to become the third-baseman for the Dodgers—I always wanted to be a newspaperman. Although my father assured me, with the certitude born of parenthood, that I would "never make any money doing that," I was unalterably convinced that journalism was my one true calling.

A feature writer with the *Los Angeles Times* since 1968, David Shaw appears to have accurately assessed his journalistic talents. Born in 1943 in Dayton, Ohio, Shaw took a full-time job as a reporter with the *Huntington Park Daily Signal* in Huntington, California, while attending UCLA.

Shaw's original enchantment with the press was reinforced by the readers of the *Huntington Park Daily Signal* when he was assigned to the "Man in the Street" section. Discovering that the American public shared his "lofty, almost awestruck view" of reporters, he had little trouble locating people "on the street" who welcomed the opportunity to be interviewed for his column.

"Few people romanticize reporters anymore," Shaw says. ". . . The role and function of the press has changed dramatically since 1963, and, to most of the general public, it has been a change for the worse. Reporters are no longer thought of as reliable and trustworthy observers and commentators but as partisans, provocateurs, collaborators, enemies."[*]

In the fall of 1973, Shaw was called in to see Bill Thomas, editor of the *Los Angeles Times.* Referred to as "T.H.E." to distinguish him from "the normal chain of command . . . one managing editor, two assistant managing editors, a metropolitan editor, three assistant metropolitan editors, and a partridge in a pear tree," Thomas suggested a specific assignment to Shaw. Unaccustomed to story assignments, Shaw preferred to remain unspecialized and free to write on any topic he chose. The topic Thomas chose for him was the American press.

"The one thing the press covers more poorly than anything else is the press," Thomas said. "We don't tell our readers what we do or how we do it. We don't admit our mistakes unless we're virtually forced to under threat of court action or public embarrassment. We make no attempt to *explain our problems*, our decisions, our fallibilities, our procedures. . . ."

In an attempt to increase the credibility, and possibly the circulation of the newspaper. Shaw set out to analyze, criticize, and make "value judgments" about the press, all in the upper left-hand corner of page one of the *Los Angeles Times.* Thomas informed him to treat the *Times* as he would any other newspaper, saying, "I hope you have a lot of friends outside the newspaper business. By the time you're through with this job, you may not have many left inside it."

Although his friends remained, Shaw did receive an abundance of complaints about his stories from the staff at the *Times*, with many reporters claiming that he was being "disloyal." Criticisms of Shaw's work were rarely referred to him personally, but words of discontent usually reached him through indirect channels. After claiming that Charles Champlin, the film reviewer for the *Times*, was "the Will Rogers of film criticism; he never met a film he didn't like," Shaw discovered that Champlin wrote a four-page memo to Thomas and that Jean Taylor, editor of the *Times'* feature and entertainment sections, let it be known that she thought Shaw had been "cruel."

Shaw, with his self-proclaimed "abrasive self-confidence," appeared undaunted by these reactions and continued his series of stories. Apparently not wishing to intimidate Shaw, Thomas did not pass along Taylor's subsequent moral outrage when Shaw described best-seller lists as "a sham—haphazard, imprecise, even dishonest, with the *Times'* list less valid than most."

In the process on researching his stories, Shaw arrived at the conclusion that newspaper reporters and editors are equally as guarded and suspicious of the press and just as likely to claim that they were "misquoted" or to reply "no comment" as the rest of the American public. When writing a story that argued "newspaper polls on political races seriously distort and undermine the electoral process," Ken Reich, supervisor of the *Times'* political polls, informed Shaw that it is "incestuous for one reporter from the *Los Angeles Times* to interview another reporter from the *Los Angeles Times* for a story to be published in the *Los Angeles Times* about polls being conducted by the *Los Angeles Times*."

Yet the strongest criticism and the harshest words were directed against Shaw when he took the initiative to praise his own paper *in* his own paper. After interviewing reporters throughout America concerning the various styles of sportswriting, Shaw discovered that the *Times* proved superior in this area. Despite a warning from Thomas that the story would appear "self-serving," Shaw replied, "If everyone said we were the worst, you'd let me use it," and he presented the facts as he found them. The deluge of complaints he received describing his writing as "highly subjective," "highly biased," "suspect," and "distorted" convinced Shaw to avoid stories that were complimentary to the *Times*.

Shaw's reports of factual inaccuracies, wrongheaded editorials, the use of fraudulent photographs, irresponsible and speculative reporting, sensationalism, a potential conflict of interest, and poor news judgment have earned him both criticism and respect from reporters and editors. As he continued his assault on both the *Times* and on the entire newspaper industry, one of Shaw's colleagues good-naturedly reflected the feelings of many reporters, "Christ, Shaw, aren't you ever going to say anything nice about us?"

—Jennifer Koch

*David Shaw, *Journalism Today* (New York: Harper's College Press, 1977).

JUSTICE: FAIRNESS FOR ALL

Justice is truth in action.

—Benjamin Disraeli

Journalists may focus on violations of truth when they discuss media ethics—but the public may be more offended by reporters' practices that involve fairness, privacy, and respect. These practices fall into a second category of ethical issues—justice—and they range from snooping to intrusion to theft of information.

Snooping. Snooping can range from rifling through people's trash cans to eavesdropping or bugging. These practices raise eyebrows, but interviewing neighbors, friends, and foes of the person is usually an acceptable journalistic tactic. Drawing the line is largely an ethical decision.

The *Miami Herald* was sharply criticized for staking out Senator Gary Hart's home in the spring of 1987 and reporting that a model, Donna Rice, apparently had spent the night there. This and a separate *Washington Post* investigation into the Senator's relationship with another woman led Hart to withdraw from the race for president. Although the *Herald* stopped short of deception or bugging, it drew attacks even from other journalists. In some cases their complaints were that such reporting made them uncomfortable. Others criticized the *Herald* for running with the story after a rather sloppy stakeout and without further checking. Yet they had difficulty pinpointing anything very unethical about it. They seemed to agree with the public that the incident demonstrated that Hart lacked the judgment or character a president should have.

When a *Washington Post* reporter asked Hart at a press conference whether he had ever committed adultery, the affair took on new significance for journalism. *Newsweek*'s Jonathan Alter said it "marked the crossing of some invisible journalistic threshhold" that opened politicians and possibly other public figures to probing questions about their character (*Newsweek*, May 18, 1987). The ethical question it raised was stated by Ron Dorfman in the June 1987 issue of *The Quill:*

> The test for journalism is the test of relevance: Does reporting on someone's secret life serve some public purpose of sufficient gravity to overcome the respect we owe to claims of privacy and human fellowship?

In Gary Hart's case, the Final Decision is Yes.

Intrusion. Intrusive practices are more controversial. In the spring of 1984, the Kennedy family held a private funeral for David Kennedy at Hickory Hill, the home of Ethel Kennedy in McLean, Virginia. The son of Robert Kennedy had been found dead in a hotel room in Palm Beach the day before. The press was out in force at the gate of the mansion's grounds to witness the event. Beyond photographing the scene with long-lens cameras, viewing the house through binoculars, and jostling to view the passing hearse, the press behaved. But reporters for both the *Washington Post* and the *New York Times* subsequently wrote of their discomfort or shame at serving what they felt was a morbid interest on the part of the public in the private grief of the Kennedy family. Their feelings were shared by many of their readers, but the readers read on because of their deep interest in this most public of families.

A few months earlier, the press was criticized for intruding on the privacy of families of marines killed when their quarters were blown up in Lebanon. In particular, critics focused on stakeouts by reporters and camera crews outside homes of families as marine officers arrived to inform them their sons or husbands were dead. The Marine Corps tried to protect the families, and, in doing so, aroused protests from the press. The problem is not an easy one to handle, but reporters learn from such experiences. One such reporter was James H. O'Connor of the *Syracuse Herald American*. He went to Camp Lejeune, North Carolina, with the mother of a marine from the Syracuse, New York, area. She had been told her son was dead and then had found out he was alive, but injured. O'Connor found her willing to talk about the affair, but it was an emotional trip for the reporter as well as for the mother.

When the marine stepped out of his ambulance, "I felt I was going to cry," O'Connor wrote in a column on November 6, 1983. But he then discovered the value of having talked with the mother. The marine "immediately was whisked into the hospital," O'Connor wrote. "I never saw him again."

The long Iranian hostage crisis of 1980 also provided lessons, though some might say the families of the hostages learned more about dealing with the press than the press learned about dealing with the families. In the early days of the crisis in the fall of 1979, the situation was much like that following the Lebanon tragedy. Robert Hershman, senior associate of the Carnegie Endowment for International Peace and a former reporter for the MacNeil/Lehrer Report, wrote in the *Columbia Journalism Review* (March–April, 1981) of the families' experience with the media.

"They were all here before we even had time to think," Hershman quotes the mother of one hostage as saying. "A camera crew approaching at full gallop can be a very frightening thing," another said. But their experience turned into a crash course in American media practice, he wrote. The families learned how the press used them and how they could use the press. "I could never shake off being considered a human interest story," the wife of a hostage said. "People kept asking me what I felt, not what I thought." They learned to word their responses to reporters carefully, but even that was problematic. "As often as not they would just paraphrase what we said and sometimes even distort it," one complained. "When we called to find out why, we were usually told, 'Your answer was too long,' but we always felt the distinctions that we made were important ones."

This may be the most common complaint against the press—that it distorts the truth by focusing only on the main point while humanizing the message. But Hershman noted another serious problem in his account: "All those months of human-interest stories didn't seem to make American attitudes toward the problem any more humane." To the contrary, he wrote, the focus on the suffering of hostages and their families may have made the idea of using force to solve the crisis more acceptable. These questions go to the heart of journalistic practice.

Theft. Stealing documents is generally considered going too far to get a story, but using documents stolen by others may seem more acceptable, particularly since the Supreme Court backed the *New York Times* and the *Washington Post* after they published the Pentagon Papers. Reporters may claim that they cannot determine the pedigree of the information, but using it because of the importance to the public may be subordinating means to the end.

Stealing information itself may be harder to define. Is a reporter stealing information by flipping over the identification tag on a person's briefcase in order to find out who it is emerging from a grand jury room? Maria Braden contended so in *The Quill* in December 1981. Is information stolen if the reporter gets it by pretending to be someone other than a reporter? American reporters routinely ferret out information the government doesn't want them to know. In the Soviet Union, where reporters work for the government or the Communist party, seeking such information would be considered espionage—the theft of information.

Overly aggressive research can divulge facts a source feels a reporter shouldn't have. The "Hildy Johnson" principle of getting a story at all costs has its followers, because being "scooped" by a colleague is even more embarrassing than not getting the story at all. But a reporter can always "update" the story with a telephone call and a little rewriting. The "all costs" theory represents the complete disregard of the means in order to reach the end.

BREACHES IN THE REPORTER'S CRAFT

Wise men learn by other men's mistakes, fools by their own.
—H. G. Bohn

Ethical encounters that raise questions of craft morality include failing to keep one's word, deceiving one's sources and colleagues, getting involved in a story, and being co-opted by one's sources.

Confidential Sources. Most cases involving keeping one's word arise in conjunction with confidential sources. Most investigative reporting and reporting on high policy matters would be difficult without them. The first involves wrongdoing; the second, top-level decision making, including "trial balloons" by those about to make decisions. A good many anonymous sources are leaking information to further their own aims.

While journalists believe they are right in keeping identities of sources secret, the courts have not always agreed. The Supreme Court, in particular, has asserted that reporters must identify their sources upon the request of a grand jury. Various states have enacted "shield laws" giving reporters limited degrees of protection, but the courts have not always been firm in supporting those laws, especially when they conflict with a defendant's right to a fair trial.

The issue sometimes comes down to a reporter's willingness to go to jail for contempt of court as the price for refusing to identify a source—and reporters have gone to jail. A recent case was that of Susan Wornick, a reporter for a Boston television station, who refused to tell in court in 1985 who told her of seeing police officers looting a drugstore. She was sentenced to three months in jail. One of the most prominently reported cases was that of Myron Farber, a reporter for the *New York Times*. He declined to turn over his notes for stories he wrote that led to a murder trial of a New Jersey physician. He was jailed until the physician was acquitted.

The question for the journalist confronted with the issue of keeping a source's identity secret is, as British journalist John Whale says, "To whom do I owe my primary loyalty—to this source or to my public?" Keeping the confidence enables the journalist to present a more accurate picture of significant news. It takes courage to refuse to identify sources, but it also takes courage to refuse information in confidence. If the journalist feels that the public will best be served by a lack of candor, he or she should at least negotiate how clearly the source can be identified and what conditions must occur before the reporter reveals the source's identity.

There are moments when the right thing might be to identify the source. A Los Angeles television reporter, Dave Lopez, heard in confidence a confession from William Bonin that he had killed 21 boys. The deal was that Lopez would have the story exclusively if he held it until Bonin, on trial for the murder of 10 of the boys, could get authorities to agree he would escape the gas chamber. When a newspaper published the basics of the confession, Lopez aired his story without identifying his source. He was summoned to the trial and at first refused to identify his source, but, on reconsideration, changed his mind on the grounds that Bonin had broken the deal and that he might escape conviction without Lopez's testimony.

Thoughtful editors are becoming more resistant to keeping a source's identity secret. While he was president of the American Society of Newspaper Editors, Richard D. Smyser, editor of the *Oak Ridger* in Tennessee, warned of the need to distinguish between confidential sources and "sorcerers" who seek to manipulate the press for political motives.

Sissela Bok offered a more substantial guideline in her book, *Lying* (Pantheon, 1978) when she asserted, "We can properly promise only what is ours to give or what is right for us to do in the first place." Reporters are not lone rangers; they need the permission of the organization that provides the reporter access to the public. It is the access, not the reporter, that interests the source. In practice, this means that the editor must assume the responsibility and authorize the reporter to make the promise.

DECEIVING SOURCES

When my love swears that she is made of truth,
I do believe her, though I know she lies.

—William Shakespeare

Journalists differ on whether it is ethical to deceive a dishonest source to get information. The staff of the *Chicago Sun-Times* once ran a tavern called The Mirage as
a sting operation. The operation produced a series of 25 articles in 1979 on pay-
offs solicited by inspectors and other officials from owners of bars and restaurants.
The series was nominated for a Pulitzer Prize, but some Putitzer Board members
objected because of the ethical implications. The reporters had been careful not to
violate entrapment laws, but critics of the operation contended that the posing by
the reporters came too close to the kind of sting the police might run.

The Final Decision is No.

A more routine kind of deception occurs when reporters do not identify
themselves as reporters when making telephone calls, or when they actually pose as
someone else. Another kind of deception, of course, is that of posing as a simple
consumer: A reporter will take, say, a car in perfect condition to garages to find
out if they say repair work is needed. Such deceptive means are justified on the
ground that they serve the good end of protecting gullible consumers.

In contrast to the above decision, the Final Decision is Yes.

Posing as an official, even one rather low in the hierarchy, is not usually
acceptable. A reporter in New Jersey was fined and sentenced to 30 days of community work after being convicted in 1983 of telling a murder victim's family she
was from the morgue to get information.

The Final Decision is No.

Another form of deception is the television ambush. Sources expect journalists to ask tough questions, but they usually don't expect to be confronted live
with charges and witnesses for which they have not been warned to prepare.
Journalists are on dangerous ground when they go beyond what courts routinely
provide to assure fair hearings.

Of course, it is easy to give advice. It is not easy for a reporter to resist temptation. A reporter striving for fame and fortune has a harder time resisting than do
successful reporters. Seymour Hersh acknowledged this when appearing on a panel
on media ethics at Syracuse University in the fall of 1983. His remarks were reported
by the student newspaper, the *Daily Orange.*

"I don't regret anything I did in the My Lai story, because I think what I did
was marginal," he said. "I think now, older and wise, I wouldn't (read the file on
the desk). I would come back again, and I would make clear that I would like to
see it."

"I'm a fat cat now," he went on. "When you're hungry you think differently
than when you're a fat cat."

Media practitioners may be stricter about deceptive reporting practices than the public. A survey of newspaper editors reported by a University of Iowa team of researchers in 1983 found that editors disapproved of hidden recording devices 7 to 1. A poll by the *Chicago Sun-Times* the year after its "Mirage" experience found the public approved recording devices 54 percent to 40 percent. The poll also found a 60 percent approval for reporters' not identifying themselves as reporters, 62 percent approving the use of hidden cameras, 55 percent approving the use of unidentified sources. The closest result was 45 percent for and 46 percent against paying sources for information.

CONFLICT OF INTEREST

We lie loudest when we lie to ourselves.

−Eric Hoffer

Journalists who appear to have conflicts of interest lose credibility, and every loss from the organization's pool of credibility is a threat to the organization's survival.

Journalists are targets for favors, if not outright bribes. When an individual reporter accepts a favor, the problem is usually obvious. When the organization accepts free or subsidized trips for its reporters and editors, the problem is less so. If the trips help journalists to meet sources and cover their beats, who loses if they refuse to go? How can a small town television critic from the midwest ever meet network stars and producers without network-sponsored trips to Hollywood? How about the editor in Alaska, where high air fares limit the visits to the oil fields of Prudhoe Bay, but the oil companies fly back and forth all the time and have spare room on the planes? What about the opportunities to fly on planes with presidents and governors at government expense?

Favors and gifts can become so influential that they threaten a reporter's portrayal of reality. The threat comes about imperceptibly. A reporter explained how it happened:

> We commonly exchange "courtesies" with the law-enforcement officials. For instance, we neglect to notice that half a dozen bottles of whiskey are not destroyed after a raid, and the police on a beat neglect to notice a reporter's car parked too long in front of a fire hydrant.

The Final Decision is No.

Anything of value that passes between reporters and their sources is potentially dangerous and limiting. The reporters may think that they can be completely objective about their news sources. But can they? That depends on the strength of the individual journalist.

Sometimes the value of the information itself can corrupt. This was the case when R. Foster Winans, a reporter for the "Heard on the Street" column of the

Wall Street Journal, told friends and others in the investment community what he was going to be writing about in the column, enabling them to make profits based on what would appear in the column. The *Wall Street Journal* broke the story on March 29, 1984, and published a long account of how it happened. This extreme case, of course, broke the law, going far beyond ethical considerations, but it dramatized the loose and casual understandings about reporter involvement in such sensitive cases.

An insidious form of conflict of interest arises when reporters become so close to sources on the beat that they start to think and feel as their sources do. They are co-opted. They lose their independent stance and become vulnerable to manipulation. They become, in effect, communications arms of their sources.

Reporters may remember that sources will still be sources after the favors are turned down. Their interest is still getting access to the public.

Another conflict of interest is through personal involvement in stories. A reporter for the *Dallas Times Herald* was charged in 1984 with conspiring to help transport illegal aliens from El Salvador into the United States while doing a story on Central American refugees. The charge alone damaged his and the paper's credibility.

What if the organization's employees are involved, even though they have nothing to do with the coverage? Critics would say that the organization's credibility is still on the line. The front-line reporter or editor may respond that publishers are often involved in community activities without drawing criticism, but even publishers don't get off completely free. John Cowles drew criticism for serving on the group that built Humphrey stadium in Minneapolis while his newspaper covered the situation. The question is not easy to answer, but it should be asked each time a journalist or publisher becomes involved in such community activities.

WHO BENEFITS? WHO PAYS?

> *When a fellow says, "It ain't the money, but the*
> *principle of the thing," it's the money.*
>
> —Kin Hubbard

What gives all these ethical questions their importance is the impact of news on the public's view of the world, on those in the news, on the sources of the information, and on the organizations that report the news.

The reporter wants to present information that will serve the public at large, but this impact is abstract. The concrete impacts are usually clearer. They fall on the people involved in the story—the participants and those behind the scenes. The questions "Who benefits?" and "Who pays?" are two of the most useful tools in the reporter's kit bag. The first may divulge the real forces behind the drama; the second reveals the characters caught up in the drama, who may be the victims of the first. Both parties are usually present in man-made events. When nature is the author, the story usually has only a victim. The ethical question, again, is whether the importance of the information justifies its impacts.

EXERCISES

1. Some newspapers have a rule that they don't mention the names of women in cases involving the lack of chastity unless the woman is a prostitute or the case is important for other reasons. The argument is that a woman has a harder time regaining her reputation than does a man. On the other hand, it is argued that the sexes should be treated alike, and the amateur prostitute like the professional. Which, as a reporter, do you favor?

2. A young woman of doubtful reputation is murdered. The police announce that they mean to question a prominent man in the case. There is no assurance that he has any connection whatsoever with the events. Should this fact of questioning be published in advance of whatever develops out of the questioning, even though some of the nastiness rubs off on the prominent man?

3. You make a practice of hiring fresh-out-of-college reporters. One has worked reasonably satisfactorily for you for fifteen months and has asked that you help her find a big-city reporting job. You write a dozen letters. She quits as your reporter, but stays around town for a week. Two days before she is to leave town, the local police charge her with possessing marijuana. If you write a story about this charge, how high do you play it in the paper and how do you identify her with regard to the paper you edit? And what do you do about the letters of recommendation you have written to other editors for her?

WORDS ABOUT INVESTIGATIVE REPORTERS

Investigative reporters have the bias of piranha fish—they will go after anything that bleeds.

—Ben J. Wattenberg

Write a sentence with the words "It is alleged" in such a manner that the reader will have no doubt that it is true.

—"Old Reporter"
Chicago Herald, 1917

I'll salute the reporter who says to me: "You've got a leak? Don't tell me. Call a plumber."

—Willard Wirtz

If you even hint where you got it, I'll say you're a damned liar.

—President Theodore Roosevelt

Journalism is not a rifleman's procedure. Journalism works more like a mortar.

—Murray Kempton

When I was an investigative correspondent in the United States for an English newspaper, I got a letter one week saying that without my work the newspaper could hardly succeed. And I got a telephone call the next week saying I was fired because I hadn't opened the door of a taxicab for one of the directors of the company visiting New York.

—Leonard Wibberly

CHAPTER 7

The Standards of Investigative Reporting

All government handouts lie. Some lie more than others.
—Joseph Alsop

Investigative reporting sounds dramatic, exciting. It can be. But it also requires persistence, stubbornness, and even a special type of personality; it is difficult, time-consuming work.

Because the investigative story is a giant step from the straight news story, we will begin this chapter with an introduction to investigative journalism.

Correspondents disagree about the definition of investigative reporting. For example, Max Frankel, who is now the executive editor of the *New York Times*, was the diplomatic correspondent on the *Times* Washington bureau staff headed by James "Scotty" Reston. They had different opinions about what kinds of news were worth digging for. At one point, Reston insisted that Frankel should invest sufficient time and energy to be able to report the identity of the new U.S. ambassador to Moscow three days before the appointment was to be announced officially. Frankel objected, arguing: "Scotty, I can find that out. It's easy. It's going to take me two days. In those two days, I might learn something far more substantial, which we would never learn if I didn't invest the two days. But the ambassador to Moscow we will find out by the announcement." Reflecting later on that disagreement, Frankel said:

> Is it important? Reston regarded me as insufficiently zealous for feeling that it isn't. Always want to be first, he argued, because vigilance resides in that instinct. He feels that if you get in the habit of waiting for government to tell you *when* it wants to tell you, you're going to lapse on more serious matters.

The "eager adversary approach" that Reston promotes should guide journalists in their daily work. Maintaining the sharp edge of vigilance is pivotal to a good reporter and a reputable newspaper. But is a story that unearths the name of the ambassador to Moscow investigative?

Perhaps, depending upon what editor or reporter you ask. One editor proclaims, "All of our reporters are investigative reporters." This is facile, of course, and misleading. Leonard Sellers, professor of journalism at San Francisco University, writes: "The investigative reporter is the one who goes after information that is deliberately hidden because it involves a legal or ethical wrong." Some investigative reporters who have been lost in the semantic swamp of defining their work have responded to this definition with, "That's it! That's it!"

By Sellers' definition, investigative reporting is the practice of opening closed doors and closed mouths. Like analysis, investigative reporting focuses on problems, issues, and controversies. In most cases, however, an analytical reporter has little trouble, because he is usually explaining public events and can find many sources who are happy to help him. In fact, one of the chief dangers of most political reporting is that too many sources want to provide too much information that will serve their own interests. In contrast, the investigative reporter tends to walk into a lot of brick walls.

HISTORY OF INVESTIGATION

Skilled writing is the art of a profound skeptic.

—Paul Valery

Are the brick walls new? Hardly. Even before the beginning of the United States, one publisher created an adversary role for himself with the government. In 1690, Benjamin Harris produced the first, and only, issue of *Publick Occurrences, Both Forreign and Domestick.* Because some of the "occurrences" were seen as criticism of colonial policy, and because he was not printing "by authority"—that is, he was not licensed by the General Court of Massachusetts—the newspaper was banned. The lesson was not lost on future publishers, and it was not until 1721, with James Franklin's establishment of the *New England Courant*, that a newspaper dared oppose government policy. Franklin, Benjamin's older brother, was the first to indulge in "crusade" journalism and refused to print "by authority." Unfortunately, his crusade was against smallpox vaccination—in retrospect, the wrong side of the issue—but, the cause became a rallying point for those fighting the local Puritan leaders. James Franklin ultimately spent some time in jail (not unlike some modern journalists), but, in the meantime, he had made the singular contribution to American journalism of establishing the principle of printing "without authority."

Clashes with authority have continued throughout the history of journalism, but an organized focus on wrongdoing did not truly begin until the opening of the twentieth century; the first decade of the 1900s was the golden age of muckraking.

Muckrakers were a salient force in American journalism from about 1902 to 1912—though there were strong examples of such reporting both before and after that period. The era began with *McClure*'s magazine trio of Lincoln Steffens, Ida M. Tarbell, and Ray Stannard Baker, who started the pattern of what historian Judson

Grenier calls the "systematic uncovery of socio-political corruption." Steffens' *Shame of the Cities* and Tarbell's *History of the Standard Oil Company* set the tone for a new literature of exposure. According to journalism researchers John Harrison and Harry Stein:

> Early in the century muckrakers had recognized that a sense of uneasiness about the malfunctioning political, economic, and social institutions which had begun to become evident several decades earlier was troubling increasing numbers of Americans. . . .
>
> They found the medium for the message—more precisely, perhaps, the medium found them—in the popular magazines that represented one current manifestation of the communications revolution that had begun at least half a century earlier. An audience was there, and the means of reaching it was at hand. The muckrakers availed themselves of that fortuitous combination.

The label "muckrakers" wasn't pinned on that small group of writers until 1906, when President Theodore Roosevelt, angered at David Graham Phillip's series *The Treason of the Senate*, borrowed the term from *Pilgrim's Progress* and castigated "the writers who raked the muck of society and never looked up." At first, upset by the obviously pejorative term, the writers soon took it as a badge of approbation, something to wear proudly. Their conversion of the term has been so complete, that Webster now defines the verb "muckrake" as "to seek for, expose, or charge corruption, real or alleged, on the part of public men and corporations."

Carey McWilliams, now-retired editor of *The Nation*, claims there is a cyclical pattern to reform journalism that began in the late nineteenth century and continues through today. "Ongoing, it seems to disappear at certain times only to surface later," he wrote in *The Nation* on November 5, 1970, adding that new communications technology and a mood of social concern usually herald an upsurge.

To emphasize McWilliams's point about reform journalism as a cyclical pattern, an episode that involves the women who were covering Eleanor Roosevelt, the wife of President Franklin D. Roosevelt, was *not* an incident of investigative (or reform) journalism. During the Roosevelt administrations, the children of all the members of the Washington press corps were always invited to play with the president's grandchildren at the White House. Moreover, all the women who covered Mrs. Roosevelt's press conferences received flowers from the White House greenhouse when they stayed home with sniffles.

One of the women, Dorothy Roe Lewis, gave this information about the women's warm relationships with Mrs. Roosevelt—which, she said, was matched by the correspondents' friendship with President Roosevelt.

> On March 3, 1933, the day before the inauguration of FDR, I was expecting Mrs. Roosevelt to drive to Washington from New York in her little sports car. That night, at 2 a.m., I was asleep when my telephone rang. Answering the phone, I heard a high-pitched voice saying, "This is Mrs. Roosevelt, Franklin says I can't do that. I have to go with the official procession. I thought you

girls would want to know right away." The women and I who would cover her joined the long procession of cars the next day to go to Washington. Mrs. Roosevelt rushed into the hotel room just before joining her husband for the new President's traditional call upon the outgoing President.

"Now girls," she said, "if you'll just wait here, I'll come back and tell you what happened."

She rushed back after an hour, bubbling with excitement, and said: "Oh, girls. I have a wonderful story for you! When we arrived at the White House, Mr. and Mrs. Hoover were waiting for us, and Mrs. Hoover poured tea, and we exchanged polite small talk. But right away, Mr. Hoover said to Mr. Roosevelt: 'Will you come into the study with me? I want to have a private talk.' So they went into the next room, but they forgot to close the door, and I could hear everything they said!

"Well, Mr. Hoover said to Mr. Roosevelt: 'Will you join me in signing a joint proclamation tonight, closing all banks?' And Mr. Roosevelt said to Mr. Hoover: 'Like hell I will! If you haven't got the guts to do it yourself, I'll wait until I'm President to do it!' Now, girls, I know you want to get your bulletins out at once, so I won't keep you."

Mrs. Roosevelt smiled triumphantly, but none of the women moved. "Why, what's the matter?" she cried out. "I thought you'd be pleased!"

One of the women responded: "Mrs. Roosevelt, you don't really want us to print that, do you? Don't you realize what would happen if that story went out tonight? The New York Stock Exchange would close. The London Stock Exchange would close. The country would go off the gold standard. There would be a worldwide panic. Besides, it's all hearsay. We couldn't quote either President directly."

She stood there, very near tears, and said: "Oh-h-h! I didn't think about all that! What are we going to do?"

The women looked at each other, then said: "It's alright, Mrs. Roosevelt. If you will promise not to tell anyone else about this, we will promise not to write it."

There they were, representing the most powerful news organizations in the world: Associated Press, United Press, and International News Service. None of the women ever wrote the story, or even told their editors. A few days later, President Roosevelt issued the proclamation. If Nancy Reagan had acted as Eleanor Roosevelt did, the woman correspondent who paused would have been knocked down and wounded by the high heels of the other women reporters as they rushed to the telephone.

ITCH FOR INVESTIGATION

> *Journalists are interesting. They just aren't as interesting*
> *as the things they cover.*
>
> —Nora Ephron

Thinking about what the modern investigative reporters do, one asks what makes an investigative reporter? What is it that directs an individual into this abrasive, frustrating, and often drudgery-filled aspect of journalism?

According to Howard Simons, former managing editor of the *Washington Post*, there is such a thing as an investigative reporter, and the creature isn't quite normal:

> I don't think everyone can be an investigative reporter. Those dozen or so successful investigative reporters I have known share some common traits, traits unshared by other competent readers. The single most important trait is the uncanny knack of linking A to Z to F to Y all by reading Yiddish footnotes or eye movements. Investigative reporters, too, all begin to mimic the persons they are investigating, that is, in my experience, they begin whispering, view the world (even their editors) conspiratorially, and write in turbid fashion.*

Simons, whose tongue may or may not have been in his cheek, was at least accurate on one point: not all journalists can or want to be investigative reporters. When Lloyd Lewis of the *Norfolk Ledger Star* was asked in an interview in April 1973 if he was an investigative reporter, he responded, "Wrong pew. I don't mind swatting demagogues, but I'm too soft-hearted to enjoy it. If the fellow isn't downright dangerous to mankind, I'm inclined to be more amused than incensed at his perfidy." Other reporters have acknowledged that they have no desire to become involved in investigations, most claiming that they don't have an "aggressive personality."

The personality required for investigative reporting goes beyond aggressiveness. The basic requirement is what William Lambert called "a low threshold of indignation," an ability to get angry. Though it might seem to be a strong term, most investigative reporters suffer from a sense of moral outrage; they do become incensed at perfidy.

When Brit Hume was asked in an interview in April 1973 why he had picked investigative reporting as a field, he began his answer with a calm explanation of the public's need to know in a democracy. "The most important thing in journalism is giving the public the information the government least wants it to know," he said. "But to get down a bit from the theoretical, I have always believed that there was more corruption and deception than most people thought. And certainly more than most reporters seem to think.

"That really alarmed me," Hume said, his voice rising. "And I *hate* it. I just hate that kind of thing. Deception and corruption, it just makes me sick. It's depressing. . . . I find it deeply troubling. I look on it as a decay, a kind of rot that is not simply unattractive, or part of the price we pay for democracy, or anything like that. I regard it as downright *dangerous.*" Hume paused for a moment and drew

*Howard Simons, "Watergate As a Catalyst," *Montana Journalism Review*, 1975, p. 14.

a calming breath. "The rot has to be dug out," he said quietly. "It's a matter of self-interest "

This small band of reporters usually lives with an odd mixture of aggressiveness and uncertainty. Committed to personal and social standards of morality, they need affirmation of those standards, if not from the public, at least from their editors. "An investigative reporter with editors who will stand behind him is a happy man," wrote Nicholas Gage in *The Mafia Is Not an Equal Opportunity Employer* (McGraw-Hill, 1971).

What satisfaction does the job offer? Are there rewards other than alleviating anger? In correspondence in April 1973, Keith McKnight listed those he found:

> I have been a general assignment reporter, a beat reporter, copy editor rewrite man, layout supervisor, telegraph editor, city editor, and managing editor. I'm not interested in being any of those things again. In each one, there seemed to be so many built-in routines or procedures that there was little time left to do something creative or worthwhile that wasn't ordinary.
>
> As an investigative reporter, I am free to explore what I please, with (at least in theory) no daily deadlines to worry me. When I report something, I can write with authority and not with the fear that my ignorance of the subject will misinform the public and make a fool of me.
>
> There are fewer rewards of course, because when you have to know what you're talking about you speak less often. But when you do, and you do it well, I suppose investigative reporting isn't much different than other professions in that the reward is the self-satisfaction you get, though others may never recognize it.

In correspondence in May 1974, Bruce Locklin emphasized the challenge involved: "I'm still doing it because it's the hardest thing I've ever been asked to do. I don't take pleasure from hurting people. I have to force myself to ask hard questions."

The asking of questions may seem to be an easy thing, but, in the domain of the investigative reporter, it can become a subtle and ingenious tool. The most basic questioning is not to treat the question as a question. That is, the information being sought should be treated as a known fact. The reporter, instead of asking "Did you go to New Orleans last month?" will ask, "Why did you go to New Orleans last month?" As simple as it may sound, it is a productive technique. Instead of giving the subject the option of denying, he or she is put in the position of explaining. If no such trip was made, the reporter, of course, will quickly be told, but if the point of the question is to get confirmation, it can be easier if the subject is off-balance.

In a somewhat more sophisticated version of this technique, the reporter hides what he considers the crucial part of the question at the beginning of the sentence, burying it under a more damaging accusation: "Is it true that when you went to New Orleans last month you spent the weekend on the Sneaky Oil Company yacht?" It is possible that the subject, busy denying or explaining the last part of the question, will unconsciously confirm the first.

An even more elaborate version, one designed to set up the entire interview, is explained by Brit Hume in *Inside Story* (Doubleday, 1974). "It is a common enough technique—you persuade the person you are questioning that you have been told a truly lurid story. In eagerness to disabuse you of it, the person will frequently tell you the truth." Hume also elaborated on why the technique works.

> A good tactic is to accuse the principal figure of something you know he can't possibly be involved in. Usually, in denying your outrageous charge, he will concede the truth. Collection agencies use this angle all the time. If they have trouble getting someone to pay a bill for $100, they'll send him a letter stating he owes $681, which must be paid immediately to avoid court action. This brings (sometimes) the debtor running in to protest that there has been a mistake, that he actually owes $100. Often he's anxious to pay on the spot. Police use similar tactics, accusing a man of deliberate murder when they know it's only manslaughter. Most people would rather tell the truth in such cases than take a chance on facing more serious charges. The same tactic works for me.

Another technique involves the sequence of questions. Jack Anderson has said that he always begins by asking a question to which he already knows the answer. "As the guy begins talking, I say, 'Now wait a minute. Court testimony indicates. . . .' That throws him off stride." It often does more than that. It can make the subject uncertain as to how much the reporter does or does not know. If the reporter leads with a series of questions to which he knows the answers, it is sometimes possible to convince the subject that the reporter knows nearly everything, and the subject may become conditioned to giving only accurate answers. Ideally, at this point, the reporter begins asking questions to which he *does not* know the answers. And if the reporter is truly Pavlovian, he saves a couple of unnecessary questions to use as reinforcers, making sure the subject is still responding truthfully.

Such interviewing tools are not so elaborate as they might sound, and some reporters use them as easily as raising an eyebrow. Indeed, even raising an eyebrow can help. As Ray Brennan said, "If you indicate you know something and ask a direct question, a man will always answer you, if only briefly. Often if you look expectant after he has finished his answer, he will keep on talking."

Even a single word can make a difference in whether a question successfully elicits information. Alex Dobish of the Milwaukee *Journal* managed to make a deliberate error work for him, when, in attempting to get a city clerk to admit he had been involved in a land scheme, he referred to the buyer as the Root River Land Corporation. "He took the bit and announced that it wasn't a corporation but a company—then suddenly knew he had stuck his foot in it."

Unfortunately, the game can be played both ways. When UPI reporter Dan Gilmore was interviewing CIA Director William Colby, his final question concerned a rumor he and other reporters had been looking into. "Was the CIA involved," he said, "in some kind of salvage operation with Howard Hughes in the Atlantic Ocean?"

"That is just not so," Colby said.

Shortly thereafter it was revealed, by other news organizations, that the CIA had been involved in a $350-million effort with the Hughes company to raise a Soviet submarine in the *Pacific* Ocean. There is no way of knowing what Colby's reply would have been had the reporter managed to place the rumor in the right ocean, but Colby is said to have told an aide after the report left: "I'm glad he didn't pursue that last question."

Some veteran reporters don't rely so much on questioning as on bluffing—on misleading or on frightening a subject with a bold front. And it is also a handy tool in the reporter's kit bag of techniques. When the investigative reporter runs a bluff, it is usually as a last resort when the standard digging methods have failed. In its simplest form, the reporter pretends to know something that he does not. But without proper preparation, it can be dangerous. The reporter who exposes his own ignorance has hamstrung himself. Some reporters refuse to use the bluffs, while others use it extensively.

"Every reporter bluffs now and then, but it's not a good policy," said Herby Marynell of the *Evansville Press*. "If you are forced to bluff then you must have failed to do enough leg work, if not for documented evidence then for statements from people who know individual parts of the story."

But Peter Benjaminson of the *Detroit Free Press* disagrees.

Bluffing is a must. . . . Quite often a diligent investigator can discover all but the final link in some train of criminal acts. That last provable link eludes him. At that point, going to the subject and accusing him of performing all the acts, while gliding over the absence of proof that he is connected with the crucial act, will often work. The subject, is his fear and trembling, may not remember how many traces he left and may assume you have all the proof you need and will admit all.

Quite often, the subjects of an investigation don't want to admit that what they've done is wrong. Bluffing works easily in these cases since after a point the subject is less interested in hiding his actions than in appearing to have disclosed them himself, so that he can argue he never did anything he thought to be wrong.

There may be an additional reason subjects will talk if they think the reporter already has what he needs. Jack Anderson, in giving advice to one of his staff about dealing with senators, said, "Pretend you know all about whatever they're doing, even if you don't. A lot of those guys don't have any news judgment and they don't know what's a story and what's not."

JACK ANDERSON

I had learned from a source that (Senator George) Murphy was collecting money from the right-wing millionaire Patrick Frawley, through Frawley's corporation, Technicolor, Inc. I learned this because Murphy had become concerned that he might be in violation of the new Senate code of ethics, so he called on the chairman of the committee, John Stennis, and described the situation in confidence. Secondhand, I got the information. I knew from past experience that Stennis wouldn't tell us anything, so I called Murphy and said, "Senator, I have evidence that you're collecting $20,000 a year from Technicolor, that all or part of your apartment is being paid for by Technicolor and that you use a credit card belonging to Technicolor. I called you as a matter of courtesy to hear your side of the story." Senator Murphy said, "You're wrong. You have been misinformed." I said, "Senator, I like you. I like your personality. I used to enjoy your movies. Because I like you, I'm going to give you another chance to answer that question. I don't think you want to go on the record with the answer you just gave. So let's do it again." "Yes," he said, "damn it, I am." Of course, I couldn't have printed it without Murphy's confession.[*]

In relating this story as an example of using manipulative tactics to trap a source, investigative reporter Jack Anderson speaks from years of experience in exposing "the bulldozers and back-scratchers, scoundrels and cheats who infiltrate the Government." As a reporter for the "The Washington Merry-Go-Round" since 1947, and owner since 1969, Anderson has been considered the most widely read political columnist in the world.

In 1972, Anderson received the Pulitzer Prize for National Reporting for reporting highly classified documents indicating a pro-Pakistan bias in the Nixon administration during the India-Pakistan war. He also appeared on the cover of *Time* in the same year for writing a series of columns charging that the International Telephone & Telegraph Corporation had pledged funds to support the cost of the Republican convention in exchange for a favorable settlement in an antitrust suit against ITT.

In his twenty-year position as the anonymous chief reporter for Drew Pearson on the "Merry-Go-Round," Anderson published a variety of sensational stories, including a series on Senator Thomas Dodd's misuse of campaign funds that led to his censure by the Senate. When Pearson died in 1969 and Anderson took over the column, he "went after everybody," checking stories thoroughly and campaigning for personal causes, eventually affecting a significant increase in the number of subscribing newspapers.

Playboy reporter Larry DuBois has described Anderson as

. . . seen by his supporters as a tough cop on a tough beat, shining a searching spot-light into all the shady nooks and crannies of official

Washington . . . seen by his enemies as a journalistic mugger lurking in the shadows, waiting to rob all passers-by, guilty or otherwise, of their virtuous public images.

A self-proclaimed "hell-raiser," Anderson has been accused of invading the privacy of public figures in minor personal matters. He justifies his actions with the response that

> I think they should be nervous. I consider it an extremely healthy exercise for an anonymous Government official to squirm just a little bit. I've seen the powerful become so godlike in their insulation that they forget they're supposed to live by the same laws and rules as the rest of us. . . . Too many bureaucrats in Washington have developed an elitist attitude. They are our servants and they want to become our masters. I just want to deflate them a little, remind them of their proper place, keep them on their toes.

The careers of many men have been damaged or destroyed in Anderson's quest to "deflate them a little." Although remorseful about some of the results his stories have produced, this has not caused Anderson to temper his writing at all. He says:

> If I started feeling responsible to protect these men from the possible consequences of their own violations of the public trust, then I'd have to quit writing the column, and quite frankly, I think our Government is a little bit better, a little bit more honest, because of the work we do. . . .
> You've got to understand the environment in which an investigative reporter functions. . . . It's a hurricane of whispers, stories, rumors, and charges. We're at the eye of this furious storm of rumors about people in power and people who seek power, because an investigative reporter has the capacity to wreck careers or to make them.

Although Anderson admitted that his credibility was lowered by his stories— "I think a lot of people will now wonder whether I'm telling the truth"—he remained confident that the American public would not doubt him for long.

> I don't think I can change the whole country, but I can sure inform the American people about the wrongdoing and hypocrisy in the dark places of the Government. . . . I think that role is a vital one. . . . I plan to sit right there in the grandstands, yelling, "Throw the bum out!" until all our public officials become incorruptible. Then I'll be out of business, and I'd like that a lot.
>
> —Jennifer Koch

*Interview: Jack Anderson," *Playboy* (November 1972), p. 237.

KINDS OF CONFESSING

Originality is the art of concealing your source.

—Franklin P. Adams

There are, however, different degrees of "confessing," as people who regularly deal with the press are aware. Reporters who are working with uninitiated sources should make clear the standard ground rules for confidentiality and anonymity. They are fairly simple:

On the Record. All statements are directly quotable and attributable, by name and by title, to the person who is making the statement. Unless otherwise agreed, all comments are assumed to be on the record.

On Background. All statements are directly quotable, but they cannot be attributed by name or by specific title to the person commenting. The type of attribution to be used should be spelled out in advance: a White House official, an administration spokesperson, a government lawyer, or whatever. The kind of attribution to be used has some importance, since sources often worry about how traceable a leak might be.

On Deep Background. Anything that is said is usable, but not in direct quotation and not for any type of attribution. The reporter is to use the information on his own, without saying it comes from any government department or official. (Reporters normally dislike this type of attribution, since officials often use it to plant stories or to float trial balloons without having to take responsibility.)

Off the Record. Information given off the record is for the reporter only and is not to be printed or made public in any way. The information is also not to be taken to another source in hopes of getting it put on the record. It is generally understood that any off-the-record arrangement must be agreed to by the reporter beforehand. (The danger in agreeing to off-the-record information is that the reporter is locked into not using it—even if it is received in another manner from another source—until someone else prints it. Most reporters automatically refuse to accept off-the-record information.)

Even supposedly sophisticated political figures who know the rules will sometimes slip up and have to be reminded. After Jeb Stuart Magruder admitted to Bob Woodward that the FBI had questioned him about a secret campaign fund, he added, "That's on background." Woodward told him that he should know better than to try to put something on background after saying it. "But you've got to help me," Magruder pleaded. "I'll get in trouble if I'm quoted." Woodward told him he might put *that* statement in the paper too.*

*Carl Berstein and Robert Woodward, *All the President's Men* (New York: Simon & Schuster, 1974), p. 78.

Once contact with a source has been made and the ground rules have been established, a reporter can find it increasingly easy to get information. A worried Brit Hume, fretting about a source, was told by his boss, Jack Anderson, "I've been through this before. Sometimes when someone opens up to you the way she did, a sort of confessor relationship develops and the person will continue to talk to you."

Even the subjects who will talk are not enough; the need for documentation can be crucial, which is the main reason that Bob Walters of the defunct *Washington Star* said in an interview in April 1973 that the growth in investigative reporting is directly attributable to a machine.

> The single most important development that reporters have taken advantage of has nothing to do with this profession—that's the invention of the Xerox machine. It has done wonders for investigative reporting.
>
> Back in the old days a guy could come to you and say "I know there's a document that says this-and-this." You, as a reporter, knew that it was classified, or administratively confidential, or whatever, and you could never see it.
>
> You always had a terrible time, saying to yourself, "Gee, can I believe this guy? Is it really there?" Maybe, if you were really lucky, somebody would flash the document at you and you could copy off a couple of phrases. And that was it.
>
> Now it's a whole new ball game. We now have available to us great masses of documentation, which for an investigative story is crucial. It's not Party X charging so-and-so, and Party Y saying it's not true and he's innocent. It's on paper and you wave it in Party Y's face and you say "What do you mean? This is your memo and you signed it."
>
> The Xerox has done wonders for us. Any reporter will tell you that one piece of documentation is worth five allegations. And that's my great Xerox theory.

But if the information is the type that cannot be photocopied—eyewitness accounts, for example—the reporter has another protection: affidavits. Affidavits are written statements under oath, sworn to before a notary public. Anyone making a false affidavit can be punished for perjury. In an interview in April 1973, Jack Nelson, the Washington bureau chief of the *Los Angeles Times*, stated his strong belief in the use of affidavits as a reporting tool.

> I've drawn up hundreds over the years, and they're very important. First, your source can't later say he was misquoted. You really have a legal document, and in all my experience with affidavits no one has ever said "That wasn't what I meant." Second, it strengthens the story. I'll give you an example: When I was with the *Atlanta Constitution*, I had an affidavit from an operating room technician who said he had seen a nurse perform major surgery.
>
> Our libel lawyer said it wasn't quite enough to go with, and asked if I could get a member of the medical staff to say, under oath, that he knew the

technician and would believe him. I got an affidavit from a doctor to that effect, and we went ahead with the story.

I drew up so many damn affidavits in Atlanta while doing an investigation of state government that people would actually call up and volunteer, saying, "I'll be willing to sign an affidavit." The paper would come out with a story saying, "So-and-so, according to affidavits from five state employees. . . ."

Although few of the Washington correspondents use affidavits, many other reporters need identification as members of the press to open doors closed to the average citizen. When those doors are supposed to be open to anyone in the first place (access to documents that by law are public), denial itself is often a news story. On the other hand, some people, particularly among high levels of government officials, have an instinctive negative reaction to reporters. Identifying oneself as a newsperson can cause some doors to close automatically. Some reporters, then, are allowed by their employers to pose as private citizens, but often only with the stipulation that, if asked, the reporter will reveal who and what he is.

Such rules, of course, have been both bent and broken. One reporter for the *Washington Post*, which requires that its reporters identify themselves, has admitted to fudging a bit, "When necessary," he said, "I go use the telephone in the press room at the State Department. That way I begin the call with 'Hello, I'm calling from the State Department. . . .'"

INVESTIGATIVE CASE NO. 1

Logic is the art of going wrong with confidence.

—Joseph Wood Krutch

The following case was written by an investigative reporter:

Robert Wright is a former FBI agent who retired after a distinguished career as a crimefighter to become a respected criminal defense attorney in your city. Over the years, he has become one of your best sources. He was the main source on several front-page stories. He introduced you to a circle of contacts in the local underworld that included his old informants and several crooks that he once arrested, but had managed to befriend. This network of sources helped you write a series of articles that won a Pulitzer Prize and made you a prominent journalist.

Wright likes to meet with you at his home, where his wife always serves you your favorite drink. You have a strict agreement with Wright that everything he tells you is off the record unless he says otherwise, and that you will never disclose to any other person, including your editors, that he talks to you or has been a source. "I only trust you," he says. You promise to go to jail rather than reveal that he is a source. You don't hesitate to make this commitment because you genuinely like and respect Wright.

Sometimes, after several drinks, Wright tells war stories. During one of these off-the-record sessions, he confides that when he first got out of the FBI he was financially strapped and one of his old informants, a convicted embezzler, gave him a break on the rent for a downtown office. He also confides that several of his underworld contacts helped him get established as an attorney by sending him clients. "You can take a different view of these things when you're a defense attorney," he says. On a third occasion, you notice a large sailboat in his driveway. He tells you that one of his clients, a known Mafia member, lets him use the boat from time to time. "He's a nice guy," Wright says.

One day it is announced that Wright has been nominated to be the next chief of your State Police, which handles major organized crime investigations. There is unanimous praise for the appointment because of his background in law enforcement and his legal skills. You smile broadly upon learning of this. Your good friend and confidential source will now be in a position to know all about the most sensitive and newsworthy investigations. You envision a long string of great stories.

That afternoon at lunch, your city editor says the newspaper must do a profile of Wright and look at his fitness for the sensitive post. "He looks like the perfect choice," says the editor. You nod your agreement. Your editor takes a slip of his gin-and-tonic and adds an afterthought: "I wonder if he has any skeletons in his closet?"

What are your obligations (1) to the newspaper and your readers; (2) to Wright; (3) to yourself? (4) What do you do if your editor assigns you to do a profile about Wright?

The following answers were written by students:

1. Your obligation to your readers is to present the whole story objectively, including Wright's crooked connections. To the newspaper, you owe the same.

Your obligation to Wright is clear. True to your agreement, you must keep his past statements off the record. You can't break this pact regardless of with whom you arrange it. A violation of this code would nullify future sources' trust in journalists.

Personally, you would want to silence Wright's connections with crooks. Wright is valuable. As your source, he would provide important story material. As a friend, his wife would provide your favorite drink.

If I had to do the profile, I would report everything on Wright that was not mentioned off the record. If other sources reveal the same information that Wright wants confidential, I would have to think twice. In that case, I would forewarn Wright that I am now obligated to report the facts. I would not ask for his opinion or his advice on the matter, but he deserves an explanation. In the profile, I would mention Wright's attempt to keep his connections hush-hush.

2. This is a tricky case that cannot simply be determined by picking from a choice of three possible obligations. A valid case can be made for each obliga-

tion: a reporter's job is to serve the public, providing the people with important information; a reporter must keep and uphold his promises to sources that are vital to him; a reporter must act in accord with what he or she believes to be right, without regard to pressures from an outside source.

I believe that as a reporter I have no specific obligation to voluntarily turn over information about Wright to my editor. In other words, if the editor doesn't ask me if I know anything, I don't know anything. It should also be noted that I do not know anything damaging about Wright—I have only heard him tell stories under the influence of several drinks in a setting in which my role was not that of a reporter. Wright was truly confiding in me as a friend, not as a reporter. Besides, he really has my word that I will not reveal anything of what he says, since it is off-the-record information.

What this means, I guess, is that my obligation to myself—the promise I made—is entangled with my obligation to Wright. By going against my promise, I would be compromising my own ideals and destroying my relationship with Wright, violating his trust. In addition, a case can be made that by not exposing the skeletons in Wright's closet, I am keeping an avenue of communication open that will likely provide a plethora of other stories in the future. Wright will undoubtedly furnish more information about other subjects that I can use in later stories.

If the editor assigns me to the story, I would tell him that my ties with other sources in the State Police would be jeopardized. If these other sources were to give damaging information against Wright, they might be identified as the only people privy to such information. If that is the case, they would probably be cut off from future information that could be vital to later stories. I would also tell the editor, in plain terms, that I have known Wright for some time and that I would probably give a report favorable to the man. Somebody else would probably be able to dig up more dirt on Wright—I just don't have the motivation. Since my reporting might be biased, then, I would not be the person most appropriate to write the story.

3. In a general sense, it seems that what is involved in this case is a decision as to the relative weight assigned to the reporter's journalistic integrity, personal success, personal relationships, and personal integrity. In fact, though, all of these elements are intertwined. While the reporter may perceive that he has a responsibility to the newspaper to contribute any pertinent information he can to a story, he also has a responsibility to maintain the integrity of his relationships with his sources so that he can be an effective investigator-reporter in the future. The choice of taking advantage of off-the-record conversations with Wright to glean disparaging information for the story is not open to the reporter if he intends on maintaining any sort of trust with sources in the future.

Moreover, while the reporter may perceive that he has a greater responsibility to his readers to expose any improprieties that would cast aspersions on Wright's fitness for the post, no such improprieties really exist, only suppositions. True, Wright may have friends in the Mob, but one cannot fault a man for his friends if he is responsible enough to keep his personal and business relationships separate. Wright seems to take a healthy, or at least "normal," perspective that one takes a "different view of these things" when he is a defense attorney. The courts are rife with attorneys who are representing clients they know to be guilty, but these attorneys are doing their jobs. Wright appears to be enough of a professional to realize what his new job, should his nomination be confirmed, will entail should he accept it. Finally, bear in mind that Wright has no criminal record whatsoever; in fact, he has done nothing even ethically wrong given his occupational circumstances for the last several years.

The overriding factor in deciding what the reporter should do in this case, though, should be his own personal integrity. He has committed to confidentiality the conversations he has had with Wright. An honest man would not break that promise. Moreover, there is no reason to believe that any other reporter has been privy to Wright's recollections, since the one in question received the Pulitzer Prize. It is entirely plausible that more such accolades will be forthcoming for this reporter if Wright becomes State Police Chief. Certainly, all of these factors should weigh more heavily than any fleeting fame that may be gained by dragging Wright's name through the mud.

Judging the moral costs involved, if the reporter is asked to do the profile, he should gracefully decline, telling the editor that he does not want to alienate one of his best sources by searching for dirt. If he has no choice but to do the profile, his privileged conversations with Wright are strictly off-limits as evidence.

4. My obligations to the newspaper and my readers are in conflict with my obligations to Wright. On the one hand I'm supposed to tell the public the truth, especially about public officials. On the other hand, I promised Wright I would never reveal him, and I wouldn't have learned all that I know otherwise. My obligations to Wright and myself—keeping my word—would win out in this case. Wright's confidences have benefitted the public in the past, and most likely will in the future.

If my editor assigned me to the profile, I would turn down the assignment. Can I do that? I hope he would respect my answer and not press for an explanation, as I don't think I could explain without giving away Wright as a source.

This is the instructor's answer:

First, although Wright can be seriously wounded by my profile, he has done *nothing illegal*, as far as I know.

Second, I could write this profile, provided I ignore everything that Wright has given me confidentially. Technically, however, I would violate my agreement with Wright because of our confidential conversations.

In trying to balance the first and the second answers, I would refuse to write this profile. I would tell nothing to my editor about Wright. Instead, I would say, " I can't." If he or she is knowledgeable about confidentiality, the editor would assign another reporter.

In both parts of this case, both would fail after the Final Decision were made.

INVESTIGATIVE CASE NO. 2

To withhold news is to play God.
                    —John Loft Hess

The same investigative reporter also presented this case:

For months there has been a secret grand jury investigation in your city of allegations of judicial corruption. Suddenly a grand jury report is released that says the local judges have been cleared of any wrongdoings. "The charges were totally unfounded," says the report.

A week later, you get an anonymous phone call from a woman who says she was a member of that grand jury. "I can be arrested for talking to you," she says. You promise her confidentiality. She says that the grand jury originally produced a report that indicted five local judges and said the local prosecutor's office was rife with corruption. But, she said, the chief prosecutor and the chief judge killed the first report. "We were told it was shredded," she says.

You and your editor are intrigued to learn that five local judges are corrupt. But she is wary. "These charges have been bandied about for months," she says. "We need something solid."

You start calling other grand jurors. Most are frightened. One of them confirms that there was a first report. "Look I can't tell you what was in it," he says, sounding a little drunk. "But it was a pisser."

You and your editor are more sure than ever. She is on your back almost every day about the story. "Find a way to get it into the paper," she says.

A month goes by. Judges in two major drug cases mysteriously dismiss the charges and set the defendants free. There is no protest from the prosecutor. In another case, a group of Mafia members receive ridiculously light sentences. You continue to make inquiries and finally you get a response. A senior partner from the state's most powerful law firm calls your newspaper's lawyer and says if you keep implying that the judges are corrupt, he'll sue you for slander. "These charges have already been investigated and disproven," he warns. You and your editor meet with your lawyer. He says that the only safe way to do the story is to get some documents backing it up. The grand jurors can't go on the record. "No way can we use confidential sources on this story," he says

A week later, a young, idealistic prosecutor calls you into his office. You chat briefly about the upcoming Super Bowl. He gets you a cup of coffee. Suddenly he stands and says, "Wait here, I'll be back in ten minutes." While sitting there, you notice a large report sitting in the middle of his otherwise empty desk. You lean forward and see that it is a copy of the original grand jury report. It looks to be about 500 pages. You realize it is no accident you've been left alone with this report.

After a moment, your friend's secretary comes in his office and says he was called away on an emergency and would be gone all day. "But he said you could finish your coffee," she says. You figure you'll have about five minutes before she becomes suspicious. What do you do next?

The following answers were written by students:

1. Chug your coffee and leave. You have never had contact with this prosecutor, and it's quite possible that he's involved in the illegitimate goings-on. In fact, it's very possible that he's tied up with the Mafia. The whole scene seems too contrived. He leaves you alone with the most valuable document to your whole investigation—such luck! The document may have been tampered with—especially if it's a copy of the original.

Later on, when the prosecutor returns, give him a call. Find out what it is he wanted to discuss with you. Ask him how he got his copy of the original grand jury report. If he had access to it, why couldn't anyone get at the original?

For now, things look fishy, and the validity of these papers is debatable.

2. Since it "is no accident" that I've been left alone in the idealistic prosecutor's office, I definitely choose to look at the grand jury report. But looking is not enough in this case—500 pages are simply 499 more pages than one can possibly digest in a five-minute period. It is clear that I have to do more than just briefly skim over the report before the secretary returns. Do I take it? Yes, I certainly do. I also leave an object of importance to me in the room—a watch or a reporter's notebook.

I slip the report under my trench coat—all good reporters in the movies wear trench coats—and walk out of the office. I immediately head for the nearest Copy Mat to make copies of the report. After making the copies, I return to the office, knowing that the prosecutor will be out for the rest of the day. As I enter the building and greet the prosecutor's secretary, I inform her that I left my notebook inside the office. This is the truth. I then tell the secretary that I'd like to enter the office for a second or two, noting that "I think I left it on his desk."

Assuming that she allows me to enter, I go in and pick up my watch from his desk and, in the process, replace the original grand jury report on the desk. Even if the secretary is in the room at the time, it would be hard for her to notice that I replaced something on the desk—the report would be inside my trench coat and would be replaced without much noticeable movement.

3. Although the temptation to use this grand jury report to build your story against the judges is extremely appealing, there are at least a few aspects of the situation that should dissuade you from any immediate action. It appears fairly obvious that you will not have the opportunity to either read or copy the report within your time limits. The choices then seem to be to steal or leave it untouched. It is not made clear how much you know about the "young, idealistic" prosecutor, but it appears that you will have to question his motives for leaving you alone with the report. If you feel that it was "no accident," then you have to wonder why the prosecutor didn't confront you

directly with the information. The situation has ideal elements for a set-up, especially when you have received threats from lawyers in the past warning you to discontinue your investigation. I think that the only legitimate choice in these circumstances is to contact the prosecutor at a later date and confront him with your knowledge of the report. If he is sincere about trying to help you with your story, then he will not be reluctant to discuss it with you directly.

4. The real issue in this case is whether the reporter is prepared to use the "young, idealistic prosecutor" as a source. The paper's attorney has made it perfectly clear that no confidential sources can be used. Under any circumstances, the origins of the supposedly nonexistent first report are going to be questioned in the courts if it is used as a source in backing up the corruption charges. Obviously, the prosecutor did not call in the reporter to discuss the Super Bowl, but neither did he intend on directly transmitting information about the corruption. He is scared, but he is trying to do "the right thing."

The reporter really has no right to remove the grand jury report from the office, and if he does so, he should be prepared for the prosecutor to charge him with having stolen it should the prosecutor's name come up as the source of the report. However, it is entirely plausible that the prosecutor should not have a copy of the report in his possession either, since the rumor was spread that it was destroyed. Perhaps, then, the prosecutor intends on shredding this copy himself once the reporter has seen it.

The only safe avenue for the reporter here appears to be to attempt to digest the information in the report in the few minutes that he has, basically to look for leads to find additional documentation for the corruption charges. If this attempt proves fruitless, as it probably will, he should take the report with him. He should then meet with his editor and the paper's attorney to determine if there is any recourse for keeping the source of the report and the method of obtaining it confidential.

This is the instructor's answer:

It *is* a felony to take or steal a grand jury report, but think for a moment about "steal." As a reporter, I would not take the report for monetary gain. Although I would benefit to some unknown degree, my stealing would probably benefit my community. I judge that the odds against me would be far outweighed by other factors.

If the prosecutor had set me up by placing false information within the pages of the report, I could protect myself to a large degree by (1) informing my editor where and how I got the report, and (2) sending myself a registered letter that tells what happened in the prosecutor's office.

Thus, I would write this story.

For me, it's a close call, but my action would pass the Final Decision.

TELEVISION INVESTIGATORS

*I can find nothing in the Bill of Rights or the Communications Act,
which says that the networks must increase their net profits each
year lest the Republic collapse.*

—Edward R. Murrow

Because the television correspondent must be on the air daily, or nearly so, he or she cannot devote the days, weeks, or even months to investigation that a print-media reporter can. Tom Pettit of NBC said that he goes ahead on a story only after he knows that he has the facts, "and that the facts can be filmed." His beginning probes, like those of almost all TV broadcasters, have to include the question of visuals: Is the story the kind that can be translated into moving film? Can it be made understandable within the framework of the medium? For the broadcast reporter, these kinds of questions often mean that the complex, abstract story, such as stock manipulations or real estate frauds, is never pursued. Any story that *is* pursued will cost the network thousands and thousands of dollars.

A network team, Brian Ross and Ira Silverman, are among the few television investigators, but they are among the best sleuths anywhere. They have been shot at, hijacked, threatened, and sued during ten years of investigating for NBC. Ross says, "It's still invigorating. In fact, it would be hard for me to envision doing anything else. It's one of the best jobs in television."

Because Ross and Silverman have proved their worth, they now have a full-time researcher working in Washington, D.C., and a second producer in Miami. Their reports sometimes run six minutes on the air—an amazing time for television reporting. Although these investigative reporters are able to appear on the air only twice a month, Tom Brokaw, the NBC anchor, says, "We'd like to see them on the air more often, but when the payoff comes, it's a bonanza."

For example, Ross and Silverman won a Dupont-Columbia award in 1985 for their "solid investigative teamwork and reporting over many years." Their investigation of payola in the recording industry showed that record companies were hiring independent promoters to get air play for new songs. The promoters were said to be bribing disk jockeys and radio program directors with drugs, women, and money.

When the NBC team first aired their findings, seven record companies severed their dealings with the independent promoters, shutting down what had been an $80 million business.

Ross and Silverman reject the name "investigative reporters." Ross emphasizes that

> We're just reporters in an area that might be more difficult to cover, but there are no special skills other than asking good questions and listening. Everybody wants to know how we do what we do. They think the FBI gives us the

whole story. Well, very few are handed to you on a silver platter. We use the most elementary, dogged techniques. It's just Silverman and Ross on the phone, night and day.

EXERCISES

1. These men pose the basic question of investigative journalism. During an interview in August 1973, Gene Patterson, editor of the *St. Petersburg Times*, laid out rules for investigative reporters:

   > Number one, no bugging. I've never wired a reporter, I never will. I've never planted a microphone; if I can't get it by other means, I just won't get it. No burglary. I fired a reporter for taking a document off the desk of a politician. . . .

   Patterson went on and on but he would not get along with the well-known Chicago reporter who quite literally has holes in his pockets from the half-dozen badges, some real, some phony, that he carries around—Patterson certainly would not have liked one of the legends of Chicago journalism, Harry (Romy) Romanoff. A master of telephone impersonations, Romanoff at various times in his fifty-year career played the President of the United States, the Chicago chief of police, a priest, a bishop, a railroad lawyer, and even a reporter for an opposition newspaper.

   Remember that Romanoff worked in Chicago. Which attitude—Romanoff or Patterson—do you favor?

2. The *New York Times* printed a story exposing the background of Daniel Burros, a leader of the Ku Klux Klan in New York, who had earlier been involved with the American Nazis. The *Times* revealed that his parents and his upbringing were Jewish. Burros asked the reporter and his editor not to print the information because he said it would ruin him in his role as a Ku Klux Klan leader. The same day the story appeared, Burros shot himself to death.

   Should the *Times* have reported this information? Did the public have a right to know about it? What would you do in similar circumstances?

WRITERS ABOUT EDITORS

Editor: he who makes a long story short.

—Anonymous

An editor is a reporter whose legs have gone back on him.

—Anonymous

An acquiring editor is someone who enjoys making love to strangers.

—Tom Congdon

No passion in the world is equal to the passion to alter someone else's drafts.

—H. G. Wells

Democracy makes a government of bullies tempered by editors.

—Ralph Waldo Emerson

The relation of the editor to the writer is the same as the knife to the throat.

—Anonymous

Perhaps an editor might begin a reformation in some such way as this. Divide his paper into four chapters, heading the first, Truths. 2nd, Probabilities. 3rd, Possibilities. 4th, Lies. The first chapter would be very short.

—Thomas Jefferson

CHAPTER 8

The Ethics of Packaging the News

The television writer must somehow cram in all the pertinent facts, often dealing in twenty seconds with events which a newspaper covers in twelve column inches.

—CBS Handbook

When an author spoke to a large audience, he ended acidly with these words: "I like to have reporters here, but some reporters know *nothing* about the people they are to cover."

At the end of the author's speech, a young reporter for a television station said, "I know what you're talking about. I agree, but consider *our* problems. The assignment editor sent us downtown an hour ago to get a few sentences from the mayor. Now we're here, and have to leave in another minute for the Sheraton Inn for a short interview. In getting ready to see you, I read the publicity release on your latest book and caught the last two minutes of your speech. I don't have *time* to get ready for one-tenth the things I cover."

To virtually 100 percent of all television and radio reporters, reporting without proper preparation is a grim necessity. Ask an assignment editor, and he or she will answer something like this: "We have absolutely no pretense of giving depth stories. Just a quick flash of what's going on. So it is that we're packaging news, not in hours, not in many minutes, just stories that run about five to eight sentences. The package will be pretty, but look elsewhere for a package that's bulky—such as newspapers."

THE EDITORS' MISSIONS

An editor should tell the writer his writing is better than it is. Not a lot better, a little better.

—T. S. Eliot

While reporters are driven to find out what happened, editors are driven to tell a story. They have nurtured their sense of the significant. Their first thoughts are

"Is it worth the space?" and "What is the lead?" Whether it is honest or fair is secondary. Editors are responsible for the content of their publication or program. They are the *gatekeepers*. It is their lot to say no a lot.

But it is also their role to *generate coverage*. This creative aspect of editing gets less attention than the gatekeeping role. In most newsrooms it is a small part of a job devoted largely to processing stories. Yet that small part can give the final product a distinctive character.

Editors also *edit* articles. Most of the newsroom's editing time goes to editing or copy editing. The accuracy and impact of the final story reflect the work of copy editors, who are detached from both the news sources and the audience, and, thus, less sensitive to the distortions in the stories.

Finally, editors *supervise*. A managing editor or news director runs the newsroom, although he or she may work under an executive editor or program director. A publisher or general manager presides at the top, although he or she may report to someone higher in the corporation. The loftier the position, the farther the employee is from the actual copy.

Editors establish the mood of a newsroom and the attitudes of its staff. In this sense, the ethics of the newsroom reflect the ethics of the editors, even when editors are preoccupied by the details of time, money, and quality. To such editors, ethical behavior includes performing well.

Editors thus fulfill four main functions:

1. Generating coverage.
2. Selecting and judging the news.
3. Processing and packaging the copy.
4. Supervising the process of gathering and presenting the news.

Each of the four functions can entangle editors in ethical snares.

EDITOR AS GENERATOR

An editor is a bit of sandpaper applied to all forms of originality.

—Elbert Hubbard

Perhaps the most satisfying accomplishment for editors is shaping the news product by deciding what to cover and how to cover it. The experience, education, and culture of each editor come into play as editors develop story ideas. It is one of their few chances to be creative in their work. They often complain of having too little time to reap its pleasures.

Newsrooms are notorious, of course, for pressures. The deadline is a recurrent rush to judgment. The right limits of space and program time impel the gatekeepers to slam the gates on information not already "credentialed" with a familiar pass. Editors have to make "creative" management decisions while looking down a gun barrel. True, newsroom experience has its techniques for handling traditional news events. But newsroom socialization takes place at a lower level in the hierarchy; managerial judgments are molded by tradition.

Editors must make judgments about such topics as these:

- Material affecting national security. Where and when does one draw the line?
- Stories that may erroneously defame public figures. Libel laws offer protection, but does that mean editors should publish possible falsehoods without waiting to check them?
- Identifying victims and survivors by name or address. Is it always necessary in order to inform the public of the crime? Is it worth the subsequent trouble it may cause the victims?
- Photographs that highlight the frailty or fragility of human life.

In weighing such stories, the editor may base decisions on the company's objectives. If the company's stated goal is to report what the journalists find out no matter what—and their publics know it—then the word on a story is usually "Go." If those publics expect the organization to show restraint, then its editors must resolve the question of "Maybe."

What journalists report, of course, helps to determine what their publics will expect.

Those who generate coverage are subject, in addition, to an elusive kind of bias: failing to cover important stories because of an editorial or reportorial blind spot. Omissions are the hardest kind of fault to notice. But one common omission that is not so hard to notice is the failure to respond to criticism or to obvious (though perhaps unintentional) imbalance in a story.

The rush to deadline is sometimes the culprit. When Alfred Jacoby,* the "reader representative" of the *San Diego Union*, criticized coverage of an appeal case of a man convicted of killing his wife, the assistant editors said the normal check for balance was not made because of the rush. The story gave full coverage to the man's side, but omitted the evidence that had led to his conviction. The paper subsequently ran another story giving the balancing material, but, of course, many readers of the first story did not see the second.

A growing threat for editors—indeed, for journalism as a whole—is journalistic excess. The most obvious form to the public is the pack of reporters jostling to get statements when newsworthy people appear in public, be it leaving their homes, catching a cab or being led into courtrooms. Pushy reporters at televised news conferences may alienate everyone involved. Even the American hostages were exasperated at clamoring reporters when their captors made them available in Beirut in 1985. Each news organization wanted its own story, no matter how similar to that of the others, and each reporter wanted a page-one byline.

Yet, it was an editor who complained about the excesses of the media in covering Christa McAuliffe's hometown of Concord, New Hampshire, after the

*Quoted in "The Ombudsmen," *The Quill*, December 1984, p. 5.

teacher died in the Challenger disaster. Michael Pride, editor of the *Concord Monitor*, told a convention of the Associated Press managing editors that he had been "disgusted" by the way the media "violated" the people of the town (*Editor & Publisher*, Dec. 13, 1986). In particular, he criticized the antics of the press in questioning students from McAuliffe's son's third-grade class as they returned home from seeing the space shuttle explode, and the disruption by photographers of services for the teacher held at a Concord Catholic church. Acknowledging that the reporters and photographers were just doing their job, Pride said a mob instinct seems to take hold in such circumstances.

Another form of excess is overextended coverage of sensational stories. The step-by-step process of the investigatory or justice system offers step-by-step pegs for rehanging the story, and often "hanging" the person involved well before he or she gets into a court of law. When to cut the coverage to the elements that are new, a factor implicit in the very word "news," is an editorial judgment. Fortunately, the journalistic community still does not equate "editorial" with "commercial," so editors are not absolutely required to repackage a sensation over and over.

When slip-ups occur, correction is in order—and a corrections policy calls for managerial direction. A forthright apology, embarrassing as it may be, goes far toward clearing the air. In May 1977, the London *Daily Mail* trumpeted that the government-run Leyland company was paying bribes to win overseas orders and that high officials of the Labor government had approved a "slush fund" for the purpose. A few days later, the paper admitted that its chief informant had confessed to forging the letter on which the story had been based. The paper's aggressive editor, David English, apologized to the wronged parties, to his readers, and to his fellow staff members—to the delight of the *Mail*'s competition, especially since English was a persistent critic of the Laborites. The paper's journalistic (and ethical) mistake was running the story before checking it with the officials involved, and it was an expensive one.

In recent years, many managers have established set times and places for providing corrections of errors. On July 13, 1987, the *New York Times* ran a two-column article at the top of page one to correct an error about the testimony of Lt. Col. Oliver North in the Iran-Contra hearings. The *Times* has run editor's notes explaining in length how something went wrong. The *Times* went to extraordinary lengths in 1981 to correct errors made in 1974 about the U.S. ambassador to Chile, Edward M. Korry. Both stories were written by Seymour M. Hersh, who uncovered evidence after leaving the staff of the *Times* that his earlier story had been wrong.

Edward Korry worked as a correspondent for the United Press, then switched to *Look* magazine, where he served as European editor. In 1962, he was appointed ambassador to Ethiopia by President John F. Kennedy, and served there with distinction. Korry's troubles began when he was appointed ambassador to Chile.

In September 1974, after the *New York Times* disclosed that the CIA had spent at least $8 million in Chile to prevent Dr. Salvador Allende Gossens, a Marxist, from assuming the presidency, Korry testified that the' U.S. maintained a "total hands-off" policy toward the military during the election. Dr. Allende won in a three-way race by 30,000 votes of three million cast. Korry denied knowledge of the ITT cablegram that became a focal point of the hearings, a report from two ITT officials in Santiago that Ambassador Korry had received "the green light to move in the name of Richard Nixon" against the new President.

Refusing to answer many questions fully from the Senators and the subcommittee staff director, Korry insisted that to describe confidential communications and official orders would be "contrary to the entire normal contract" he had entered into with the Presidents (Kennedy, Johnson, and Nixon) under whom he had served. Korry, along with then CIA Director Richard Helms and two State Department officials, was accused by members of the Senate staff of providing misleading testimony to a subcommittee of the Senate Foreign Relations Committee.

When the *New York Times* account of CIA involvement was published, Korry sent many letters to reporters and editors protesting what he cited as errors in the newspaper's coverage. He also insisted that his testimony was honest and that his reluctance to testify more fully was not based on inside knowledge of CIA and ITT activities. Korry emphasized that the inability of the press and the Senate investigators to reach the truth about his involvement tells something "about our country and the way Washington really works when the ambitions of its most important people and the interests of its most powerful groups come into conflict with the national security interests."

The assumption that Korry was not telling the truth persisted in the 1975 investigation by the Senate Select Committee on Intelligence, which was devoted to probing the illegal activities of the CIA. Korry was permitted to testify for only a few moments before a public hearing, and his testimony was not sought until the committee had published two reports on CIA activities in Chile, both of them critical of his term as ambassador. His pleas of innocence and his protestations against unfair treatment by Congress and the press had been ignored.

Who was responsible for Korry's nightmare years? First, Jack Anderson published in 1972 the ITT papers which said that Korry was following White House orders in Chile. Next, Seymour Hersh of the *New York Times* had written in 1974 that Korry was involved in the CIA effort to defeat Allende. After Korry learned during the 1975 hearings that many operations had been going on in Chile, he talked to Hersh at length, attempting to convince Hersh that he knew nothing of the operations. Hersh later wrote that Korry's "account was too self-serving to be credible."

Not until February 9, 1981, was Korry exonerated by Hersh. On that day, Hersh's 3,000-word story ran on the *Times* front page. It was headed, "New Evidence Backs Ex-envoy on His Role in Chile."

"I didn't need Hersh to tell the world I was innocent," Korry shouted to an interviewer seeking his reaction to the article.

> That's old news. The Senator Frank Church Committee made it clear five years ago. I wanted Hersh to tell what really happened down there. It wasn't the CIA that got Allende—it was 500 percent inflation and Soviet double-

dealing and the Allende government's own corruption. But Hersh doesn't want to hear that.

Then Hersh was intent on writing a positive article on Korry. It was apparently not from a pure desire to do justice. Thomas Bray, the associate editor of the *Wall Street Journal*, wrote in the issue of February 15, 1981, that "The story apparently arose out of a series of conversations in which Mr. Hersh was seeking help with a new book taking a negative view of former Secretary of State Henry Kissinger. . . ." Hersh had hundreds of thousands of dollars in advance from the publisher.

THE ETHICS OF NEWS SELECTION

> *An editor is someone who knows what he wants,*
> *but sometimes doesn't know what it is.*
>
> —Walter Davenport

The greatest influence on how editors handle the news, be it "generating" or "gate-keeping," comes from those editors' experience in the newsroom. From their supervisors and colleagues, from their knowledge of what has been done in the past, from the bruises and rewards of their years of rushing to deadlines, they have learned what is news for their papers and programs. True, their experience is built on their education, upbringing, and life experiences, but the influence of the newsroom is paramount. Furthermore, editors are apt to reflect their company's culture and ethics, for how well they "match" the company influences whether they advance within it.

Gatekeepers must choose among the many stories clamoring for space or airtime. It is a difficult task and it requires good editorial judgment, a subjective quality at the heart of the craft of journalism. Although editorial judgment is seldom studied, editors surely value newsworthiness and public appeal over concern for fairness or the individual. Even so, both the public and the profession expect editors to pay heed to those lesser concerns.

THE JUSTICE OF EDITING

> *Everyone needs an editor.*
>
> —Tim Foote, commenting on the
> fact that Adolf Hitler's original
> title *Mein Kampf* was *Four-and-*
> *a-Half Years of Struggle Against*
> *Lies, Stupidity, and Cowardice*

Fair news coverage, especially concerning reports of alleged crimes, is a tricky matter. Publicity is sometimes the price for wrongdoing, but publicity must not

SEYMOUR HERSH

He has been called the "unrivaled master of the government expose" by *Time* magazine and labeled a "sleazy goon and a heinous hack" by a fan commenting on his writing. Seymour Hersh refers to himself as an investigative reporter. ". . . It's like being a freak," he says. "You're trying to get information other people don't want you to have. I don't make deals, I don't party and drink with sources, and I don't play a game of leaks. I read, I listen, I squirrel information. It's fun."

The source of many front-page stories in the United States, Hersh has uncovered stories in every possible area of government secrecy, including the massacre at My Lai, the secret bombing of Cambodia, and the military's unauthorized bombing of North Vietnam. He was also the first to report on the wiretapping of aides by Secretary of State Henry Kissinger, the theft of papers from Kissinger's office by the Pentagon, the CIA's involvement in the Chilean coup against President Allende, and the CIA's operation of domestic spying.

Hersh originally worked as a police reporter for the *City News Bureau* in his hometown of Chicago, Illinois, following his graduation from the University of Chicago. He also held the position of correspondent for United Press International in Pierre, South Dakota, and for the Associated Press in Chicago and Washington, D.C. In 1968, Hersh served as press secretary to Senator Eugene McCarthy during his presidential campaign. Hersh, at age 35, accepted a position as a *New York Times* reporter in the Washington bureau and transferred to the New York City office in 1975.

Hersh's relentless news-gathering methods have earned him a reputation as an incredibly thorough, if somewhat intimidating, reporter. Jack Nelson of the *Los Angeles Times*, after competing with Hersh for a story, commented, "Every place we went, Hersh had been there." Stating his motives simply—"I just want people to know the truth"—Hersh does admit the tedious amount of work necessary to reveal and produce his stories.

In addition to the obligatory background reading, Hersh conducts interviews with anyone who might know anything about his topic. His persistence and badgering tactics on the telephone have been chronicled by more than one source, as well as his sarcastic exclamations of "Ah, come on; come *ooon.*"

Hersh has received numerous awards for his investigative reporting skills, including the George Polk Award, the Worth Bingham prize, the Sigma Delta Chi distinguished service award, and the Pulitzer Prize for international reporting in 1970 for his stories on the My Lai massacre. In addition, *My Lai Four: A Report On the Massacre and Its Aftermath* was named as one of the best nonfiction books of the year by *Time* in 1970.

While a reporter for the *Times*, Hersh received the Front Page Award, the Scripps-Howard Service Award and the George Polk Award in 1973 for his stories on the bombing in Cambodia, and the Sidney Hillman Award and the George Polk Award in 1974 for his articles on CIA domestic spying. In addition to his first book on the My Lai massacre, Hersh wrote another account in 1972, entitled, *Cover-Up: The Army's Secret Investigation of the Massacre of My Lai Four* (Random House, 1972). Hersh's first book, *Chemical and Biological Warfare* (Bobbs-Merrill, 1968), while criticized for an indiscretion in relation to national security, gained respect for the accuracy of the information as well as for the research it represented.

The reviews for Hersh's *The Price of Power: Kissinger in the Nixon White House* (Summit Books, 1983), covering the initial phase of Kissinger's diplomatic ascendancy and his role as national security adviser, all attest to his unrelenting methods of gathering information. Bruce Manuel of the *Christian Science Monitor* called the book a "jolting account which penetrates deep into the hidden processes of policymaking." Hersh is praised for "producing an exhaustive treatment of a difficult subject, and managing to sound like a historian instead of a muckraker."

Peter S. Prescott of *Newsweek* was slightly less complimentary. Although he called the book a "bombshell," he claims that "the ferocity of Hersh's assault on his subject may prompt even Kissinger's detractors to scratch for a word in his defense. . . . He allows no scurrilous remark, however gratuitous, about his man to go unreported." The *Commentary*'s review, written by Michael Ledeen, makes no attempts to convey subtleties in its criticism, called *The Price of Power* "seven hundred pages of gossip which should stand as an ironic commentary on the effects of megalomania on Washington journalists."

Apparently undaunted by those who oppose his methods of gaining or presenting information, Hersh continues his quest for "the truth" as well as his disregard for the secrecy surrounding governmental policymaking.

"I hate secrets," Hersh once explained to an audience at the University of Michigan. "I don't think there should be secrets. I'm awfully tired of people in Washington telling me something is secret in the name of national security. I happen to believe that making sure that every car gets twenty-five miles to the gallon is the most important kind of national security."

---

impinge on a fair trial. If the story will cause harm to the victim, the editor must weigh the harm against the benefits of publishing the story. Editors may have some uncomfortable soul-searching to do. Merely recognizing the issue or putting themselves in the victim's place may help them face it, but all such difficult decisions transcend the mechanical, unquestioned rules of the craft.

The hardest part of being fair is making sure the story gives the full picture. Reporters may not see gaps, so the editors must.

The editors are also responsible for the quality of the stories they select—that is, for seeing that the system for gathering, selecting, and processing the information provides enough doublechecks to ensure accuracy. Journalistic validation falls short of scientific validation, but the editor must be sure that reporters go to several sources, ask questions in various ways to assure that their answers are understood, and check the answers against relevant documentary sources. It takes courage for an editor to hold a good story for further checking, and fortitude if the competition tells the story first; it also takes quick thinking to make such decisions under deadline.

THE ETHICS OF EDITING COPY

The one thing I have learned about editing over the years is that you have to edit and publish out of your own tastes, enthusiasms, and concerns, and not out of notions or guesswork about what other people might like to read.

—Norman Cousins

The line between competent journalism and ethical behavior becomes blurred for copy editors and tape editors. They are usually not involved in the coverage and selection decisions, yet they determine the form of the final stories. Their main concern is in doing a competent job. But implicit in their work is an ethical standard based on four major responsibilities: checking accuracy, condensing stories, writing accurate headlines, and remaining sensitive to the impact of stories.

The first responsibility is that of making the stories as accurate as possible by checking the information for possible errors. It takes a respect for facts, for credibility, and for those affected by the errors.

Condensing is a second responsibility. It obviously calls for good judgment about what information is necessary. News sense goes into play here, but so does a moral sense of balance and fairness. Omissions can distort a story's meaning or significance.

The editor should also preserve the presence of the writer, for "butchers" cut into morale as well as prose. Respect for colleagues is part of an editor's ethics, as is respect for the truth and the public.

Perhaps the biggest complaint by the public about copy editing is that headlines distort the facts. Headlines that hype are the equivalent of misleading labels on food packages. Unless the purpose of a media enterprise embraces hype, its public expects straightforward headlines. More often, perhaps, the offense to the public's expectations results from a slip-up on the part of a harried headline writer. Writing headlines under pressure is one of the most demanding tasks in journalism, and bad headlines are nearly always the result of restricted space coupled with restricted time. A headline that miscommunicates misserves the public as much as errors in the story. One solution is simple: supervisory editors can revise a page layout that puts a complicated story under a too-brief headline.

Of all those in the mass communications process, the copy editors and tape editors may be the most remote from the people in the news and from the public for that news. To remember the potential harm to those remote people calls for sensitivity beyond any that could be expected of an individual. Management must help by encouraging such sensitivity as well.

THE ETHICS OF SUPERVISION

An editor is one whose profession is arguing with writers.

−Anonymous

In addition to shaping content, editors also direct the performance of others. Some supervision consists of straightforward orders from the boss, some involves give-and-take discussion between media professionals, and some comes from the editor's example. In their supervisory capacity, editors set the policies that guide ethical concepts such as truth, justice, and craft standards.

Editors also establish the psychological mood that prevails in a newsroom. Perhaps more than anything, this determines the attitudes of staff members. In this sense, the ethics of the newsroom reflect the ethics of the editors, even though the editors are mainly concerned with staff performance.

Performance in a typical media office is determined to a large extent by tradition. Pride is one factor—pride in one's medium and the role it plays in society, and pride in the quality of the news operation. There is an element of mystery as well. The mystery lies in the usually unquestioned news judgments of higher-ups in the editorial hierarchy. There is typically no rejoinder to "the managing editor says so." A system that operates on deadline obviously must adhere to production-line discipline. But deadline discipline may spread to other situations as well. The imperative is to do what the boss wants and not raise awkward questions.

Even so, editors have the responsibility for developing their staff as part of their supervisory role. This is a demanding job, for staff members can be perversely resistant to their own development, especially when risky decisions must be made. Still, informing the staff members of what is to be done, listening to their opinions, acting on worthy suggestions, and explaining decisions are all parts of productive management communications. In the process, the supervisor may have to bring up the questions about behavior: What are we doing? How does it fit our mission? Are we doing anything questionable? Are there adequate justifications for doing it? Could we do it in some less objectionable way? Obviously, the questions must be asked before the deadline crunch.

Time consuming? Yes, but important. Behavioral questions can affect efficiency just as operational questions can. Involving staff members in planning is one good way to get their support in carrying out editorial plans.

The editors are the guardians of media content, a powerful role that editors too often make trivial by acting on trivial concerns. They may act as if their job is merely to screen out what doesn't fit the organization's criteria and to trim what does, but the integrity of the editors affects the integrity of that content. Distortion, untruths, fabrication, abuse of the power of communication—all these can tarnish that integrity. As guardians, editors must know the pedigrees and the implications of the stories that get space or air time. The essence of guardianship is responsibility for what one is guardian over. The guardianship is the editor's and is not to be abdicated to reporters. The danger is that editors will forget the organization's key purposes and the journalist's mission of disseminating truth—uplifting goals that give editors a prestigious character.

Of course, editors cannot insist that every reporter tell them every source for every item of information. Reporters also have integrity. But trust is built through familiarity and experience: A beginning reporter must earn it. Editors and reporters are human beings and are engaged in complex human relationships. The system works best when all involved respect the others for what they are—human beings with human strengths and weaknesses.

EDITING A MILITARY NEWSPAPER

> *Editor: a delicate instrument for observing the development and flowering of the mediocre and encouraging its growth.*
>
> —Elbert Hubbard

When an excellent student, Julie Jacobs, began editing a military newspaper, she was elated. In a short time, she was dejected. Here are her words:

> My guess is that my short career as an editor has been an unusual one, because of the nature of the paper I worked for, its location, and some of the ethical problems I faced there.
>
> I worked as a student intern for *Pacific Stars and Stripes*, the U.S. military paper serving personnel in Japan, South Korea, Guam, Okinawa, Diego Garcia, the Philippines, Hong Kong, and other areas in the Far East. The paper is based in Tokyo, with correspondents in most of the above circulation areas.
>
> My job was exciting for several reasons. First, I enjoy copy editing, and appreciated having responsibilities essential to the paper from the first day I arrived in Tokyo. Second, I had never lived out of the country, and was very glad to be able to observe the nation that Americans are probably the most curious about right now.
>
> Third, I felt I needed to see the military firsthand, to understand more about how it operates without making judgments based on ignorance. As it turned out, the military was so foreign to me that getting used to operations at *Stripes* was at least as challenging as adjusting to life overseas.
>
> I had worked on three papers in the States as a reporting intern or stringer;

Stripes' first difference from these papers was that very little of *Stripes* is staff-written. Most of the staff are editors: they choose, edit, and "shape" wire copy. I put the word "shape" in quotes, because *Stripes* has a new pagination system that allows us to determine the shape of stories with computer instructions and then lay out the paper on a computer screen. The problems of using a system that is revolutionary and that doesn't work very well were daily issues at *Stripes.*

Stripes has two types of problems, in my opinion. Because it is a military paper, certain items are censored, for various reasons. Often, our colonel would pull a story because he had moral objections to it; in my opinion, these stories were not in bad taste and his actions would have been inappropriate on a "real" paper. One such story, for example, involved Japanese Turkish baths, or "turkos," which are allegedly run by the Japanese organized crime syndicate, the Yakusa. The Yakusa closed the turkos, which are, in actuality, brothels, to foreigners because of the fear of AIDS. The colonel did not let us cover this story, which I feel is certainly more newsworthy than stories on promotions of various generals and other officers, stories that always got great play. We were, ultimately, a large, daily, Pacific-wide equivalent of a base paper.

Additionally, certain stories judged offensive to "host country sensitivities" were often pulled. For example, a story critical of the Marcos regime might be pulled off the front page of the Philippines edition. I didn't understand every decision, and I disagreed with some, but I soon learned not to expect *Stripes* to be a "real paper," despite the fact that its Department of Defense mandate establishes it to be more than an arm of DoD propaganda.

That certain items were censored by the military was a fact I could live with; I was, after all, observing from within. Journalistic offenses perpetrated by civilians were problems I ultimately could not tolerate. I quit *Stripes* after eight months, although my three-month contract had been extended to a year, because of ethical problems I had with certain practices.

One day, for example, shortly after I arrived on the news desk, the executive editor gave me a story to rewrite from one of our military correspondents in Guam. The story was of very low quality; I did what I could with it. The writer had held very few interviews, had an awkward and ungrammatical style, had omitted a lot, and had turned in a story worthy of a high-school paper, in my opinion. I was nervous when I gave the story back to my editor.

He told me I had done a bad job, that the story had no punch. He then referred me to his revision. In the lede, he had included a quote that had not been in the original—that he had made up. I pointed this out to him, and told him I didn't think that was a good idea. He asked me, brusquely, if I didn't agree that we could infer that quote from the story as was originally written. I said that we could not. He informed me that as long as I was the intern and he was the editor, etc., etc.

This editor's equivalent of a teacher's pet was a young man fresh from J-school. He was given the run of the newsroom, over people with much more experience, much better news judgment, and much better managerial skills. This young man wrote a story based on a speech he heard on the radio from

Washington. Although he wrote it in Tokyo, he gave himself a Washington dateline. This was our star, our golden boy.

The longer I was at *Stripes*, the more I saw both trivial and major examples of this type of behavior. In one case, I was told of the executive editor retouching a photo of a golfer, putting a tiny dot of white-out in the photo to simulate the golf ball. It was unbelievable to me—according to the golfer's swing, the ball should have been someplace over Pittsburgh, but my editor had drawn in the ball about five feet away from the golfer. On numerous occasions, I watched him rewrite the ledes of wire stories, adding "facts" out of his head without doing any additional research.

Our editor's headlining is notorious among the staff. There's the time he took a story about a hijacking, where it was mentioned in the last graf that two GIs were on board the plane, and headlined it: "GIs fail to avert hijacking," on page one. The headline was designed to draw in enlisted readers, a big part of our audience, but it in no way reflected the story.

At any rate, I enjoyed the job I performed, but ultimately could not work for an editor I did not respect. For about six weeks, I carried out the role of features editor, because in-house politics were so paralyzing that no one would step in when the real features editor was sick. I very much enjoyed the role of gatekeeper; my job was to choose the stories for about six pages a day from the day's wire service offerings, in areas such as education, health, and Hollywood news, and then lay out, choose photos for, and assign these pages to other staffers. That's the job I ultimately want to do, for a paper I respect.

After I quit *Stripes*, I immediately fell into a copy editing job at a New York ad agency's Tokyo office. Although I never wanted to "sell out" and work for an ad agency, the move was a good one. Office politics were minimized; amazingly enough, my co-workers actually thanked me at the end of each day for a job well done. This is certainly not something I'd expect from an American paper, but nonetheless it improved my morale substantially.

Although I don't plan now to work for the ad agency for very long, I do plan to return to Tokyo when I graduate for the job they're holding for me, in copy editing and teaching English to the Japanese executives. I feel I'll be able to do good work for an organization that gives me both responsibility and support. My salary is three times my *Stripes* salary, and will be even higher when I return. Money isn't my primary goal; I hope to return to newspaper editing, to someday edit at least a section on a metropolitan daily. But I never want to work for an employer I can't respect again.

EXERCISES

1. You are the editor of a small-town weekly newspaper, and most of its profits come from the newspaper's print shop that does commercial work. Your biggest customer is a hometown company plant publication. As editor, you learn that the company plans to build a new plant elsewhere. The deal is not final and it does not mean the company will move out of your town. Company managers ask you to delay printing the story. Although they make no threats, you know they could easily take the company's own publication

elsewhere. It's Tuesday afternoon, and your weekly comes out on Wednesday morning.

What do you do?

2. The executive editor of a newspaper chain was interviewed by two new reporters from one of the chain's papers. When the editor read the article that resulted, he realized that his quotations had been shortened and changed. He called in the two reporters and asked them why they had changed his quotations. Their answer amounted to this: "They didn't fit." The editor was almost apoplectic. Was he right?

WORDS ABOUT PICTURES

This is not I . . .
Retouched and smoothed and prettified to please;
Put back the wrinkles and the lines I know;
I have spent blood and brains achieving these,
Out of the pain, the struggle and the wrack,
These are my scars of battle—put them back!

—Berton Braley

The imitator is a poor kind of creature. If the man who paints only the tree, or flower, or other surface he sees before him were an artist, the king of artists would be the photographer. It is for the artist to do something beyond this: in portrait painting to put on canvas something more than the face the model wears for that one day; to paint the man, in short, as well as his features.

—James Whistler

Private faces in public places
Are wiser and nicer
Than public faces in private places.

—W. H. Auden

CHAPTER 9

Visual Communications

There are three forms of visual art: Painting is art to look at, sculpture is art you can walk around, and architecture is art you can walk through.

—Dan Rice

Photojournalists and camera crews may be the most maligned of journalists, and sometimes for no good reason. William Anders, who was on the crew of the Apollo 8, was hounded by the press and the public after his return from the moon. He and his wife finally escaped to a hotel in Acapulco for a quiet vacation, but were exasperated when a photographer knocked on their door and asked to take pictures. "Okay, come on in," Anders sighed. "Thanks," the photographer said enthusiastically. "You've got the best view of the bay in the whole place." Anders, of course, assumed that the reporter was merely callous—insensitive to his need for privacy. It is the kind of assumption that may dog those who practice visual journalism.

Many of the more emotional confrontations over ethics arise over photographs. A writer can often cover a situation in great detail without provoking a response, while a photograph accompanying the story will stir a storm.

The "best" pictures, even prize-winning pictures, are especially likely to draw criticism because they so often reveal human emotions. Critics, who may not know the subjects, may be driven by compassion for their apparent embarrassment or the invasion of their privacy.

Pictures are powerful. They shape the vision of the world in people's minds. But photographs are even more powerful than drawings or paintings: They are more natural, more independent of the artist—in a way, more real. Susan Sontag, in her book *On Photography* (Farrar, Straus and Giroux, 1977) contends that qualities like this help to give photographic images "virtually unlimited authority in modern society."

Many editors close their eyes to the impact of photos. When they see a dramatic photograph, they may display it on the front page, but they often see it as a supplement to the news story. They may think more about page-design criteria or the news in the story than about the impact of the photo. Yet the impact of the

SUSAN SONTAG

Writing is a mysterious activity. One has to be, at different stages of conception and execution, in a state of extreme alertness and consciousness and in a state of great naivete and ignorance. Although this is probably true of the practice of any art, it may be more true of writing because the writer—unlike the painter or composer—works in a medium that one employs all the time, throughout one's waking life.

The writer of numerous novels, screenplays, short stories, essays, and reviews, Susan Sontag is well qualified to speak about the "mysteries" of writing. Her talent is displayed in topics as diverse as the effects of illness on cancer patients and the importance of photography in society, leading Maureen Howard of *Saturday Review* to refer to her as "our most celebrated woman intellectual."

To reach Sontag's high status, she was born in New York City and later attended the University of California at Berkeley and the University of Chicago, as an undergraduate. She received master's degrees in English and philosophy from Harvard and was a Ph.D. candidate there from 1955-57. Her employment history includes a position as an English instructor at the University of Connecticut at Storrs; the editor of *Commentary* in New York, New York; and a lecturer in philosophy at City College in New York and Sarah Lawrence College in Bronxville, New York. In addition, Sontag was an instructor in Columbia's department of religion and a writer-in-residence at Rutgers University.

Sontag's publications include *The Benefactor* (1963), *Against Interpretation, and Other Essays* (1966), *Death Kit* (1967), *Styles of Radical Will* (1969), *Trip to Hanoi* (1969), *The Temptation to Exist* (1970), *On Photography* (1976), *Illness as Metaphor* (1978), and *I, et cetera* (1978). Her work has also appeared in the introductions of several other books as well as in magazines such as *Atlantic Monthly, American Review, Playboy, Partisan Review, Nation, Harper's* and the *New York Review of Books.*

Sontag also demonstrated her diverse writing style in *On Photography,* believing that photographs "give people an imaginary possession of a past that is unreal, and help people to take possession of space in which they are insecure." She claims that "It all started with one essay—about some of the problems, aesthetic and moral, posed by the omnipresence of photographed images; but the more I thought about what photographs are, the more complex and suggestive they became."

A collection of short essays, the book explains the impact of photography on tourism, stating that "it seems positively unnatural to travel for pleasure without taking a camera along. Photographs will offer indisputable evidence . . . that fun was had." Sontag also discusses the immortality of photography and the ability of the camera to "create an image-world that bids to outlast us all."

The last explanation Sontag offers for her interest in photography appears easily generalized to all forms of art, especially to her devotion to writing:

> The final reason for the need to photograph everything lies in the very logic of consumption itself. To consume means to burn, to use up—and, therefore, to need to be replenished. As we make images and consume them, we need still more images; and still more. But images are not a treasure for which the world must be ransacked; they are precisely what is at hand wherever the eye falls. The possession of a camera can inspire something akin to lust. And like all credible forms of lust, it cannot be satisfied: first, because the possibilities of photography are infinite; and, second, because the project is finally self-devouring.

—Jennifer Koch

story is more often determined by the photograph than by the story itself. Studies show that about twice as many people look at the picture as read the story. No wonder intrusive pictures arouse protests.

THE PRIVACY ISSUE IN PHOTOJOURNALISM

History is little else than a picture of human crimes and misfortunes.

—Voltaire

Photographing another human being is almost always intrusive. Photographers are often torn by guilt, especially when others are angry at them for taking the photos. Bill Welch, a photographer for the *Nashville Tennessean*, wrote in the *Editorially Speaking* feature of *Gannetteer* (April 1982), of "a sense of intruding on an almost embarrassing intimate time" when he photographed a crying Vietnamese veteran. He became aware of people glaring at him as if he "were committing some obscene act." Sontag likens taking pictures to voyeurism, and asserts that the act of photographing a person has a "semblance of rape."

"There is an aggression implicit in every use of that camera," Sontag says. Just as the camera is a sublimation of the gun, she explains, "to photograph someone is a sublimated murder—a soft murder." In this predatory aspect, a photographer cruelly ravages the subject and carries away the subject's image as loot. "To photograph is to appropriate the thing photographed," says Sontag.

Primitive people (and some not so primitive) see photographers as stealing part of their being from them by making away with their image. If a person's picture is widely published, that person has lost some element of his or her private life. The words "taking a picture" reflect this sense of appropriation. Photographers are familiar with such feelings. David Perdew, photo editor for the Gannett Rochester Newspapers, tells of turning away from what would have been a dramatic picture of a woman pinned inside a wrecked car, her face pressed against the windshield, her eyes looking at Perdew. "Was I intimidated by being caught in the act of stealing a person's image—invading her privacy (dignity)?" he wrote in *Editorially Speaking* in April 1982.

The invasion of privacy hangs constantly over a photographer's conscience. His problem is not so much legal as it is moral. An editor's instruction to "shoot first and we'll worry about it later" may relieve the photographer of the legal question, but cannot eliminate the ethical torment. The privacy issue is always there. Harry Marsh, head of the department of journalism and mass communication at Kansas State University, wrote a letter to *The Quill* (February 1972) commenting on a picture of a grieving family, "I don't know how we can demonstrate reality other than by invading people's privacy."

Demonstrating reality is what photographers are trying to do. In *Editorially Speaking* (April 1982), photographer Bill Welch says the point of his assignment, to photograph the veteran crying over his lost comrades at a ceremony in a park, was "to give thousands of newspaper subscribers, through their viewing of photographs, a means of understanding and even sharing what this event was all about." There is no joy in photographing violence or crime or tragedy, Welch explains, but news about it depicts society as it is. "Pictures that vividly portray real-life scenes of tragedy are part of that news," he says. "They tell us how acts of violence threaten to consume us."

All reporters face ethical questions about how they get their information. A photographer faces these questions with special intensity. Suppose that your newspaper/magazine is planning a hard-hitting report on heroin use. The picture editor says that he or she will settle for nothing less than a tough photo of someone "shooting up," i.e., injecting heroin. No faces, please, but the editor reminds you that the picture can NOT be staged.

From your research and your contacts with the joint state-federal drug strike force, you know that heroin use is a felony. However, it is a crime in your state to be a party to someone using a prohibited substance even though you are NOT the one using the illicit narcotic.

What do you do—resign, saying that you will not be party to anything illegal? Hit the streets, looking for the drug subculture that you have heard about? Call a friend who once hinted at being a heroin addict? Ask the reporter with whom you are working for help?

More often, though, the dilemma arises from knowing that one is capitalizing on the trauma of one clearly identified person to convey the story to a faceless public or be immune to the pain one causes.

Of course, some of the public outcry may seem overmuch, even to the sensitive photographer. Sometimes photographers might wish they could follow the example of John Bright, a British orator and politician. Bright was once at the scene of a serious traffic accident. He put ten pounds in his hat and went around the crowd that had gathered, saying, "I'm ten pounds sorry. How sorry are you?"

Readers are, in fact, quick to protest when they perceive that pain. Tim Bunn, managing editor of *The Syracuse Herald-Journal*, wrote a column on February 5, 1984, in response to such reader protests. The paper had printed a large, dramatic picture of the limp form of a man being taken from a flooded manhole, where he had been trapped in cold water for half an hour. The man survived, in critical condition, but that did not stop the protests. Bunn defended the use of the picture as "a vivid and dramatic image of humankind at its best," with "firemen and policemen working frantically to save a fellow human being.

"There is legitimate news in a man's being able to survive for half an hour under frigid water," Bunn went on. "We did what professional news editors do. We presented it to our readers."

The Final Decision is Yes.

But editors don't confront the subjects of the pictures. True, editors could never get the paper out or the program on the air if they had to think through every decision. But too many editors operate entirely by hand-me-down rules. Ethical editing requires thought. When a columnist in a photographic magazine, Howard Chapnick, urged photographers to work to change the thinking of editors because they are making newspapers too superficial, he talked about something more basic than photographs. His column that month was on journalistic ethics.

Photojournalism has its own version of the conflict between public and professional standards. In *On Photography*, Susan Sontag, writing about photography as an art, identifies this conflict. "The history of photography could be recapitulated as the struggle between two different imperatives: beautification, which comes from the fine arts, and truth-telling." The latter, she says, is a legacy from conscience and the "profession of independent journalism." The differences in perspective are most clearly evident in the desire of the people photographed to be "photogenic" and look pretty or handsome while the photojournalist wants to film them as they actually look. But the differences go beyond photogenic beauty. The public expects journalists in general to serve a community's purposes by portraying it positively.

Death and grief may be the most sensitive issues for picture editors and photographers. Grief communicates powerfully through pictures. The guideline for using such pictures is usually whether the event causing the grief is newsworthy. But the dramatic quality of the picture can sometimes overwhelm an editor's news judgment. A good example was provided by a picture in 1985 of members of a family in Bakersfield, California, at the painful moment of shock as they saw their drowned son revealed when a bag containing his body was opened.

The picture was taken by a photographer for the *Bakersfield Californian*, despite mild efforts to keep him from shooting the scene. It captured the essence of the human emotions involved. The picture was distributed by the Associated

Press and caused more than 500 protest letters and telephone calls to the news-paper. The managing editor, Bob Bentley, later said the decision to publish the photograph had been a mistake. *Editor & Publisher* (June 21, 1986) quoted him as saying:

> The reaction was too intense and widespread to shrug it off and say we're just doing our job. We encroached on the private grief of a family. If we don't hear those protest voices, we're playing right into the hands of our critics who say we are insensitive, intrusive, arrogant, and have lost touch with our readers.

Brian Steffens, news-graphics editor of the *San Diego Union*, offered a guide-line in a discussion of the Bakersfield and other questionable photographs (*Editor & Publisher*, June 21, 1986). While warning against any absolute decision against the use of such pictures, he reminded those at a meeting of the California Society of Newspaper Editors, "we're in the business of news, not drama."

The tendency of editors, however, is to consider the human drama an im-portant attribute of the news. A few years ago, members of the Associated Press Managing Editors organization were surveyed about two photographs. One showed the ruins of a house after a fire that killed six members of a family, and the other showed the father of the family sobbing in the arms of a neighbor. Eighty-six per-cent of the editors polled thought the picture of the grieving father was the better picture, fifty-five percent saw no invasion of privacy; and twenty-five percent said they saw some invasion of privacy, but would publish the picture anyway.

In both cases, with some qualms, the Final Decision is Yes.

One of those surveyed was Donald Gormley, then editor of the Chicago *Daily News*. Later Gormley, as editor of the Spokane *Spokesman-Review*, ran into hot public criticisms over a photograph. It ran on page one and showed a dramatic pic-ture of a woman apparently resisting arrest after driving her car into a river. She was a public defender whose client had that day been sentenced to 75 years for rape. As reported in *Editor & Publisher* (Oct. 3, 1981), Gormley responded to protests over publishing the picture by explaining, in an editorial, the journalistic criteria for publishing the photograph.

> First, . . . it is a splended news picture. It has action, emotion, composition, and a strong focus of attention. And it tells a story, better than words could possibly do. Readers see the picture and literally "feel" the story. That doesn't happen to readers very often.
>
> Second, it is clearly news. A driver zipping off a bridge into the Spokane River is not a common occurrence. When the driver then struggles with police, that makes it a little better story. When the driver turns out to be a public defender in a widely publicized and important trial, the story gets more com-pelling. Let it happen on judgment day for her client and it becomes very touching. It was really a rotten day for Julie Twyford (the public defender).
>
> Third, the photo was not obscene, filthy, or abhorrent in moral content.

It did not titillate or arouse base passions. By objective standards, it was not in bad taste.

Fourth, we do not think publishing the photo was unfair. The picture was made in a public place of a public incident. The information in the picture and the cutline were accurate. With its cutline, it was complete and it was certainly timely.

The photo met every one of the exacting standards set by the management of this newspaper. So, it belonged in the paper; there was no reason to bury it inside.

Gormley then asked readers to mark ballots to show whether they would have printed the picture. The resulting tally was 1,231 in favor of publishing it and 545 opposed. Gormley later said the sobering aspect of the experience came from the intensity of feelings expressed by those opposed. He said it made his staff more sensitive to the need for compassion in news judgments.

Gormley's criteria offer points for consideration of ethical implications involved.

The pictorial quality of the photograph. Most journalistic photographs show what happened, or rather, one instant of what happened in a news event. They are normally undramatic and are selected for their role in telling the story. Outstanding pictures are likely to be more dramatic because they show the climactic action of a news event or depict an emotional situation. These pictures, at least, will be published prominently by newspapers. These are the pictures most likely to raise ethical questions. When pictures show only what a person's face looks like or only record some ceremonial action, editors may still use them to solve layout problems and please participants in the news. Pictorial quality moves newspaper editors less than it does television producers: Dramatic pictures nearly always get on television.

The news conveyed by the photograph. A picture alone is largely meaningless, no matter how good its pictorial qualities. The story of the woman in Spokane provided the context for the picture. If a photograph is staged well, or if it shows the visible result of an event, it might tell a good part of the story. But pictures with emotional potential are more likely to be unplanned glimpses that convey little but drama. The story crystallizes the emotion—the picture gets its news quality from the words that accompany it. In fact, one picture can be given different meanings with different cutlines. More can be read into a picture than the news justifies.

Since a dramatic picture is thus independent of the news, the news quality of the photograph is a slippery basis for ethical decisions.

The taste displayed by the picture. This subjective quality can be the source of endless disagreement. Gormley's criteria of obscenity, filth, or moral abhorrence don't satisfy everyone, but they do at least constitute guidelines. Disputes over good taste may involve ethical issues, but often they result from differences in background and experience. The journalist should look clearly at the nub of the dispute to determine its nature.

The fairness of the photo. Photos, like news stories, can distort a situation. So can cutlines. Secretary of State George Shultz was once photographed with his face in his hands at a hearing in which the Marine commandant in the picture inadvertently called Lebanon "Vietnam." The Associated Press cutline said Shultz was reacting to the general's slip of the tongue. The television tape of the hearing showed that the still photograph had been taken before the general's miscue and Associated Press subsequently sent a correction. This was a misjudgment by a picture editor and the Associated Press acted ethically to clarify the matter. Yet, it shows how easily pictures could be unfairly used. Obviously, editorial criteria for avoiding distortion in news stories also apply to photos.

A similar error involving pictures of the family of teacher-astronaut Christa McAuliffe was shown in the *Boston Herald*. The cutlines with pictures distributed by the Associated Press and published in the *New York Times* said they showed family members reacting to the explosion engulfing the space shuttle Challenger. The *Herald*'s photographer caught the same shot at liftoff, nearly a minute before the explosion. After a *Herald* story pointed out the discrepancy, the Associated Press and the *Times* checked video tapes and issued corrections.

What about staged photos of dramatic events? If a photographer misses a dramatic moment, the temptation to add a prop or pose the characters may be irresistible. Consider this case:

At a photojournalism clinic in North Carolina, a long-time photographer made this recommendation to editors: "Always carry a broken tricycle in the trunk of your car. Then, if you come to a fatal accident involving a child, you can use the trike to provide foreground interest."

One editor reasoned this way: Certainly the picture will be of more interest because of the tricycle as a prop. But should I promote this? Of course, if I say it's fine to carry a tricycle, so what? But as an editor, I'm an authority figure, so the photographer will think I approve visual fiction. The editor said no—agreeing with the Final Decision.

A similar question, this time without human beings:

Not long ago, a photographer with artistic pretentions went to Portola State Park in search of scenic pictures. Glancing down, he noticed an interesting arrangement of dead leaves and rocks along a stream. It occurred to him that the scene would be better if he moved two leaves and added another. But then he began to wonder if it were ethical to modify the arrangement he found. Most photographers would say yes, but editors must be wary: To condone visual fiction, even in a trivial situation, has serious implications.

To alter photos is even more tempting since the development of electronic machines that can convert photographs into digital data. Developed for retouching photographs, the machines can also rearrange the elements of the picture, moving them or even eliminating or adding elements. The changed pictures show no evidence of having been changed.

As an example, suppose that your newspaper (or magazine) has just acquired a dazzling SCITEX machine, something probably better suited to cut "Star Wars" than your publication. However, the executive editor thinks of himself or herself as a knowledgeable "picture person" and can not wait to retouch photos (and eliminate a costly art department) with this $250,000 piece of gear.

By way of background, the SCITEX machine analyzes a color transparency or black and white negative, then digests it and turns the negative into billions of bits of digital information. A technician, not an editor, can use a little computer "mouse" to retouch a photo, doing something as innocent as zipping the fly of someone in a photo to editing out unwanted persons or superimposing parts of the picture in another part of the frame—all without the faintest trace of hand retouching.

One of your most able—and principled—staff photographers returns from Cairo, Egypt, with smashing photos of the Pyramids to accompany a long article on the changes taking place in this important Arab state. Unfortunately for the layout staff, the best photos are all "horizontals" and your art director/graphics editor wants a vertical photo for a full-page takeout.

No problem—the SCITEX machine can neatly tuck one Pyramid behind another, making a tidy vertical out of a pecky and irksome horizontal picture. The photographer, however, protests.

Not surprisingly, most editors say the only thing accomplished by the SCITEX machine is to change the camera angle of the photographer, not the essential content of the photograph.

You are not so sure, knowing that by changing the camera angle you would also change the background, the angle of the sun—certainly change the orientation of the Pyramids to a camel driver who so conveniently appears in the foreground of the photo.

Is the photographer just being a tiresome artist, or does he or she have a point? Have we tampered with reality? Will the readers ever know—or care? Is this just a twentieth century (maybe twenty-first century) form of cropping a photo? Should you spill everything you know to the *New York Times*?

The Final Decision is No, because the credibility of pictures may soon be lost—and the potential for ethical problems is immense.

TELEVISION

Television's strengths are its immediacy and its ability to deliver both pictures and sound to a very wide audience. Its weakness is that it cannot deliver anything like the volume of news found in good metropolitan newspapers. But that is what we are, an orange, and it would be pleasing if our critics would stop complaining that we are not an apple.

—William McAndrew

Much that has been said about still photography applies also to the moving photography of television. But the visual impact of television is so great that it raises even more ethical questions. Television pictures can be "live," and, even on tape, they often seem live to viewers. The seeming reality speaks directly to the viewers' emotions, so that many viewers will react strongly to an invasion of privacy. When television reporters interviewed the families of Marines killed in Lebanon or of hostages held in Iran, the video pictures aroused protests from viewers who felt the families were being abused. Picturing grief on television angers people for whom grief is an intensely private matter. Similarly, pictures of bodies of the victims of accidents, violence, or crime, even if not particularly gory, are often too strong for the public, and a picture of a person threatening to jump off a bridge seems to many to be an invasion of privacy.

Editors and producers in such cases must decide. They draw the lines of acceptability. By far, most of their line-drawing is based on newsworthiness, not on ethical factors. The danger is that editors and producers will become so callous that they will consider only news criteria. Their sensitivity can be sharpened by articulating their policies, as Donald Gormley did in Spokane, so that they and their staff members have a shared understanding of the guidelines they will try to follow.

Assignment editors play an especially sensitive role in how camera crews cover the news. Pressed for fresh shots or action, they may ignore, say, the statement by the mayor that is the heart of the news. Photographing activists only when they are demonstrating in the streets deprives the public of ever thinking of them as having any reasoned arguments.

The sheer size of the television audience multiplies complaints of abuse. At least some of the millions watching a network program will be easily offended by the intrusions of the camera. Television producers and advertisers may beg the question by blurring TV coverage, affecting accuracy. Once again the importance of good judgment is clear, for both ethical and professional reasons.

The need to maintain large audiences also affects editors and producers. To do this, they exploit human curiosity, which can range from the sublime to the base. Editors draw their line between the two. Appealing to the baser forms of curiosity attracts the biggest audiences: People are drawn to neighborhood fires or automobile accidents and they want to hear about them. Journalism has to keep its feet in the streets and even tread judiciously in the alleys and sewers if it is to keep the public properly informed. To draw interest, editors tread dangerously close to drawing ire.

However, the media must neither augment events to make them more interesting, nor allow others to augment events for publicity. A demonstration staged by a group with limited access to the media is one thing; a terrorist group is another. People have long accepted what Daniel J. Boorstin terms "pseudo-events"—news conferences, for example—yet journalists are too often aware of being used for purposes unrelated to the mission of informing the public. The ethics in such situations are mixed. Perhaps the best guide for journalists is to make clear to the public where the information comes from and whose interests it serves.

Like print journalists, television journalists select stories from among many subjects, but the events are much more fleeting and fragile. A few stragglers watching a parade can seem like a throng if a clump of observers is photographed. What happened before and after a picture was taken did not happen as far as the viewer of the picture is concerned. Yet the event photographed may have been building up for a long time.

Should photographers drop their roles as recorders of events to help a person in danger? The reporter can help the person and still get the story, but the photographer might miss the picture. The ethical guideline is fairly clear. If no one else can help, the photographer must—and be satisfied with whatever pictures are then possible. If others are helping the victim, the photographer might take the pictures, then join in their efforts. A tougher decision is when it is unclear whether the aid is necessary, even if others are present. The best guide is for photographers to think about the possibility before it occurs so that they can act quickly—and ethically.

EXERCISES

1. Read again the case of the photograph on Page 141 in which a woman apparently resisted arrest. Although 1,231 readers favored publishing the picture and 545 were opposed, what do *you* think of publishing that picture?

2. Read again about the photojournalism clinic in North Carolina on Page 143 in which a photographer recommended that other photographers should carry a broken tricycle in the trunks of their cars. What do you think of this suggestion?

3. A film crew from a large metropolitan TV station was assembling a documentary on campus protests, and, in particular, on the "Out of South Africa" movement. On the day selected to shoot the group scenes, including marching, the crew was not certain that sufficient signs and placards would be in evidence; consequently, they manufactured and took along additional placards for use by available students. At the time of the shooting, there were not enough placards for the film crew's purposes. They distributed the signs they brought and filmed the scene. What do you think of this action?

WORDS ABOUT ADS AND PR

Advertising may be described as the science of arresting the human intelligence long enough to get money from it.

—Stephen Leacock

Unmentionables—those articles of ladies' apparel that are never discussed in public, except in full-page, illustrated ads.

—Changing Times

You can tell the ideals of a nation by its advertisements.

—Norman Douglas

I don't care what is written about me so long as it isn't true.

—Katharine Hepburn

The art of publicity is a black art.

—Judge Learned Hand

Nothing's so apt to undermine your confidence in a product as knowing that the commercial selling it has been approved by the company that makes it.

—Franklin P. Jones

CHAPTER 10

The Ethics of Persuasion

I do not read advertisements—I would spend all my time wanting things.

—Archbishop of Canterbury

Critics who question the ethics of advertising contend that advertisers make a virtue of lying. Yet advertising seems as amenable to treatment as the news stories, and the sins no worse. A distortion in a news story, where the public does not expect it, may be morally worse than a distortion in an advertisement. Neither is it virtuous, but most members of the public are on guard when they are exposed to an advertisement.

By the time students reach college, they have spent more time watching television commercials than they will spend in class in their four years as undergraduates. One would think they should be thoroughly brainwashed, but many are skeptical unbelievers when it comes to commercials. They have learned to function in that bazaar in which Sissela Bok finds justification for white lies—the area of hard selling in which the advertisers pit creative message-makers against blasé sophisticates hardened by thousands of commercials. Each side knows what the other is doing. Of course, these students are influenced by advertising and by messages relevant to their own desires and needs. That those desires and needs have been significantly shaped by advertising is beyond question. However, this deeper kind of influence is no more clearly the work of advertising than it is of journalism as a whole. The news editor exploits the public's needs and desires just as the advertising professional does.

The role of advertising has been described by Frederick R. Gamble, former president of the American Association of Advertising Agencies as follows:

> Advertising is the counterpart in distribution of the machine in production. By use of machines, our production of goods and services has been multiplied. By the use of mass media, advertising multiplies the selling effort. Advertising is the great acceleration force in distribution. Reaching many people rapidly at low cost, advertising speeds up sales [and] turns prospects

into customers in large numbers and at high speed. Hence, in a mass-production and high-consumption economy, advertising has the greatest opportunity and the greatest responsibility for finding customers.*

Advertising is criticized because selling carries a stigma. Centuries ago, Anacharsis said, "The market is the place set aside where men may deceive each other." Frederick Gamble's comments suggest that many buyers are not particularly on guard against deception, despite the rise in consumerism and efforts to counter market deception.

In writing about the ethics of the mass media, one does not take on the entire burden of advertiser morality. Philip Kotler, in his book *Marketing Management* (Prentice-Hall, 1980), a standard textbook, holds top management responsible for developing policies that define proper marketing conduct. He lists fourteen morally difficult situations in marketing, of which only five deal with advertising messages; the rest involve such things as spying on competitors, bribing purchasing agents, and lobbying. Kotler's message-related moral questions range in seriousness from calling a modernized, but basically unchanged, product "new and improved" to advertising a product that research shows is harmful to a person's health. He does not include outright lying in his list. The ethics—if not the law—are so clear in that case that it should not present a "troublesome" issue to a respectable marketing manager.

Advertising operates under stricter legal controls than other forms of mass communication. Commercial speech is protected by the First Amendment, but not as fully as political or religous speech. Federal and state governments regulate advertising, and the media also set standards that limit advertising abuses. The guidelines for the CBS television network, for example, fill more than forty typewritten pages and are applied by a staff under the supervision of a vice president for program practices. Every commercial must be cleared before it can be scheduled.

Like journalists, advertisers confront ethical decisions by considering their mission, best viewed from the perspective of the potential consumer. The mission, from that angle, is to provide information that will help consumers to satisfy their needs and wants—that is, accurate and relevant information. The information can also create needs and wants, which may benefit the advertiser, but which also raises ethical questions. There is no easy answer.

ADVERTISING AND MONEY

> *Of all the possible values of human society, one and only one is the truly universal, truly sound, truly and completely acceptable goal of man. That goal is money.*

> —C. Wright Mills

*Edwin Emery *et al.*, *Introduction to Mass Communications* (New York: Dodd, Mead & Company, Inc., 1960) p. 308.

The measure of advertising's success is the extent to which it increases demand. Competition or declining profits can blow good intentions out of the board room. In such cases, the perspective shifts from what is best in the long run for society to what is best in the short run for the company. Ethics are fine for the secure, but a greater market share is what the slipping company needs.

The potency of market share was shown a few years ago in Dallas. Lee Guittar, publisher of the *Dallas Times Herald*, decided in 1980 to replace press releases as news copy in the paper's Sunday real estate section, with real news coverage of real estate. The advertisers were furious and the *Times Herald*'s share of the real estate advertising market dropped from rough parity with the *Dallas Morning News* to 27 percent of the market.

"For our bold and gutsy move, we just generated angry advertisers, and we never got any credit in the newspaper industry," Guittar said. In 1983, the *Times Herald* quietly resumed running press releases in its Saturday edition.

If one thinks that Guittar changed from gutsy to gutless, one should consider that the *Times Herald* and the *Morning News* are in a battle for survival. Most cities that had competing daily newspapers have become one-ownership markets. Between 1980 and 1983, the advertising market share of the *Times Herald* dropped from 46.9 percent to 45.5 percent. In view of such figures, was the *Times Herald*'s move back to press releases unethical?

The mass media depend on advertising for most or all of their revenues, but many journalists try to disassociate themselves from the advertising department. The public seems to see a difference, too, and puts up its guard for advertisements. So one simple kind of right behavior is to identify advertisements so they won't be taken as news. One gray area is editorial copy that appears between the ads in special advertising sections. This is often "fluff" that praises the products being advertised, although typographically it looks like news. The more inserts, the more fluff—which, in inserts, is written by advertising writers rather than by reporters.

Advertising, like editorial content, reflects the people who produce it. Its business leaders represent the full range of ethical perspectives. To the extent that managers' motives shape their advertising, their adherence to the standards of practice of the American Association of Advertising Agencies (AAAA) will differ.

Even the most ethical advertiser wants to emphasize the attractive qualities of a product and detract attention from its negative side. "Weasel words" that hide the truth arouse little condemnation. Respected advertisers often associate a product with attributes that have nothing to do with its quality. Ads that disparage competing products by name, even if they are fair, may bother some consumers. Wise advertisers do not usually mislead and trick potential buyers, because they want long-term acceptance for the product. The profits come from the repeated purchases. Most advertising, in fact, is designed to keep customers buying what they are already buying. This may be the greatest force for ethical advertising.

One advertising-related issue for journalists is the influence advertisers have over editorial content. This is an arena where expectations clash. Editors and producers are expected to guard their domain from influence, yet businesses expect friendly treatment. When they don't get it, they are quick to threaten to withdraw advertising. Here is a case related by a reporter:

> The advertising manager came to me today and asked me for heaven's sake to give G— — a break. He said G— — was sore as the devil and ready to pull out his advertising. He said we were not being fair to him in reporting a lawsuit against him. The ad manager said, couldn't we ever run a story favorable to one of our advertisers? The city editor said to me, "Call 'em as you see 'em."

One may applaud the city editor, but wouldn't the reporter have been surprised if the editor had waffled and looked for a way to run a story favorable to the advertiser? If the editor had, the Final Decision would have been No.

Another case: On penalty of canceling all their advertising, theater owners in a small town demanded that the editor treat them "fairly." Specifically, (a) cease to publish news of theaters closing on Sunday, (b) cease to publish letters to the editor complaining of the quality of pictures currently being shown, and (c) support candidates for city offices who are opposed to increasing the cost of theater licenses. The advertising involved was a considerable amount of the paper's weekly revenue. The editor compromised.

A more courageous response would have been to check the news and the letters. If they proved accurate and fair, the editor should have continued them: The editor's obligation was to the public, not to the theater owners. If the news and letters were inaccurate or unfair, his obligation to the public would require that he correct them, not omit them. If the theater owners' demands had been more clearly in the community's interest, the ethical decision might have been more complicated.

This example raises a practical question about the cost of behaving ethically. If the publisher backed the theater owners against the editor, the editor's options might have been to yield or give up his job.

A reporter for a metropolitan paper tells of an instance that illustrates how it may be easier for a big paper to handle advertisers.

A large corporation withheld for 24 hours the announcement of a dividend increase on its common stock, enabling some company executives to profit substantially on the resulting market fluctuation. An enterprising reporter discovered and wrote the story. His boss, the financial editor, took him to confer with the managing editor. The three agreed to run the story as written and to run an editorial as well, criticizing the company's "reprehensible behavior."

A high corporation officer called the reporter into his office and protested that the story was unfair. He threatened to pull the company's advertising out of the paper. The reporter replied, "What an interesting story that threat would make for tomorrow's paper." The advertising stayed.

The reporter could be criticized for overstepping his powers; an editor, after all, would decide whether the threat was a publishable story. But the case illustrates that small media companies are more vulnerable than large ones.

When *Reader's Digest* decided in 1955 to accept advertising, it worried David Ogilvy, a leading advertising man. Some years later he wrote, "I was afraid that the *Digest* editors would start pulling punches in deference to advertisers and even give editorial support to advertisers—an obvious temptation to magazine editors. But this has not happened. The *Digest* has remained incorruptible. No log-rolling, no back-scratching."

Reader's Digest passed the test. But many other magazines are more susceptible to pressure from the advertisers, on whom they are so dependent. A magazine's success often depends on its choosing the subjects of articles out of the air, in contrast to a newspaper editor's chronicle of daily events. Small magazines' cash flow makes them vulnerable. In addition, the specialized nature of most magazines means their readers are less likely, in any case, to distinguish between editorial and advertising content.

ADVERTISING AND BROADCASTING

> *A professor at the New School of Social Research said, "Advertising is a profoundly subversive force in American life." Holy smoke, is that what I do for a living?*
>
> —David Ogilvy

Broadcasters are especially sensitive to the needs of advertisers, because their audiences hinge on the message they send at any moment. If the message is not attractive, they may lose the audience—and the advertising revenue.

Interestingly enough, in the early days of radio, nearly everyone thought there should be no place for advertising in broadcasting. Even David Sarnoff, who later became chairman of the Radio Corporation of America, saw broadcasting as a public institution free from commercialism.

The trade publication *Printer's Ink* asserted in 1923:

> An attempt to make radio an advertising medium. . . would, we think, prove positively offensive to great numbers of people. . . . Imagine the effect, for example, of a piano sonata by Josef Hoffman followed by the audible assertion, "If you are under forty, four chances to one you will get pyorrhea." Or, "Pickle Bros. are offering three-dollar silk hose for $1.98." Exaggerated, no doubt, yet the principle is there. To break in upon one's own entertainment *in his own house* is quite likely intolerable, and advertising as a whole cannot be the gainer by anything of the sort.

By the end of the 1920s, radio was big and costly enough to dash the hope that the industry could remain free of advertising. Merchants were quick to use broadcasting to sell their goods.

Sponsored programs were first broadcast experimentally in 1922 on station

WEAF. Thereafter, they developed rapidly—though not without protests from government officials and the public. For example, at the first annual Radio Conference in Washington, Herbert Hoover, who was then Secretary of Commerce, declared, "It is inconceivable that so great a possibility for service . . . be drowned in advertising chatter."

When Congress finally passed the Radio Act of 1927, the broadcasting industry began to develop its four main contemporary characteristics: (1) submitting to legal and administrative control by federal licensing, (2) providing mass entertainment, (3) acting as an adjunct of the marketing system, (4) and concentrating its operational control in network organization.

After World War II, television stations scrambled to affiliate with the national networks that dominated the industry. By the summer of 1955, there were 432 television stations, including 13 noncommercial educational stations. The costs of broadcasting became enormous.

COSTS OF BROADCASTING

Advertising is one of the few callings in which it is advisable to pay attention to someone else's business.

—Howard W. Newton

The smallest regular-powered television station on the air requires an investment of $2 million in buildings and equipment. A medium-sized station costs more than $5 million. The costs of programming are also impressive. When the astronauts on Apollo 11 landed on the moon in July 1969, it cost the networks an estimated $11 million in expenditures and lost revenue to cover the spectacle. Production costs of a 60-second black-and-white commercial was $12,595 in 1969, and that figure can now exceed $100,000.

If television sometimes appears to be "a collection of hollow men trying to fill a vacuum tube," in Leon Gerry's description, it is because it cannot afford to offend either viewers or advertisers. The very form of television drama is governed by advertising—by the need for commercial breaks. Even breaks in football games are scheduled for television commercials.

Substance, too, is governed by advertising considerations. The chairman of the Writers Guild of America, testifying at FCC hearings, said that "sponsors' fears of the unknown" contributed to the death of original TV drama. The late Rod Serling told how advertising considerations affected the treatment of his play based on the story of Emmett Till, a black youth from Chicago who was murdered in Mississippi. In Serling's version, the entire cast was white. At the insistence of the advertising agency, he had to move the locale from the South to New England, delete every suspected Southern colloquialism from the dialogue, and delete all references to Coca-Cola because it was "a Southern drink." Said Serling: "When the show finally hit the air, it had been so diluted and so changed . . . that the central theme I had my characters shouting about had become too vague to warrant any shouting." In a drama about the Nuremberg trials, the word "gas," a cause of death in Hitler's concentration camps, was blipped because the sponsor was an association of natural gas interests. In a Chrysler-sponsored program about the Civil War, all references to President Lincoln was deleted because a competing automobile is named Lincoln. Presumably, no one would ever ford a stream in a program sponsored by Chevrolet.

MEDIA ABUSES OF ADVERTISERS

Advertising is legalized lying.

—H. G. Wells

The abuse of power does not always come from the advertisers. The media can be guilty of what Louis W. Hodges and his colleagues at Washington and Lee University call "moral imperialism" by refusing to accept ads for purposes the media managers oppose. They quote Gene Patterson, editor of the *St. Petersburg Times:*

> A newspaper that chooses not to print news or lawful advertising simply because it editorially disagrees with the thrust of the information is, in my judgment, irresponsibly blinding a community to what is going on in its midst. . . .
> I do believe the reader's thought most dangerous to an ethical free press would be: What is the newspaper NOT telling me? So I believe the ethical policy is, so far as possible, to tell it all.

The First Amendment that the journalists hold so dear also protects advertisers' freedom to publish honest advertising that meets the industry's acceptable standards of taste.

Some media refuse ads that promote ideas rather than products. The Mobil Corporation regularly runs ads in newspapers and magazines supporting views that contrast with the views in editorials in those publications. The broadcasting industry, because of legal requirements to air various sides of controversial issues, has won Supreme Court approval of its right to turn down such editorial advertising, but the time limitations of broadcasting do not apply to advertising space in the print media.

Political campaign advertising also raises ethical problems. Leonard S. Matthews spoke out in 1983, as president of the AAAA against what he termed the "low ethical level" of political campaign advertising in 1982. With the approach of the 1984 presidential election, he urged broadcasters to insist that candidates live up to the code of fair campaign practices adopted by the AAAA. It is designed to prevent personal vilification; character defamation; whispering campaigns; and personal, scurrilous attacks on candidates or their family life. Matthews attributed much of the 1982 mudslinging to political action committees more interested in defeating particular candidates than in electing others. With political advertising campaigns playing an even greater role in the 1984 election, the potential for negative advertising was greater, but there was less criticism. Presumably, the AAAA efforts, and those of other critics, were effective.

PUBLIC RELATIONS

Planned public relations is usually a stepchild of conflict.

—Kinsey M. Robinson

Like advertising, public relations differs from journalism, but there is some overlap. Reporters must assess public relations works and recognize that "public relations" and "publicity" are not synonymous: Not all PR is devoted to placing news releases.

When Paul Garrett went to Detroit to work for General Motors in 1931, he was the only public relations employee on the company payroll. When he retired as a vice president twenty-five years later, General Motors was spending more than a million dollars a year on a public relations program involving more than 200 employees.

Garrett's early experiences with GM are typical in one respect. He was asked when he arrived, "How do you make a million dollars look small?" The management was then acutely sensitive about the company's size. Garrett said that he not only had no answer to the question, but that he did not consider it his task to provide one. Public relations is the practice of winning confidence, he insisted, not of putting on an act. Now, GM's public relations program attempts to convince everyone that General Motors is a desirable company, even though it is huge.

Garrett followed a pattern that the public relations field encourages—that of persuading employers and clients that good behavior, and publicity about it, is the best public relations policy.

Nevertheless, a basic difference in perspective separates PR practitioners from journalists. The difference is like that between community boosters and small-town journalists. The PR aim is to promote the client; the journalistic aim is to find out the news, which often emphasizes the negative.

What one early public relations specialist, Edward L. Bernays, called the "engineering of consent," the journalist may call "space-grabbing." The journalist's view is largely shaped by encounters with press agents or PR campaigns. Bernays, himself, criticizes publicity stunts. Addressing members of the Public Relations Society of America in Syracuse, New York, in the spring of 1984, he called for legal sanctions to keep PR people from misbehaving. The ninety-two-year-old pioneer of PR recalled that in the early days "we never sent out releases," which are perhaps the main space-grabbing technique of today.

The Public Relations Society of America, whose members Bernays addressed, works to improve the professionalism of public relations practitioners, largely through a well-regarded accreditation program. It also strives to bring about a better understanding of what "public relations" means.

DEFINING PUBLIC RELATIONS

> *Radio sets are like continuously firing automatic pistols*
> *shooting at silence.*
>
> —Max Picard

One of the most comprehensive definitions of public relations was formulated by Cyrus W. Plattes, former manager of the department of public services for General Mills:

> Public relations is that responsibility and function of management which (1) analyzes public interest and determines public attitudes, (2) identifies and interprets policies and programs of an organization, and (3) executes a program of action to merit acceptance and good will.

Obviously, more than "publicity" is involved. In fact, many public relations practitioners see publicity as only one of many tools. A news story, a speech, a film, a photograph—each is a tool of public relations. The channels that carry the tools—a newspaper, a club meeting at which a film is shown, a magazine, a television or radio program—are media.

None of these terms, however, obscures an obvious fact: The mass media are important to public relations people, and, to the extent that they can use them, they will.

Public relations, in a vital sense, involves social consequences of an organization's behavior. As Harwood L. Childs puts it:

> Our problem in each corporation or industry is to find out what these activities are, what social effects they have, and, if they are contrary to the public interest, to find ways and means of modifying them so that they will serve the public interest.

What is the public interest? In effect, says, Childs, it is what the public says it is.

In practice, few corporations subscribe to these objectives of public relations. Nugent Wedding of the University of Illinois studied 85 representative business firms and found that only about 35 percent saw public relations as forming proper policies and then interpreting them to the public. Almost 11 percent regarded public relations solely as a publicity activity.

PR AS BUSINESS

> *Business? It's quite simple. It's other people's money.*
>
> —Alexander Dumas, the younger

Because American business persists in emphasizing words, rather than deeds, it wastes enormous amounts of money trying to convert the public, according to Bernays. Public relations, he believes, must emerge as a form of social statesmanship. Its practitioner, with the full cooperation of his clients, must have four objectives:

To define the social objectives of his client or to help him define them.

To find out what maladjustments there are between these objectives and the elements in our society on which his client is dependent. These maladjustments may be distortions in the mind of the public due to misinformation, ignorance, or apathy, or they may be distortions due to the unsound action by the client.

To attempt to adjust the client's policies and actions to society so that the maladjustments may be resolved.

To advise the client on ways and means by which his new policies and actions, if it is deemed advisable to retain them, may be understood by the public.*

Apart from the 35 percent that had a concept roughly equivalent to Bernays', the firms surveyed by Wedding had narrow views of the objectives of public relations: To create favorable public opinion and good will, 29.4 percent; to help sales, 10.6; to interpret business to the public and the public to business management, 8.2; and to whitewash business when business is under fire, 1.2.

HOW A UNIVERSITY PR MAN CAN WORK

> *Slogans are both exciting and comforting, but they are also powerful opiates for the conscience.*
>
> —James B. Conant

A journalist in university news and publication is usually labeled a "flack" by other journalists. Robert Beyers, director of news and publications at Stanford University, says, "Think like a journalist and you'll serve your institution well. Write like a journalist and you'll do even better."

---

*Edward L. Bernays, "The Philosophy of Public Relations" (Women in Communications, Inc., Professional Papers), undated.

ROBERT W. BEYERS

One senior student at Stanford describes Bob Beyers, Director of News and Publications at Stanford University, as "the man who works 24 hours a day, every day." Although anyone may doubt this statement, it is almost true. Beyers is working whenever anyone sees him—night or day, anywhere.

Fred Hechinger, the former education editor of the *New York Times*, wrote in *Change* magazine, these words about Beyer's operations: "The guidelines are simple: openness and accuracy; professionalism on the staff; no barriers between those who want news and the university; confidence, speed."

José Steinbock, Assistant Vice President of Rutgers, says, "Before I visited the Stanford News Bureau, I was somewhat skeptical of what I had read about its fierce independence. I am now convinced that Beyers has great freedom and that he uses it in ways that support Stanford enormously over the long term."

Nearly all Stanford alumni, faculty, and staff applaud Beyers and his staff, but, of course, a few read negative news about Stanford and vent their opinions. Here is a man who stressed that Stanford's reporting needed a lot more development "on the positive side." While acknowledging that Beyers's credibility with the media was a plus, he commented that he was frustrated by Beyers's tendency to present an "unbalanced" picture in the name of news.

For such critics, Beyers has one answer, just as he has for everyone, "In times of crisis, candor pays." He continued with these words:

What held true during the period of student demonstrations remains true in an era of financial crunch for the nation's colleges. And, to paraphrase Charles Wilson, what's good for the colleges might eventually be good for the country. Back in 1967—about a year before he urged university endowment managers to move into common stocks rather heavily— Ford Foundation President McGeorge Bundy gave a national convention of educators a piece of advice which may stand the test of history a bit better than his portfolio management advice.

Bundy said—and I quote—"We have no choice but to seek a drastic increase in the levels of public support for both private and public institutions. But the consequences for us all is a new requirement of candor. . . .

"The tension and the turmoil of the present may yield in the end to increased openness, at every level and in all direction. . . ."

Throughout the 1950s and early 1960s, most college presidents, their publicists, and catalogs fostered the happy assumption of unmitigated excellence in higher education. That assumption was shaken by Berkeley and shattered by Harvard and Columbia—to say nothing of San Francisco State or Stanford.

Parents, taxpayers, and donors who had worshipped at the feet of alma mater suddenly discovered that the grand old gal had warts.

Politicians quickly made colleges their whipping stock, especially in this state, and students returned the compliment in kind.

Since 1966, it's hardly news but it's worth remembering, public confidence in colleges plummeted. The same thing happened with other social institutions—business, labor, government, the military, banks, you name it—as the easy rhetoric of promises met the hard and devastating reality of Vietnam, both abroad and at home.

Unfortunately, many colleges persist in wanting their "news" operations to conform to the stereotype of PR—boldly projecting what's "good" about the place and downplaying or forgetting what's "bad."

The need for changes to bring America's practices into accord with its professed ideals is both great and urgent. Openness and candor are important elements in helping achieve such change.*

The few who oppose Beyers's truthfulness find they face a man who retaliates, not with physical force, but with so many facts from so many disciplines that they are stunned. Dazzled by Beyers's intelligence and ability to use numbers and statistics, they asked, "Who is he?"

Beyers, now a pleasing bear of a man, was born in New York City in 1931; attended 20 schools before college; and majored in sociology at Cornell, which Beyers calls "the Stanford of the East." After serving as editor-in-chief of the *Cornell Daily Sun*, he worked as a reporter for a Texas daily; in advertising; in public relations; and as editor of a weekly in Michigan, then found his niche at the University of Michigan News Service. He landed at Stanford in 1961, and he has spurned many opportunities at advancement to continue at his home: Director of News and Publications.

Thinking about Beyers's duties and his staff, he outlined the tasks they must accomplish:

Our coverage responsibilities include about 75 teaching departments, about 25 organized research units (including several located in other parts of the state), a teaching and research staff of about 2,000, and all the branches of the campus administration. Although we still consider news initation (i.e., via press releases, press conferences, television newsfilms) to be the prime focus of our efforts, we devote a great amount of our time in responding to the needs and demands of the news media. We often get as many as 50 media requests in a day. . . .[†]

Faced with such responsibilities, many a person would give up, but Beyers was the second to receive the highest award at Stanford: The Kenneth M. Cuthbertson award for exceptional service to Stanford.

*Robert Beyers, "Outline for a Case Talk," July 14, 1982.
[†]Robert Beyers' talk at Cornell, June 5, 1985.

COPING WITH HIGHER-UPS

Imitation is the sincerest form of flattery.

—Charles Caleb Cotton

Beyers is forthright and certain, but he is skillful in balancing his commitment to the university and to journalism. Here is an example:

> One part of the university was upset over a state safety inspection, but re-
> fused us permission to write about the criticism and the university's response
> to it. After the basic findings leaked, they were promptly clobbered by the
> outside press, and no mention was made of our corrective efforts. About a
> month later, we sat in during the "exit" interview with another set of safety
> officials, turned out a story summarizing their concerns and our intentions—
> and got a much smaller, more balanced story, with lots of praise from the
> press. In the process, we automatically informed our workers that safety was
> an important matter for the university, and, in effect, urged everyone to be
> more concerned about safety.*

A CONFRONTATION

*Fanatic love of virtue has done more to damage men and society
than all the vices put together.*

—Raymond Bruckberger

Beyers sometimes faces much more serious confrontations, but once decided, he never blinks. Here is one such case.

Beyers' boss professes support for open reporting within the university, in-cluding spreading news releases when appropriate. When his boss submitted a report to the federal government on higher education, Beyers prepared a routine summary of its contents. The boss said it was an excellent summary, but that it should also be submitted to the federal agency.

The agency agreed that the release was accurate, but opposed any "official" release. The boss then said there should be no story, but he and the agency agreed that the full report could be published in a widely circulated education newspaper.

What did Beyers do?

> I wrote a letter of resignation, but left it unsigned. I went in for a final dis-
> cussion, pointing out how ridiculous it is not to have a release on a totally
> public report. This proved persuasive, and my boss never learned of my letter.
> Had the decision been different, my letter would simply have been signed and
> handed over. You never threaten to resign—you do it or you don't.

*Robert Beyers' "Ethical Choices for Flacks and Journalists," speech before an ethics class, September 30, 1985.

Of course, we looked rather stupid coming out with a release after most of the media had published a story on our own story, but at least the principle of disclosure ultimately was sustained.*

EACH CASE IS DIFFERENT

Every concrete situation is unique.

−E. C. Curran

Another lesson from Beyers: When *Time* magazine planned a profile on Stanford, Beyers suggested that the *Time* reporter interview various professors, including Sandy Dornbusch. Although Dornbusch was a good selection, he said the Stanford library was "the worst at any major American university." This upset many of Dornbusch's colleagues, who chastised Beyers for putting *Time* in contact with Dornbusch.

Said Beyers:

Recognizing problems is the first step in their solution. The *Time* story contributed directly to the decision of the distinguished librarian, Rutherford Rogers, to come to Stanford. He enlisted the help of Dornbusch, and we have a far better library today.

SCIENCE AND PR

A cynic is a man who knows the price of everything and the value of nothing.

−Oscar Wilde

Even science stories can present ethical problems in public relations. Beyers told of the following case.

Two scientists discovered a new particle, a finding clearly of Nobel Prize significance. The physics world spread the news quickly—by telephone, in classes, and in cocktail party conversations. Stanford wanted to spread the word rapidly, but four institutions were involved, each with a stake in the story. A university science writer fashioned a first-draft story and circulated it for comment. A nationally prominent scientist at another institution said the lead of the story must be based on Einstein's theory of relativity. Meanwhile, the leading newsletter in physics said it would not publish a report of the finding if it were leaked to the press first.

The story began to break, however, first in a student newspaper, then in questions from students in physics classes, and then the science editor of the *New York*

*Robert Beyers' "Ethical Choices for Flacks and Journalists," speech before an ethics class, September 30, 1985.

Times called to ask for confirmation. Beyers argued for time and won an hour or two. He reached one of the two scientists involved. Beyers said:

> I asked the scientist to tell the story in lay terms because I was not very knowledgeable about physics, then asked him to contact his colleagues to make certain they agreed. We made the deadline with several minutes to spare, and the quotes were used everywhere.
>
> The key here was not to be thrown off the track by a bunch of institution-conscious administrators. After all, who could deny either of the two scientists their right to describe what they did in their own terms? That is, just think like a journalist.*

PR BATTLE ZONES

That favorite subject. Myself.

—James Boswell

Public relations people work in a battle zone between clients and public, between corporate obedience and telling the accurate story. Many came out of news jobs and have journalistic values; they are buffeted by ethical conflicts unless they can get their employers to consent to telling the story as it is. Beyers's unsigned letter of resignation illustrates why ethical thinkers include courage in their ethical codes.

EXERCISES

1. Claude Hopkins, an ad copy writer for Albert Lasker's agency, was assigned to do the new Quaker Puffed Wheat and Puffed Rice account. Hopkins toured the Kellogg plant and did his reportorial research on the products in 24 hours. He came up with the "Shot from Guns" campaign. Lasker held it for six weeks, and the client was impressed. Lasker said later that their client would not have been impressed if he had known how quickly the work had actually been done. Did Lasker do the right thing?

2. You're the editorial page director of a major Washington newspaper. You have been highly critical of the "obscene" profits of oil companies, in person and in print. Your paper reports the increases on page one and hammers away editorially. Then a reader sends you a letter to the editor pointing out that your paper's profits are about twice those of the oil industry by any of the standard measures. Would you publish the letter? Would you do anything more, such as suggesting that the news side do a piece on publisher's profits nationally?

---

*Robert Beyers' talk at Cornell, June 5, 1985.

WORDS ABOUT LOVE

To love is to admire with the heart; to admire is to love with the mind.

—Theophile Gautier

If two people love each other, there can be no happy end to it.

—Ernest Hemingway

Love is the word used to label the sexual excitement of the young, the habituation of the middle-aged, and the mutual dependence of the old.

—John Ciardi

Only little boys and old men sneer at love.

—Louis Auchincloss

People who are sensible about love are incapable of it.

—Douglas Yates

Take away love and our earth is a tomb.

—Robert Browning

No woman ever falls in love with a man unless she has a better opinion of him than he deserves.

—Ed Howe

Love does not consist in gazing at each other but in looking outward together in the same direction.

—Antoine de Saint Exupery

CHAPTER 11

Dealing with Sexism

*Love is the whole history of a woman's life; it is
but an episode in a man's.*

—Madame de Stael

A noted author, Sloan Wilson, included this paragraph about children in his book,
What Shall We Wear to This Party? (Arbor House, 1976):

> The hardest part of raising children is teaching them to ride bicycles. A
> father can run beside the bicycle or stand yelling directions while the child
> falls. A shaky child on a bicycle for the first time needs both support and
> freedom. The realization that this is what the child will always need can hit
> hard.

Is teaching *boys* to ride bicycles "the hardest part"? Almost all fathers will
respond that teaching boys about sex is by far the hardest part. In nearly all cases,
if boys are taught by their fathers, boys will learn more about sex from their peers.
For example, in his article "The Dirty Play of Little Boys" (*Society*, November-
December 1986), Gary Alan Fine wrote these sentences:

> Whatever latency might have been during Freud's childhood, in contem-
> porary America preadolescence is a period of much sexual talk and some
> sexual behavior. . . . A boy must walk a narrow line between not showing
> enough involvement with girls, in which case he may be labeled effeminate,
> immature, or gay, and showing too much serious, tender attention, in which
> case he may be labeled "girl crazy". . . .[I]t is common to hear boys saying
> things like "You're a faggot," "What a queer," and "Kiss my ass." . . . Al-
> though sometimes morality does not change, if the new "improved" morality
> is supported by the subtle reward structures of adult society, we can say with
> a fair measure of confidence that dirty players emerge into saintly adults—at
> least adequately saintly adults.

To probe boys and men further, we will next consider two stories—one a short story, the other, a novel—by J. D. Salinger.*

TWO TALES BY SALINGER

From a mere nothing springs a mighty tale.

—Propertius

Salinger's short story, "A Perfect Day for Bananafish," begins with a daring conception: He has beautiful Muriel, wife of Seymour Glass, speaking on the hotel telephone from Miami with her mother in New York for more than four pages. In each sentence or half-sentence their exchanges fill in both characters.

Muriel's mother is apprehensive about Seymour, because she is certain that he is nearly insane. Mother and daughter speak almost interminably, but their exchanges tell readers this: Mother is a typical, rich mother, deeply distraught about her daughter and her husband—but not so involved that she can't ask about dress, tourists, and fashion in Miami. Near the end of the conversation with her mother, Muriel says she isn't afraid of her husband. By this time, readers are certain that she is as tough as old leather.

The first scene is grim—with a dash of humor—the second scene, a delight. It begins with a four-year-old girl, Sybil Carpenter, discussing Seymour Glass with her mother. This dialogue tells readers that Sybil is entranced by Seymour Glass. Her mother dismisses her, she runs toward the flat part of the beach, sees Seymour alone, and they engage in conversation that is nothing but rapture for the little girl and the adult man.

The last, short scene begins with Seymour riding the elevator to return to his room. A woman is also riding, saying nothing, and Seymour goes into a rage at the woman because he says she is looking at his feet. The woman—confused, fearful, and angry—disembarks from the elevator. Seymour gets off the elevator at the fifth floor, goes to Room 507, sees Muriel asleep on the bed, opens one piece of luggage, takes out an Ortgies calibre 7.65 automatic, aims the pistol at his head, and fires a bullet through his right temple.

You may suppose that this story is to prove that Seymour is fed up with his life, but you must think further. When you are assigned to read one story by a serious author, always read another story by the same author to understand either story. We will explain "A Perfect Day for Bananafish" by explaining *The Catcher in the Rye*. Both stories say exactly the same thing.

The Catcher in the Rye begins with Holden Caulfield being kicked out of Pencey Prep, an expensive school in Pennsylvania. It was the fourth school from

*J. D. Salinger, "A Perfect Day for Bananafish," in *Nine Stories* (Bantam Books, 1953) and *The Catcher in the Rye* (Bantam Books, 1964).

J. D. SALINGER

J. D. Salinger, author of *The Catcher in the Rye* and other works, started writing when he was in prep school. At night, tenting a blanket over his head to hide his flashlight, he wrote his first short stories. In 1937, at age 18, he went to Vienna with his father, who tried unsuccessfully to interest him in the Polish ham business. Salinger then returned to America for a lackadaisical half-semester at New York University.

During World War II, Salinger was an aloof, solitary staff sergeant whose job was to discover Gestapo agents. Salinger carried a typewriter in his Jeep, and an Army acquaintance remembers him typing, crouching under a table while his area was under attack. In France, he met Ernest Hemingway, then a war correspondent, who read some of Salinger's writing and said, "Jesus, Salinger has a helluva talent."

In 1946, having divorced his European wife, Salinger moved back to New York. He was gentle and humorous, and, though he lived with his parents on Park Avenue, he spent his nights in Greenwich Village with women he lured away from a drugstore in the chaste Barbizon Hotel for Women. Soon Salinger began the first of several retreats from his friends and fellow writers. He withdrew to a cottage 24 miles away and finished *The Catcher in the Rye.* Eventually, he moved to New Hampshire, where, for a time, he had many teenagers visit his home. Salinger learned what he could from them. Then, he married, had two children, and became a recluse.

Before Salinger became reclusive, he wrote a reluctant statement about himself in *Harper's* (July 1965), which is quoted in part:

> In the first place, if I owned a magazine I would never publish a column full of contributor's biographical notes. I seldom care to know a writer's birthplace, his children's names, his working schedule, the date of his arrest for smuggling guns during the Irish Rebellion. The writer who tells you these things is also very likely to have his picture taken wearing an open-collared shirt. . . .
>
> I've written biographical notes for a few magazines, and I doubt if I ever said anything honest in them.
>
> . . . I won't say I'm a born writer, but I'm certainly a born professional. I don't think I ever *selected* writing as a career. I just started to write when I was eighteen or so and never stopped.

Like at least a few other writers, Salinger has long prized solitude. In fact, when several critics contributed to a book entitled *Salinger*, it began with an essay called "The Invisible Man." Many critics wondered in print why Salinger loved nonpublicity, while at the same time still other critics wrote that Salinger's nonpublicity stance was actually a bid for publicity; the more he was a recluse, the more writers attempted to see him—and wrote about Salinger.

> Nonetheless, Salinger has always opposed publicity for himself. In 1951, when *The Catcher in the Rye* was published, the *New Yorker* published a note from Salinger. He wrote that when a writer is asked to talk about his craft, he should only call out the names of the writers he respects. Salinger listed among the writers he loves, Flaubert, Tolstoy, Proust, Emily Bronte, Jane Austen, Henry James, and others—all of them dead. He added that he wouldn't name any living writers, because "I don't think it's right."

which he had been expelled, having failed four out of five subjects. During the following hours, Holden has the miseries and ecstacies of a half-convinced rebel. He is a tall, crew-cut 16-year-old.

Afraid to go home, Holden checks into a Manhattan hotel and takes on a man-about-town role, never knowing that his role is much too large for him. After wandering about the city, Holden returns to the hotel and the elevator man says he will send a prostitute to his room. Holden is grateful to the elevator man.

Later, Holden sneaks into his home, and, while talking to his beloved ten-year-old sister, Phoebe, reveals what he wants to do; talking only about small children, who are playing in a field of rye, which is near a "crazy cliff," there stands Holden Caulfield catching all children before they fall off the cliff.

What is below Holden's cliff? Adulthood. If all the kids become adults, they would become "phonies" (Holden's favorite word).

For those of you who have read *The Catcher in the Rye*, think for a moment about how many adults receive friendship from Holden: None. In fact, Phoebe is the only person in this book whom Holden loves without hesitation.

Now, think again about the precisely planned "A Perfect Day for Bananafish." Salinger shows in the first scene how the web for Seymour is woven, first, by his wife, then by his wife's mother—both of whom stand for other adult women. The second scene, which involves Seymour and Sybil, is nothing but delight. The last scene shows Seymour lashing out at an adult woman, then killing himself.

Thus, both stories carry one message: Never grow up to become an adult.

We are conjecturing that, in nearly thirty years, Salinger, as far as anyone except Salinger knows, has written nothing. Why? He is giving us one message: "I've grown up."

So far, we have quoted only male writers. Although Salinger is almost always obscure to casual readers, the women we will quote are vindictive, perhaps because these writers are outraged.

WOMEN ABOUT SEXISM

> *Men who flatter women do not know them;*
> *Men who abuse them know them still less.*
>
> —Madame de Salm

A Feminist Dictionary carries many definitions, by women, of sexism. Here are four of them:

> Sexism is a social relationship in which males have authority over females—Linda Phelps.

> Sexism is stereotyping people by sex, just as racism is stereotyping people by race—Sara Delmont.

> Sexism is no bias which can be eliminated but is the foundation stone of learning and education in our male controlled society—Dale Spender.

> Sexism is the oldest form of institutionalized oppression—Betsy Warrior.

As if responding to Warrior's definition of sexism, Eva Keuls wrote and had published *The Reign of the Phallus: Sexual Politics in Ancient Athens* (Harper & Row, 1986). The first paragraph is a barrage of feminist artillery:

> In the case of a society dominated by men who sequester their wives and daughters, denigrate the female role in reproduction, erect monuments to the male genitalia, have sex with the sons of their peers, sponsor public whore-houses, create a mythology of rape, and engage in rampant saber-rattling, it is not inappropriate to refer to a reign of the phallus. Classical Athens was such a society.

This paragraph and much of the rest of this book is so evidently the work of a woman, that the editors of *Atlantic Monthly* magazine retained a man, Bernard Knox, the director of Harvard's Center for Hellenic Studies, to write a review of her book. In his review (April 1986) Knox wrote:

> In this book, written with great verve and a laudable desire to make it "accessible to the general reader," Professor Keuls assembles an enormous body of evidence for the case against Athenian men. Most of the passages that she produces from the literature of the fifth and fourth centuries have not previously been cited in the context of social history. The most original feature of the book, however, is the exploration of the pictorial record: "[T]he panorama of ideals, myths, fantasies, and, above all, scenes of daily life that appear on the tens of thousands of Greek vases, scattered in museums all over Europe and the United States." She reproduces more than three hundred of these paintings from the classical period, many of them erotic, some grossly obscene.

Although much of Knox's reviews challenges Keuls's observations, he ends with these words: "In this case, once the wilder flights of speculative imagination are discounted, a solid core remains, a rich and memorable survey of the abject condition of women in a society that for creative brilliance in art, literature, politics, and philosophy has hardly a rival in the history of Western culture."

As for a modern treatment of sexism, *Against Our Will: Men, Women, and Rape* by Susan Brownmiller (Simon and Schuster, 1975), is still the best study among the many books written by women. She begins her massive study with a personal statement:

> The question most often asked of me while I was writing this book was short, direct and irritating: "Have you ever been raped?" My answer was equally direct: "No."

From this point to the end of this 541-page masterpiece is, to put it bluntly, mind-boggling. Rather than attempting to sum up her arguments, we will present here the reactions of two prominent reviewers, both men, and *Time* magazine:

> May significantly change the terms of the dialogue between and about men and women—*Time*; it also named Brownmiller as one of the Women of the Year.

> EYE-OPENING . . . *Against Our Will* is a history of rape in all its overt and subtle manifestations.—Christopher Lehman-Haupt, the *New York Times*

> GET INTO THIS BOOK AND HARDLY A SINGLE THOUGHT TO DO WITH SEX WILL COME OUT THE WAY IT WAS. . . . A most important eye-and-mind-opening book—Eliot Fremont-Smith

The rest of this chapter will deal with the attitudes toward *Playboy*, which will be the subject of an ethics class session.

PLAYBOY, MEN, AND WOMEN

> *If it is not erotic, it is not interesting.*
>
> —Fernando Arrabal

The following article was written by a student, Christine McCulloch:

> "We like to visit the campuses of the PAC 10. Nowhere else in America do you encounter such extreme examples of the dualism of mind and body." This statement was used to introduce *Playboy* Magazine's October 1985 pictorial, entitled "Girls of the PAC 10."
>
> The series featured 25 women, both clothed and unclothed, from each school of the Western athletic conference referred to as the PAC 10. The controversy that erupted over *Playboy*'s arrival at the campus last April is a particularly powerful example of these turbulent reactions that the magazine's editors describe.
>
> The publicized group actively opposing *Playboy* magazine and its advertisements in the *Daily* soliciting female students to pose for their October issue, is called STOP. STOP is an acronym for Students Opposed to Pornography. Several protests were held both on and off the campus last spring, while in-

dividual members of the organization sought to hinder the selection process by using a more direct approach.

According to the September 25, 1985, issue of the *Daily, Playboy* photographers stated, "Some people tried to tie up hotel switchboards by phoning in fake appointments. Others pushed computer-printed handbills "under the doors of guests at the Holiday Inn to warn them of what was going on down the hall." A petition against *Playboy* was also circulated around campus, expressing the main ideal behind STOP's protests: "*Playboy* reinforces sex stereotypes by portraying women as sexual objects and thus furthers inequality in society." This phrase was to be repeated often during the spring and again in the fall, when the issue was released for sale.

On the other side of the spectrum were the women who wanted to pose for the magazine. Photographer David Chan reported that at least 75 women were interviewed in his hotel room with serious aspirations of appearing in the publication. During the interview, Chan took several Polaroid pictures of each woman and asked her to fill out a form of basic information. He also required that she bring her I.D. with her so that there would be no question of her enrollment at the university should she be chosen as a model. "It is not necessary to be a full-time student at any University where we are photographing," explained Chan. *Playboy* only requires that a woman follow at least one course there in order to be eligible.

Ramona Turner, a senior majoring in computer science last year, took full advantage of those minimal requirements. She decided to see "how far she could get" with the *Playboy* offer, "just for fun." Ramona was one of the two women chosen to represent the campus, along with C. C. Shanahan, then a freshman. C. C. explained that she responded to *Playboy*'s advertisement, mostly out of curiosity. At the time, she was doing some other modeling and the opportunity of appearing in a major national magazine lured her to David Chan's door. C. C. appears fully clothed in the pictorial and Ramona is wearing only a shirt, which is completely unbuttoned.

An advance copy of the "PAC 10" issue was released to newspapers in the Bay Area in late August to promote a publicity tour featuring the models. On August 22, the *San Francisco Chronicle* printed an article which bore the headline, "Cal, Stanford Show Their Class." The article which followed applauded the fact that only two out of the seven women representing the Bay Area schools appeared "semi-nude." The reporter continued that "Stanford and Berkeley women are better educated and have more respect for themselves than women at the other schools." The sentiments which are expressed in this article, while complimentary to the morals and values of both Stanford and Cal women, are exemplary of the elitist attitude which is often associated with both of these universities.

Laurie Wedemeyer, now a sophomore and a member of STOP, appeared on the Channel 4 afternoon talk show with the Bay Area models in August. Wedemeyer echoed the elitist perspective of the *Chronicle* when she stated that she was "offended" that *Playboy* came to the university in the first place. She believed that the atmosphere was not an appropriate breeding ground for the values which *Playboy* magazine contributes to American society. Shanahan challenged her by asking why their university should be so different than any other university with respect to the controversy stimulated by the presence of *Playboy* magazine on college campuses. Wedemeyer did not respond when Shanahan asked "where the line was drawn" that separated Stanford from all other institutions.

The issue of pornography was a focal point of STOP's argument and protests against *Playboy* magazine. *Webster's Dictionary* defines pornography as "the depiction of licentiousness or lewdness or the portrayal of erotic behavior designed to arouse sexual excitement." Consequently, it is the responsibility of each individual to determine whether the material printed in *Playboy* is pornographic or not. Elaine Fox, a public relations executive for *Playboy*, told *Oakland Tribune* reporter Harriet Swift that "*Playboy* has never been proven guilty of pornography in any court of law." In addition, each model from the Bay Area schools maintained that she did not consider *Playboy* magazine to be pornographic. Berkeley model Leslie-Ann Chamberlain described *Playboy* as "erotic and sensual," but not at all pornographic.

Vanessa Poster, who is a graduate student associated with STOP, had a comparatively different conception of pornography, which she explained to reporter Harriet Swift. "We are not bothered by naked women or nudity; pornography is about violence, not sensuality."

The idea of violence was a powerful central force around which protesters built their argument that pornography contributes to the physical as well as the psychological abuse of women. Swift explained that today's women's movement links pornography with "battered women, rape, incest, child abuse, and harassment."

Protesters were questioned as to why *Playboy* magazine, which is considered to be not only the softest of the so-called porn editorials, but a highly acclaimed literary journal as well, is considered to be so dangerous to society. Their general response was that *Playboy* is a threat "because it is so widely accepted in American culture."

Wedemeyer added that society's acceptance of *Playboy* magazine encourages other more sexually offensive and abusive publications such as *Hustler* to be circulated.

Valerie Miller, a mass communications instructor at Berkeley, stated that "the soft core porn of *Playboy* gives permission for the hard core porn to get harder, to release it into the mass media," thus establishing the link between *Playboy* and other nude magazines. Miller believes that these magazines "make it easier for him (the male reader) to consume pornography than to experience sex."

The two Stanford women who appeared in the October issue had very different reactions to the turbulence caused by protesters which rocked the Bay Area. Ramona Turner who was seen baring all, expressed no feelings of regret or embarrassment for her appearance in *Playboy*. "I have a beautiful body," she stated. "I just wish the picture could have been bigger." Turner actually attended an anti-*Playboy* rally last spring, but it did not convince her to change her decision to pose. She described *Playboy* magazine as a "cultural artifact" filled with pages of gorgeous women. Turner is proud to be recognized as "one of those gorgeous women," and she firmly believes that she is not hurting anyone by appearing in *Playboy*.

Shanahan and Turner both agreed that everyone was entitled to express his or her opinion concerning the issue. Shanahan, however, was a bit more wary of her adversaries, especially when she returned to campus in the fall. She appeared completely clothed in the issue, explaining on a television interview that she "couldn't walk through campus with everyone knowing what she was under her shorts and t-shirt." Shanahan said that she didn't even consider posing nude for many reasons, which included the possibility of future repercussions in the professional world, reactions of family members and schoolmates, and, as the *San Francisco Chronicle* quoted, "because I didn't have the guts."

Reactions of the protesters frightened Shanahan who took their opinions ". . . very personally. I finally realized that it was not *me* they were against." Weidemeyer even explained that STOP members were trying to protect her, if anything. Shanahan explained that she had very few problems from students. The harshest reaction was voiced in a letter to the *Daily*, which criticized her motives for appearing in the magazine. Actually, it was fun being recognized at all the parties," she said. "Lots of people still call me C. C., even though it's not my real name."

As with many issues that American society is faced with every day, there is no right or wrong answer to settle the controversy over *Playboy* magazine's recent invasion of their campus. The members of STOP are fighting a battle against pornography and the sexual abuse and discrimination of women. The women who appeared in *Playboy* were not necessarily attempting to counter their efforts because they viewed *Playboy* magazine and its objectives in a different perspective. The final line is in *Playboy*'s introduction to the pictorial states: "Freedom of expression is easy to defend." On this point at least, all would agree.

STUDENTS' ANSWERS

One good head is better than a hundred strong hands.

—Thomas Fuller

The following questions about the above article are answered below by two male students:

1. Students Opposed to Pornography (STOP) is a group that is against *Playboy* and its advertisements for women to pose for *Playboy* pictures. Because each student is presumably intelligent, why should any student join STOP?

A. STOP was formed on the premise that students are intelligent—despite its acronym, STOP's major efforts are directed at sparking thought, discussion, and debate. STOP can't keep *Playboy* from publishing, and it can't really prevent women from posing, but it can encourage people to re-examine their values and actions, and the possible effects of those values and actions. It is STOP's hope, because members of the Stanford community are presumably intelligent, that they will recognize the benefit of such thought and discussion. Even intelligent and supposedly enlightened individuals require a little prodding now and again, if only to think about that which they normally take for granted.

B. I believe the reason why students join STOP is to display, in public, their anger over pornography and pornography's effect on the behavior of members of society. These students likely believe that it is not enough to feel that pornography is a vice—they have to take action against pornography, even if it is only as symbolic as joining an organization.

There is really no practical reason for somebody to join STOP, however. Any woman—a woman with intelligence and fully capable of reaching her own conclusions about posing for *Playboy*—is going to act on her own volition. One of the true tests of a person's character is to stand up against the pressure of peers, and, in doing so, express his or her individuality. The chances that STOP is going to change the mind of a woman who has made her own decision are slim.

It seems, then, that the reasons for joining STOP are chiefly symbolic. I guess the people who join the group also hold out the hope that sometime in the future their actions will have an impact on pornography. If this is the case, then the reason behind joining such an organization is long-term—the immediate situation at Stanford might not change, but in the years to come the event will be remembered and the turmoil again will be brought before the student body.

2. If *Playgirl*, a magazine published for women, should have a photographer visit this campus looking for handsome men to photograph nude for *Playgirl*, would STOP attempt to halt the photographer's effort?

A. There is a line in feminist and minority theory that goes something like this: Sexism and racism only have an adverse effect on society as a whole when they are directed toward the oppressed by the oppressor, toward the minority by the majority. That is, if a black manager who is hiring denies a white man a job because the man is white, society is not harmed, because society (and history) has put all the power behind the white man. According to this line, racism and sexism work only in one direction—blacks can't oppress whites, and women can't oppress men. So *Playgirl* doesn't count.

However, I don't know how popular that theory is, and I would expect STOP to protest *Playgirl* as well, if only because it serves to legitimate pornography that centers on women. The question, in fact, is evidence of this function: "Is *Playboy* ok as long as there's a *Playgirl*?"

B. My first reaction is that STOP would not try to halt the efforts of a *Playgirl* photographer. The issue is less immediate to the female members of the organization, since men, not women, are the people involved. The group might also argue that exposing the bodies of men does not create violence against men, as they claim the exposing of women's bodies does. An interesting tautology.

After looking at the situation more closely, however, I believe that STOP would protest *Playgirl*'s efforts—purely for political reasons. The members of the organization would recognize that it would appear hypocritical not to protest the *Playgirl* photographer. The group, then, would almost be forced to protest in order to protect its validity as an organization against pornography.

3. Are the members of STOP informing students on pornography? Or are the members of STOP warning students who might pose?

A. It's a dual function. STOP hopes to convince women not to pose with the same reasons it uses to convince people not to purchase pornography. If no one buys a magazine with pictures of naked women, the magazine will go away; and if no women will pose, there is no magazine. Apart from that, STOP's expectation is that while such magazines exist, they will not be endorsed by educated people, either as models or as buyers.

B. While I believe that members of STOP would probably state that they are only informing women about pornography and its dangers, the real intent of the organization is to prevent women from posing. The group, then, is warning the women on campus that what they are doing, should they choose to pose, is wrong and there will be negative consequences from the action later. These consequences are both *personal*, such as the possibility as always being known as the woman who bared it all for a couple of bucks or as the loose woman on campus, and *societal*, such as the reasoning that the exposure of one's body naturally leads to violence against women.

I want to note here that I believe the societal warning is amazingly off base. The organization, if it really believes this, then supposes that the bullet theory is operative—a person sees a picture of a naked woman and immediately goes out to attack a woman. Something is missing in this logic. Where does the personality of each reader/looker come into play? Are all men really inherently evil and do they turn toward thoughts of violence when they see a naked woman? You cannot go immediately from a stimulus (a picture) to a response (violence) without first considering the organism. All men are not alike, just as all women are not alike—some choose to pose for *Playboy*, others choose to protest *Playboy*.

4. Ramona Turner, one who posed for *Playboy*, said, "I have a beautiful body. I just wish the picture could have been bigger." She also said that she believes that she is not hurting anyone by appearing in *Playboy*.

Is she right or wrong about not hurting anyone?

A. I think her comment does more harm than her picture. Personally, I find it hard to believe that *Playboy* leads to serious pornography or to violence against women. I *do* think the magazine perpetuates distinctly American values and ideals that are, perhaps, undesirable, or at least questionable.

Turner's comment is indicative of our belief that young/fit/beautiful rules. There are not fat or old women in *Playboy*. I'm not saying there should be, but it seems that, if *Playboy* hurts anybody, it is the woman who doesn't look like the centerfolds.

B. If you buy the logic that women who pose naked lead to violence, then you might believe that Ramona Turner's action is hurting the cause of all women. I don't buy this.

The actions of Turner helped her make a few dollars. Perhaps she really needed the money, maybe even needed the money to help her pay for tuition. Undoubtedly, some women in this country pose for magazines such as *Playboy*, or appear in X-rated films, because it is truly the only means they have of making a living.

The action of Turner did not hurt the men who purchased the magazine. Maybe they did get what STOP would probably call "a cheap thrill" when they saw Turner's body. God forbid that some boys out there probably masturbated upon seeing her body. I just can't equate the act of masturbation with violence.

5. What do *you* think of *Playboy* as a publication?

A. As I've said, I don't buy into the *Playboy* perpetuates rape and other horrors theory. I do find the values it celebrates reprehensible. Well, maybe not reprehensible, but they're certainly nothing to be proud of. Still, can we blame *Playboy* for giving us something we want? The fault isn't *Playboy*'s. I think the people who don't think *Playboy* should publish basically want to smash the mirror because they don't like the reflection. You can't eliminate sexism by banning its manifestations.

B. I really don't know what I think of *Playboy*. I've seen copies of the magazine and looked at the pictures several times. And, gosh, I didn't read about the lust in former President Jimmy Carter's heart. I haven't picked up a copy of the magazine in at least a year, and I've never actually purchased the publication.

I guess that I think of *Playboy* as a magazine that runs pictures of naked women. I think of Hugh Hefner and his mansion that everyone hears about when I think of *Playboy*. I don't think of violence when I think of the magazine.

6. What do *you* think of STOP?

A. I didn't follow them that closely during the *Playboy* affair, so my understanding of what they've done and what they wish to accomplish isn't quite as complete as it could be. But I think, apart from a basic holier-than-thou attitude some members display, their aims and methods are fairly intelligent. I said in the last question that *Playboy* isn't really the issue, and I think STOP recognizes that.

B. STOP is a great outlet for women to vent their frustration over pornography. Women and men can express their dissatisfaction with magazines such as *Playboy* and maybe even change the future of pornographic publications in this country. The magazine might also receive increased revenue generated from the attention *Playboy* gets in the course of STOP's protests, probably something not given much consideration by STOP.

When an organization like STOP prevents women, against their will, from posing for the magazine, the organization has overstepped its bounds. Keeping phone lines busy with the intention of preventing a woman from carrying out her own will to pose for the magazine is a violation of that woman's rights. The woman has every right to pose for the magazine if she wants to.

These same questions about the above article are answered below by two women students:

1. Students Opposed to Pornography (STOP) is a group that is against *Playboy* and its advertisements for women to pose for *Playboy* pictures. Because each student is presumably intelligent, why should any student join STOP?

   A. STOP is an organization just like any other—it formed to protest against an action that it feels is wrong and to convince others to share these views. Students join STOP because they believe in the principles that it presents, namely, that *Playboy* "reinforces sexual stereotypes." STOP presents a united front against an action that it feels is unjust. The members of STOP, just like the members of [Students] Out of South Africa (SOSA) organization, hope that if enough people join their organization, if enough people take notice of their cause, then the public will begin to rethink its previously unquestioned values.

   B. Students Opposed to Playboy (STOP) is a group, which is not only opposed to *Playboy*, but to the right of individuals as well. Each student is presumably intelligent, and, therefore, can presumably make educated decisions. Yet, STOP, an organization of students, assumes superiority over other students in its attempt to make decisions for the rest of the university. STOP is an infringement upon the rights of intelligent, reasonable individuals.

2. If *Playgirl*, a magazine published for women, should have a photographer visit the campus looking for handsome men to photograph nude for *Playgirl*, would STOP attempt to halt the photographer's effort?

   A. STOP is specifically opposed to the sexual stereotypes of women. They are not representing sexual discrimination in general. STOP believes that *Playboy* promotes sexual inequality by portraying women as sex objects, thereby encouraging an image of women as inferior and subject to harrassment. Women have traditionally been looked upon as the passive sex, submissive to the whims of men. STOP wants to promote a public awareness that the broad acceptance of *Playboy* in society is perpetuating that stereotype.

Any exposure by men in a magazine would contradict, rather than continue, the subjugation of women.

B. According to STOP, pornography "reinforces sex stereotypes by portraying women as sexual objects and thus furthers inequality in society." STOP feels that by portraying females as objects, males assume dominance. Because men are considered the actors and women the objects acted upon, *Playgirl*'s objectification of the male body would not be viewed as offensive by the members of STOP, because it does not further sexual inequality in society.

3. Are the members of STOP informing students on pornography? Or are the members of STOP warning students who might pose?

A. STOP probably intends to promote a little bit of both, with a heavy emphasis on informing students and the general public. STOP realizes that it has little chance to dissuade a student who has made up her mind to pose, unless it indirectly does so by convincing others and making it difficult for the girl to resist peer pressure. I think STOP's main objective is to state their views to others. STOP believes that *Playboy*'s widespread acceptance encourages sexual inequality, and they are trying to encourage the public to understand and accept this point of view, rather than directly discourage a girl who is determined to pose for the publication.

B. Members of STOP are certainly not informing students about pornography, especially about such a long-standing and well-established magazine as *Playboy*. The majority of students is exposed to some type of pornography or has been informed of it before entering college. Furthermore, rather than warning students who might pose for *Playboy*, the members of STOP simply condemn them: "Reactions of protestors frightened Shanahan who took their opinions 'very personally.'" The members of STOP neither inform nor warn, but rather act as judges of the actions of their fellow students.

4. Ramona Turner, one who posed for *Playboy*, said, "I have a beautiful body. I just wish the picture could have been bigger." She also said that she believes that she is not hurting anyone by appearing in *Playboy*.
   Is she right or wrong about not hurting anyone?

A. The obvious answer is no, she is not hurting anybody directly.
   However, she is indirectly harming two distinct groups of people. The first group is the entire community, which Turner has chosen to represent. Her attitudes about the publication and her morals about undressing for the enjoyment of others is a reflection of all students at Stanford. Stanford students may very well have their own opinions of her actions and do not feel personal harm by them, but from a detached point of view, the representatives of Stanford appear unconcerned with issues of sexual equality.

The second group that Turner is hurting is women in general. A successful woman at an elite institution undressing for a magazine sets the women's movement back a great deal. Turner is proclaiming, by her behavior, that even intellectual women can be sex objects for men. Turner is making a statement with her picture, and that is that sexual stereotypes are acceptable.

B. *Playboy* is considered by many to be the class of men's magazines. The articles and pictures, which are supposedly less explicit, are thought to be of higher quality than those of other magazines. Much of the pornographic ring is composed of magazines which show women being harmed or in dangerous positions. These magazines and their models act as detriments to the morality of society. Society, however, overreacts when it comes to simply exposing the human body, which *Playboy* does without hurting anyone. As the saying goes, "If you've got it, flaunt it!"

5. What do *you* think of *Playboy* as a publication?

A. *Playboy* is said to have excellent articles and interviews, and that aspect of the magazine seems entirely valid. I am tempted to say that *Playboy* is only "soft-porn," and, therefore acceptable, but I agree with the argument that *Playboy* poses a great threat to women merely because it is so accepted in society.

I believe *Playboy* has the right to publish the stories and pictures due to laws regarding freedom of speech and expression, and I do not feel that the publication should be prohibited from operating. The owners and editors of *Playboy* are not to be blamed for running what has turned into an extremely lucrative and successful business. Rather, the girls who pose for it can be regarded with disrespect. C. C. Shanahan states several reasons why a girl would not want to pose nude—fear of professional repercussions in the future, reactions of family and friends, and the knowledge that everyone would know what she looked like "under her shorts and t-shirt." Then why pose at all? Having her name associated with *Playboy* is going to produce negative and/or erotic images in future employers looking for models, anyway. If she was a good enough model and wanted to stay clothed, why didn't she approach some less controversial publications? And given all the negative reasons for undressing for everyone to see, what exactly are the positive aspects? Did Turner do it for fun, or for her ego, so that she could say "they picked me"? This hardly seems to counteract the negative consequences. Finally, *Playboy* is not exclusively a magazine showcasing beautiful women. Their system of payment—$100 for a clothed picture, $200 for semi-nude and $300 for completely nude—is not the value of how beautiful a girl is, but of how much she's willing to take off.

B. The fact that *Playboy* is a generally accepted magazine (e.g., the existence of the Playboy Channel, Playboy Bunny appearances on network television, and performances at the Playboy Club by such stars as Bill Cosby) means that it is not viewed as a harmful publication by society as a whole. Although I am not one of *Playboy*'s readers, I feel that, as a publication, it has the rights of such. Yet, *Playboy* also has the responsibility to ensure that its publication does not become harmful to society.

6. What do *you* think of STOP?

A. I think STOP has some excellent points in regard to pornography and sexual equality, but I don't think they will have enough support to have their views heard or accepted. I think many of their actions—such as tying up the *Playboy* switchboard—are ineffective ways to express their position, but neither can I think of a better way. The failure of the women's rights amendment is symbolic of the atmosphere of negativity associated with equality for women and the ideals of feminism. STOP does not yet have enough acceptance, male or female, for the organization to make any impact or impression. To sum this up, I suppose I feel that the organization is futile, but this does not imply that they do not deserve to exist.

B. STOP has the right to express its opinions, according to the Constitution of this country. Yet, STOP does not have the right to infringe upon the rights of others. STOP is judgmental and imposes its beliefs on other people. Not only do I disagree with STOP's stance concerning *Playboy*, but I also disapprove of the manner in which the members of STOP went about expressing their beliefs.

HOW TO REFER TO WOMEN

> *Inconsistency is the only thing in which men are consistent.*
>
> —Horatio Smith

During the last two decades, the position of women in the United States has changed—and is still changing—all for the better. In referring to women in writing, remember these rules, all of which are compiled by several adult women:

1. Do not use prefixes indicating marital status. First reference should include a person's title (if any) and given name; later references should include last name only. For example, Secretary of Defense Caspar Weinberger held a news conference. . . . Weinberger stated; Senator Paula Hawkins said today. . . . Hawkins replied. Use of Mr. and Mrs. is limited to discussions that include a married couple, where the last-name-only rule might cause confusion. Miss and Ms. are not to be used at all. First names alone are also not appropriate for adults.

2. Females over the age of 18 are "women." They are not "girls," "gals," "ladies," "chicks," "broads," "lovelies," "honeys." Words like "homemaker" and "housewife" are also not synonyms for "woman"; check carefully for

accuracy before they are used. "Coed" does not mean "woman" any more than "ed" means "man"; persons who attend school are "students."

3. Gratuitous physical description, uncommon almost to the point of absence in news stories about men, should also be eliminated from such stories about women. If you would not say, "The gray-haired grandfather of three was elected senator," then do not say, "The gray-haired grandmother of three was elected senator." This rule does not apply with equal force in feature writing, especially profiles, in which physical description is often an essential aspect. However, care should be taken to avoid stereotypical description in favor of describing an individual's unique characteristics.

4. Similar considerations apply to the mention of an individual's spouse and family. In a news story about a man, his wife and family are typically mentioned only in passing and only when relevant; the same practice should apply to news stories about women. See the examples above. Again, this practice is slightly different for feature profiles, but the test of relevance should also be applied.

5. Most achievements do not need sexual identification; those that do should be identified for both men and women. If you would not say, "Dan Rather is a male reporter," do not say, "Helen Thomas is a female reporter." Instead of "John McEnroe is one of the best American tennis players and Pam Shriver is one of the best American women tennis players," say, "John McEnroe and Pam Shriver are two of the best American tennis players," or, "John McEnroe is one of the best American male tennis players and Pam Shriver is one of the best American female tennis players."

6. Avoid sins of omission as well as those of commission. If, for example, an expert is sought in a given field, or if an example is needed to make a point, women should be used in these cases as a matter of course—not simply as "oddities" or representatives of "a woman's viewpoint."

7. "Man," used alone and in words like "chairman," is a sexually exclusive term and should be avoided when possible. "Man-on-the-street," for example, can easily be changed to "person-on-the-street" or "ordinary person"; "chairman" to "chairperson." The federal government has begun to change its job titles to reflect this problem; persons formerly called "mailmen" are now called "mail carriers."

8. Women's professional qualifications or working experience should always be acknowledged, to forestall the common (and incorrect) expectation that most women are full-time housewives.

9. "Feminist" is the correct term to describe a woman committed to equal rights for women. "Women's libber" is an unacceptable pejorative.

10. Headlines seem to be particularly susceptible to the use of stereotypical, simplistic language. As in other areas, play on these stereotypes is to be avoided.

11. When you have completed a story about a woman, go through it and ask yourself whether you would have written about a man in the same style. If not, something may be wrong with the tone or even the conception for your article. Think it through again.

EXERCISES

1. A female student came into the college daily's office, upset that a professor of physics posted a *Playboy* centerfold in his class as a joke. When she said she was offended, he refused to take the picture down. She thinks the incident deserves a story, but she's not willing to take the matter to the university for action. Is this a story?

2. Larry Flynt, publisher of *Hustler* magazine, offered CBS videotapes which showed auto mogul John De Lorean involved in a cocaine deal. CBS officials knew that if these tapes were aired, De Lorean would be essentially tried by the public, but they believed the news value of the tapes superseded this concern. CBS aired the tapes, and the De Lorean drug trafficking trial was postponed indefinitely because of prejudicial pretrial publicity. Were Flynt and CBS right or wrong?

3. Read the eleven rules about "How To Refer to Women." Then add another rule that is *not* covered in the eleven rules.

WORDS ABOUT THE PRESS

Along with responsible newspapers, we must have responsible readers.

—Arthur Hays Sulzberger

If a newspaper prints a sex crime, it's smut, but when the New York Times *prints it, it's a sociological study.*

—Adolph S. Ochs

The things that bother a press about the President will always bother the country.

—David Halberstam

News is the first draft of history.

—Benjamin Bradlee

Newspapers always excite curiosity. No one ever lays one down without a feeling of disappointment.

—Charles Lamb

The only authors whom I acknowledge as American are the journalists. They, indeed, are not great writers, but they speak the language of their countrymen, and make themselves heard by them.

—Alexis de Tocqueville

CHAPTER 12

Editorial Leadership

The strongest man in the world is he who stands most alone.

—Henrik Ibsen

It is appropriate to begin with college editors, and then editors of professional newspapers, magazines, and television.

COLLEGE EDITORIAL LEADERSHIP

Originality does not consist in saying what no else has ever said before, but in saying exactly what you think yourself.

—James Stephen

These words come from a college editor:

The primary problem that faces every editor of student newspapers is that they are editing *student* newspapers. The staff members are students who happen to be journalists, or if the editors are fortunate, journalists who happen to be students. The students are never just journalists, and, consequently, many problems arise.

Some problems are obvious. Students have time commitments beyond the newspapers. They go to classes (some more regularly than others), the library, parties, football games, and everywhere else students wander. Student reporters do not always have time, especially during peak academic periods, to do their jobs as, and especially when, editors would like them to. Beat reporting, in which the journalist must check in with sources and must always be ready to write if news happens, is especially difficult for a college paper. And when students *can* devote time to reporting, it often comes at night, after classes but also after sources have left their offices—and, of course, after the deadline, which editors wish the reporters had met. But these obvious problems are relatively easy to solve—provided student reporters are relentless. An editor must have a staff twice as large as he or she

184

expects to need, and an editor must become used to the idea that the paper will come out late a good percentage of the days it is published.

More subtly, ethical problems also plague student newspapers, though; problems much more difficult than schedule conflicts to solve. The most common problem is that student reporters tend to be involved in activities on which student newspapers report. College editors have a reasonably small pool from which to attract staff members, so some student reporters will inevitably belong to fraternities and sororities, play on varsity teams, run for student-government offices, support political causes, and work in outside jobs. If a given reporter does not do any of these things, it is likely his or her best friend does. The possibility of a conflict of interest—or at least the appearance of one—is great, and that makes an editor's job difficult.

Students seldom want to see a news story hurt an organization in which they are involved, so an editor has to watch carefully to see that all matters are treated fairly and correctly. Here is an example:

The editors of a college newspaper learn that a number of dormitories are conducting a gambling scheme in which groups of students "buy" college basketball teams in the NCAA Tournament. If a student buys a team that does well, he or she can win thousands of dollars. The total pools are as high as $10,000. An editor calls residential education, but a man answers that they do not know about the games and "have better ways to spend our time, anyway." The county district attorney's office, however, says that if prosecuted, the gambling could bring a serious fine and up to three years in jail. But the district attorney does not have time to deal with it, either. Is this a story? Certainly. Students have been acting illegally, but no one in authority seems to be concerned. The paper runs the story; sportswriters, many of whom were involved, are furious.

Student reporters will, understandably, use many kinds of excuses as to why a certain story should not run:

> "It will make the Betas look bad, and they're really a bunch of nice guys."

> "We're a student newspaper, so we can afford to be more understanding and not print the name of the student who was arrested for sexual assault. He is pretty young to be deprived of the chance to make a new start."

> "If you print the fact that the Senate is losing money with the Coffee House, Servomation might take it over. You don't want that to happen, do you?"

> "My friends will hate me forever if you run this story."

Usually, the arguments themselves are easy to dismiss, but reporters themselves are the problem. Sometimes it takes careful diplomacy to keep them working for the paper.

Another vexing problem for almost any editor is that he or she has a certain obligation to allow any student to write for the paper. Given that editors feel this way, what can be done with students who simply are not qualified to be reporters? The sincere commitment of a novice simply does not make up for a complete lack of talent or ability to learn about basic journalism. Not many students completely lack ability, but enough do to present a problem.

Job performance as a whole is a problem area for college editors. Because student reporters are not employees—in the true sense of that word—there is little an editor can do to keep his staff in line. Salaries are generally so low already that docking them is not a practical form of punishment for poor work, and there are never enough staffers that an editor-in-chief can afford to fire an editor. When a staff member fails to do his or her job properly (which usually means failure to do the job on time), there is little the editor can do beyond appealing to the offending party's sense of responsibility—or sense of guilt.

Another major set of problems comes about because the role of an independent college newspaper is often misunderstood. Readers and others are seldom perfectly clear on what an independent newspaper is and is not, and that presents a constant stream of annoying problems. Faculty members occasionally call the paper to explain that they have sent over a certain announcement which, of course, will be published. They do not often realize that what is published in the paper is not their decision, but is the decision of the student editors. "But students really need to know this information," they inevitably say. When they are right, a story is published; but when they are wrong, which is usually the case, they are told politely to buy an ad. They are seldom happy with this suggestion. Fortunately, most college administrations seem to understand the importance of student newspapers' independence. When the president of a university has a complaint about a story, he usually writes a letter to the editor as anyone else would.

This problem is not limited to the faculty. At one college paper, the Senate candidates pledge every year to "have the paper print" this or that information about the Senate, just as they promise to make other changes over which they have no authority—like forcing banks to open automated tellers in all dormitories and requiring the post office to make its lines shorter.

Many readers of one student paper say they feel the paper has an obligation, as the community newspaper of the college, to print everything written by members of the community. One graduate student has submitted a half-dozen opinion pieces, and he is beside himself that the paper refuses to print a 40-page thesis he has written on the health of ideas at the university. "You give three or four pages to sports each day. Why not run my piece?" he has asked over and over. He has gone as far as recruiting faculty members to call in their support.

One history professor called, shouting, "You have space for all those pizza ads, and you're trying to tell me you don't have space for this?" The distinction between revenue-producing advertising and editorial copy was lost on him.

Finally, the perceptions about what the college paper's role should be occasionally cause problems. Student newspaper staffs generally agree, though, that their papers should be primarily local. In a newspaper market flooded with giant dailies, all of which have the staff and money to cover national and international news better than the college paper can, it would be foolish to compete. The college daily, however, can cover the campus better than any other paper.

Coverage is at once one of the most frustrating and most exciting aspects of college journalism. Because of the nature of news, no single issue of a college daily is the perfect one, and no single issue is the worst; there is always tomorrow's issue. This knowledge that the news changes, that the next issue might be better than this one, and that the decision made today will be remade tomorrow, probably keeps all the staff members from collapsing under the weight of their jobs. At one paper, a fraternity president stormed out of the college daily's office last year, promising to "spend the rest of my life shutting down this liberal bullshit." He hasn't been back.

PROFESSIONAL EDITORIAL LEADERSHIP

> *My interest is in the future, because I am going to spend the rest of my life there.*
>
> —Charles F. Kettering

When a new managing director joined the *London Times* some years ago, he became curious about an obscure little man carrying a black satchel who entered the building every Friday and left on Monday morning. Old-timers had seen the man come and go every weekend for years, but no one knew who he was or what he did. One day the director noted a curious expenditure in the ledgers. Bookkeepers told him it was for meals that a nearby restaurant sent in to the little man on weekends. Eventually, the director tracked down the intruder. The little man was from the Bank of England, and his little satchel contained five thousand pounds in cash.

On a Saturday afternoon decades earlier, during the Boer War, the *Times* had wanted to send a reporter to cover a big story on the Continent. Boat traffic was halted by a storm, and the man could not charter a boat because there was no cash in the office and the banks were closed. To make sure it would always have cash on hand for such contingencies, the *Times* arranged for the Bank of England to send a representative each weekend with five thousand pounds in cash.

The story may be apocryphal, but it epitomizes how one leader of newspapers can become set in its ways—ways unthinkingly perpetuated long after the reasons for them have vanished.

THE BLINDNESS OF ROUTINES

> *If the blind lead the blind, both shall fall into the ditch.*
>
> —Matthew 15:14

Defining a mission may seem more creative and destiny-shaping than day-to-day operations, but operations can also be creative, for they shape the company's environment. Yet, the creative aspect of operations can quickly be lost as routines take over. One part of editorial leadership is to monitor the routines to see that they serve the organization's purpose, and to ensure that not only operational glitches but ethical ones get the attention they deserve.

Managers constantly offer directions for dealing with the operational problems, and they need to do the same for ethical problems. The existing ethical routines are in the form of codes of ethics, which may be posted on newsroom walls.

There is a danger, however. As frequently stated here, the dominant imperative operating on journalists is to publish or broadcast what they have found out, as long as it is news. Translated to ethical issues, this means publish, no matter what the impact. There is an automatic drive to do so. The routines support this ethical position. Fortunately, in most cases, a routine decision to publish probably is the ethically correct decision. However, routine can lull editors into inattention.

Journalist-Researcher Philip Meyer was disturbed by this finding in a study of more than 300 newspapers he conducted in 1982 and 1983 for the American Society of Newspaper Editors.* "The knee-jerk response to publish at all costs may not always, or even often, lead to bad outcomes," he wrote, "but it does prevent the question from ever rising to the level of an ethical issue." Meyer was impressed with his finding that staff members tended to follow traditional newsroom values more strictly than their editors and publishers did. But his additional finding—that ethical decisions were often arrived at viscerally rather than rationally—gives a clue to the nature of such knee-jerk ethics. Two major lessons stand out. First, the staff members are more rigid and less sensitive to competing standards than the supervisors. Second, the decisions are made without thought—no doubt as a result of time pressure and the obvious need to rely on routines.

Successful managers make time for thought, but reporters and copy editors cannot do this. Since ethical problems take time to resolve, decisions about ethical behavior must start with management. This does not mean that staff members should be excluded from discussions of ethical standards. It is the responsibility of management to initiate and crystallize them in a clear expression of the organization's purposes, the values that flow from those purposes, and the latitude employees have in fulfilling those purposes and values. Managers must be missionaries for the organizational values that operational routines slight.

CONTROL BY PRESSURE GROUPS

> *A man convinced against his will*
> *Is of the same opinion still.*
>
> —Samuel Butler

An editor of a strong newspaper once described the leading pressures on him and his staff:

Editors, Publishers and Newspaper Editors, ASNE, 1983, p. 34.

1. *Liberalism vs. conservatism.* "The strongest pressure that operates on our staff is one of liberalism vs. conservatism. Some of our staff members go to the clubs and they get this sort of pressure."

2. *Labor unions.* "We're careful about unions because their feelings are hurt so easily. I was a union member for seven years. I lean to management's side because their arguments are better. But I'm conscious of that. So we lean over backwards to be careful about the union side."

3. *Organizations.* "All the organizations want more publicity for whatever cause they're supporting."

4. *Religion.* "We get some pressure from the Protestants when we run news about the Catholics."

5. *Politics.* "We don't pay much attention to that. As long as the Democrats and Republicans squawk about us, we're all right."

6. *Advertising.* "We've made about a dozen mistakes in news about a major advertiser in the last year, and he thinks we're against him. For example, one of the government agencies fined him on some technical violation of the law. We ran the story. He thought it should have been left out. We couldn't do that, so he thought it should have been played down—a smaller head."

How do the pressure groups operate to influence newspapers? By almost any means: sending committees to call on publishers and editors: telephone calls; letters; personal influence at social or business occasions; favors, parties, or entertainment; threats; and arguments made to editorial writers, reporters, or editors.

Managers absorb most of these pressures, which fall within the community-relations function of management. Good managers can use such conflicts to get employees to improve their decision-making processes. Employees cannot be shielded from all pressure—and some complaints *should* pass through management to the people involved in causing them.

BIGNESS MEANS WEAKNESS

Few rich men own their own property. The property owns them.

—Robert G. Ingersoll

Michael Frome was fired in 1974 as conservation editor of *Field & Stream* magazine. It seemed that he was fired after he began to rate U.S. senators and representatives according to their voting record on environmental issues. Was that the reason for his firing? It could have been because he had reported questionable land transactions conducted in New Mexico by officials of the Bureau of Land Management of the Department of the Interior, a report that Frome's editors chose not to publish. Or, he could have been fired because he filed a criticism of the Forest Service's Environmental Program for the Future. Should one blame the publisher or the editor of *Field & Stream*? Perhaps—or perhaps not. After all, *Field & Stream* was the property of CBS.

"Today," Frome wrote, "when every company appears to be owned by some other company, it is virtually impossible to say anything of importance without stepping on somebody's toes and irritating the financial nerve, directly or indirectly."

Eric Sevareid, the retired CBS commentator, said, "The bigger our information media, the less courage and freedom of expression they allow. Bigness means weakness." He then went on:

> Courage in the realm of ideas goes in inverse ratio to the size of the establishment. The investment in any given item that is produced—whether it is a TV program or a Hollywood movie or a big mass magazine—is so enormous that they must find a great denominator in terms of audience, whether it is the lowest common denominator or not. The risk is too great. This is not true of the small-capital media, like the stage or book publishing or a small magazine.

One might ask: Would most journalists be happy as cogs in a great magazine if it is controlled by a tire manufacturer?

In a world of conglomerates, it may be more difficult for editors to protect journalistic judgments against marketing judgments. To do so may be an act of courage. True, the source of the pressure often has no bad intent. When the Xerox Corporation paid Harrison Salisbury to write an article about the state of the United States and agreed to buy advertising space in *Esquire* so that the magazine could publish the article, it saw the act as one of public service. It convincingly asserted that it would not have tried to influence either what Salisbury wrote or the editing by *Esquire*. Yet the idea provoked controversy because it raised questions of credibility and conflict of interest.

Even issues that involve a nonprofit source—one not usually considered a special interest—can require courageous editorial stands. John Fischer, the late editor-in-chief of *Harper's*, told of such an incident involving Robert Hutchins, head of the Fund for the Republic and once president of the University of Chicago. Fischer wrote in *Harper's* (May 1968):

> Over lunch, Dr. Hutchins explained that the thoughts of the Fund's staff and its grantees were not getting the public attention they observed. Indeed, the pamphlets it issued sometimes were ignored entirely by the American press. To remedy this lamentable situation, he proposed that the Fund should take over each month a section of *Harper's*—say, 32 pages—and fill them with articles of its own production. In return, it would pay *Harper's* $500,000 the first year, and, if the results were satisfactory, the arrangement might be continued.
>
> Did Dr. Hutchins mean that he would like to buy 32 pages of advertising

space each month? No, no, that wasn't the idea. The space to be filled by the Fund would not be labeled as advertising. In fact, the name of the Fund would not appear at all. The articles it provided would seem to be a normal part of the magazine so the readers need never know that they had not been developed by the regular editors. The impact, he suggested flatteringly, might be greater that way.

Should Fischer have accepted the money from Hutchins in return for surrendering 32 pages a month?

Although Fischer was aware that *Harper's* was losing money, he declined. He told about it:

> I assured Dr. Hutchins that I was in favor of both ideals and a democratic society, and would probably agree heartily with most of the causes he wanted to promote. But, I added, the primary responsibility of all editors was to their readers. In good conscience, therefore, an editor could not surrender control over the editorial content of his publication, even for the best-intentioned of purposes. Neither could he offer the readers somebody else's product under the guise of his own.
>
> All this sounded pretty stuffy, I'm afraid; but I still believe that the role is a sound one. It is some protection, moreover, against all the dangers. So long as an editor remembers that he is working, first and last, for his readers—who are, ultimately, the people who pay him—he usually should be able to resist most temptations, even those of his own ego.

Life magazine, however, part of Henry Luce's powerful Time, Inc., empire, published a piece critical of the Christian Anti-Communist Crusade, a right-wing organization led by a former Baptist revivalist named Frederick C. Schwarz and backed by West Coast industrial leaders. The earth seemed to shake when the magazine reached the Schwarz group in Los Angeles. An article in the *Saturday Evening Post* (June 6, 1963) discussed the affair:

> "Whoever pulled that sleazy stunt," roared Schwarz, "is working for the Communist criminal conspiracy." Raging protests, many from big businessmen, overwhelmed the magazine. . . . Large corporations were threatening to withdraw millions of dollars' worth of advertising. Reluctantly, Luce, the pragmatist, conceded the need to make handsome amends. Westward winged *Life* publisher Charles Douglas Jackson to appear on the same platform with Schwarz at a Hollywood Bowl rally. Before 15,000 cheering crusaders, he not only made an abject apology, but aligned *Life* with Schwarz in the fight against Communism.

Two weeks later, *Life* repaired its tattered pride in an editorial reaffirming its hostility to the radical right. But for Schwarz, it reserved a pat on the head.

JOHN FISCHER

The late editor of *Harper's* magazine, John Fischer, once wrote that the easiest styles to master are "the Murky Academic, as found in practically any doctoral dissertation, or the Rococo Breathless, typified by Tom Wolfe (the youth culture kid, not the novelist), and the Long-Winded Profound, a specialty of the *New York Review of Books*." Fischer's tone displays his distaste, but the styles he identifies with such names are certainly familiar.

Writers of the "murky academic" style use long and abstract words in long sentences like these:

> The second issue is whether or not the classical conditioning paradigm is indeed the correct one for research procedures such as those of Staats and Lott. The epistemological importance of definitely evaluating the appropriateness of the classical conditioning paradigm. . . .

The "rococo breathless," an ornate style that may produce strong effects but sometimes makes the reader work too hard, is typified by this passage written by Tom Wolfe:

> But she is not alone in her thrill as the Black Panthers come trucking on in, into Lenny's house, Robert Bay, Don Cox the Panthers' Field Marshal from Oakland, Henry Miller the Harlem Panther defense captain, the Panther women—Christ, if the Panthers don't know how to get it all together. . . .

The "long-winded profound" style is represented well by this paragraph from the *New York Review of Books:*

> We can also say, more importantly, that when he traces the lines linking Rousseau's thought to the tyrannies of our century, Crocker is extrapolating and giving reality to themes which in Rousseau remain in the realm of imagination or of historical reminiscence. . . .

A professor who had chosen the above illustrations of Fischer's distaste showed them to Fischer, who said, "Those items are what I was writing about."

Fischer is a tall, spare man, who in the 1950s and 1960s had immense power. He was born in one of the least likely places—Texhoma, Oklahoma. Although Fischer was an extremely talented student at the University of Oklahoma and later became a Rhodes Scholar at Oxford University, he chose to become a reporter. Eventually, he became a government administrator, but Fischer finally found a home, not as editor of *Harper's*, but as the columnist who occupied "The Easy Chair." Here is the beginning of a column

Fischer wrote in August 1966:

> The columnist's job calls for something more than responsible reporting. It requires taking a position. It is not enough for the writer to say, "Here is a bunch of facts. Make what you can out of them." He is obligated to go a step further and say, "I have examined these facts as best I can, discussed them with other knowledgeable people, and arranged them in some kind of order. Here, then, is a conclusion which common sense might draw from them, and a course of action which a reasonable man might follow. . . ." The real function of such analytic reporting is to help readers arrive at conclusions of their own. Here, I believe, is the chief justification for any column, in newspaper or magazine. It offers the reader a chance to become familiar enough with a given point of view so that he can use it to work out his own intellectual bearings.

No doubt this quotation from Fischer seems to define in few words what a columnist is to do. Certainly, Fischer's intelligent, plain style will live for a long time.

DEVELOPING A COMPANY CODE OF ETHICS

The moral obligation is to be intelligent.

—John Erskine

If management articulates a clear mission, clear values, and clear limits, a collaborative kind of discussion about standards can prove productive. Their value in making staff members feel they have a say in their own fate makes the time worthwhile. These talks encourage understanding among all parties, for the goal should be to consider all significant views about guidelines for behavior within the organization.

The discussions may not result in the standards themselves; that may be up to the managers. But the managers should respond to staff's views with comments that clearly reflect organization's mission, values, and limits. The process should offer the opportunity for further discussion and for some flexibility in applying the standards. If the discussion results in a framed code of ethics, fine; but the real value may lie in the understanding that comes from the process that produces the code. Codes of ethics tend to fail if they are overly specific—they may be inflexible and they may encourage rote applications.

It is ongoing communication between managers and staff that best resolves behavior issues. A publisher who takes part in thoughtful decisions is more likely to give the standards life than is an absent publisher who expects the staff to live up to the code on the wall, as Philip Meyer reported.

Discussions of standards also lead to a better understanding between management and staff. Take as an example how money is viewed in a media company. Meyer found strong suspicions on the part of staff members about money because they saw it in terms of power and influence. Publishers were more likely to see money as a tool to be used to achieve the company's goals. The framing of standards that work will be responsive to such differences and may even help to narrow them.

In setting a course through the conflicting pressures from the community, editorial leaders need constantly to recall who has first claim on their loyalty. Even in issues involving advertisers, audience is paramount: After all, the quality of the media product affects the audience attention the advertiser is buying.

In short, management plays a big role in shaping the expectations of its staff and a not-insignificant role in shaping those of its publics. Success hinges in part, then, on developing expectations or discerning them, and then fulfilling them. The general guideline is this: Respect the people and their interests.

THE IMPORTANCE OF PURPOSE

> *Leaders have a significant role in creating the state of mind that is society.*
>
> —John Gardner

This book has stressed the importance of knowing one's purpose in order to make good decisions about how to behave. A clear mission is more than a tool for deciding right and wrong, however. As Peter Drucker and others have written, effectiveness depends on setting and monitoring goals. Defining the organization's mission is a basic function of top management and a primary responsibility of the board of directors.

An organization's mission reflects its history. The founder of a newspaper, a radio station, or a public relations firm had purposes beyond making profit. True, money *is* a primary motive for some publishers. Once, George Gordon, Lord Byron, gave his publisher a beautiful Bible. The publisher was proud of the gift and displayed it on a table—until a visitor pointed out that the sentence "Now Barabbas was a robber," had been changed to "Now Barabbas was a publisher." But usually a founder's other purposes were more important—the desire to influence people, to inform them, to join in community development, to provide a service needed at the time, to exploit a technological breakthrough, to enhance the founder's public standing. The original goals changed along the way.

If the organization thrived, its success likely involved an understanding of the publics it served. Some owners and managers may have had the power to be ruthless in pursuing other goals. But over the decades, as better-prepared practitioners and better-educated publics have pushed for better performance, economic success has gone to those organizations that best responded to high public expectations.

EXERCISES

1. Is the editor of your college newspaper
   a) elected? If so, by whom?
   b) appointed? If so, by whom?

   Write a 500-word paper as to whether the editor carries out his or her function admirably, passably, or any other description that suits your opinion.

2. A business editor decides that his paper's finance section would be improved by the presence of a local stock column. Writing the column involves talking to local stock analysts, following developments in local companies, and predicting what stocks will do. Should the editor choose a staffer who holds no local stocks? Or, can he solve the problem with a disclosure line at the bottom of the column indicating that the writer does hold stock in the subject of a column?

3. A high-echelon federal manager says that all news media are largely responsible for the negative image public employees have. He says that most public employees are competent and dedicated, but few people know this because of all the negative stories in the media. Is he right or wrong?

WORDS ABOUT MOVIES AND TELEVISION

The only -ism Hollywood believes in is plagiarism.

—Dorothy Parker

It was a hideous and untenable place when I dwelt in Hollywood, populated with a few exceptions by Yahoos, and now that it has become the chief citadel of television, it's unspeakable.

—S. J. Perelman

I'm a Hollywood writer; so I put on a sports jacket and take off my brain.

—Ben Hecht

No one can write a script for a spontaneous demonstration.

—Anonymous

Television is a nasty business to write about—especially if you identify with Diogenes.

—Gary Deeb

Television is a device that permits people who haven't anything to do to watch people who can't do anything.

—Fred Allen

If there are only two good programs on TV on a given evening, they'll be televised at the same time.

—Anonymous

CHAPTER 13

The Media Codes

Women no longer talk about the hairdresser, the maids, and the manicurist. Now they all talk about the movie they want to produce.

—Lynn Wasserman

When a professor was lecturing a college class on movie ethics nine years ago, he commented that movie ratings—X, R, PG, and G—seemed to be working. He was astonished by the response. Although everyone in the class was at least eighteen years old, *all* of them had bitter memories of the time when they were excluded from movies several years ago. "How could *they* close us out?" asked a student, almost shouting.

A bit taken aback, the professor responded with a question: "Would you like your nine-year-old sister to go to *any* movie?"

"Well . . . well, no," a student said. "But the age will have to be lower than it is." Luckily, the professor had asked perhaps the *only* question that would cause his students to pause. Those who had younger sisters understood. They then decided that 13 is the only reasonable limit.

This incident suggests how all the codes have been adopted by the media and its adjuncts, advertising and public relations. All codes have been subjected to acrimonious arguments. Nonetheless, even though the codes have been changed at least slightly every few years, the various media codes in the appendices are the industries' own definition of what constitutes good or bad practices. We will begin by looking at each of them.

Unlike the other industry codes, the Statement of Principles of the American Society of Newspaper Editors (ASNE) has nothing to say about decency and morality. It is concerned with information rather than entertainment, and assumes the foundation of a free, self-righting process in society and a public able to distinguish between good and bad, truth and error. If it makes any assumption about morality, it prefers a moral to an immoral society. The topics of the statement are responsibility, freedom, independence, truthfulness, accuracy, impartiality, and fair play.

The following analysis of the ASNE code, the code of the Society of Professional Journalists-Sigma Delta Chi, and the *Washington Post* code was written by Deborah Shannon, a student and former Associated Press reporter and editor:

> There is no doubt the three newspaper codes expect journalists to exercise impartiality, fair play, and accuracy. But to what degree?
>
> The codes differ dramatically in how much (or little) leeway they give. The American Society of Newspaper Editors (ASNE) code gives few "thou shalls," and, potentially, has the most ambiguity. The Sigma Delta Chi (SDX) code has black-and-white rules, such as "nothing of value should be accepted." The *Washington Post* has, by far, the most explicit rules:
>
> > There is such a thing as a free lunch, under some conditions; if you're unsure what those conditions are, ask a managing editor.
>
> There's a reason why the *Post* code is so explicit and comes across as being the best. The other two codes were written for journalists who work at hundreds of papers, and this undoubtedly was taken into account by the ASNE and SDX authors. If you work at an ASNE-member paper or if you belong to SDX, you could break a rule and be rendered odious, but you wouldn't necessarily be fired. The *Post*'s rules are just that: the paper's rules. Those who break them can expect to be fired, or at least chastised, so it is in the paper's best interest to define each provision as carefully as possible.

HOW THE CODES STACK UP

The man who makes no mistakes does not usually make anything.

—W. C. Magee

The ASNE code says journalists must "avoid impropriety and the appearance of impropriety" and should "neither accept anything nor pursue any activity that might compromise or seem to compromise their integrity."

What does that mean, though? Should a reporter owning stocks in companies be allowed to write a column about those companies, and should the column note that the author owned the stocks? Under the ASNE code, would it be acceptable to own the stocks and acknowledge it in the column? It is hard to tell what action the reporter would have to take to be considered ethical.

The code says the journalist must avoid impropriety, but what if the reporter's spouse is a teacher and the reporter has the education beat? What if the spouse protests a nuclear power plant and the reporter regularly writes about the local power utility? The code mentions nothing about relatives, a weakness that would be easy to remedy.

Much of the ASNE code referees outside conflicts—those between the newsperson and the world. One excruciating conflict took place inside the newsroom, though. It was between the Houston religion reporter and the Catholic editor, who, it seems, had an interest in how certain diocese affairs were publicized. A stronger code, perhaps, would have been more specific about what constitutes a conflict of interest.

The ASNE code says significant errors of fact or omission should be corrected promptly and prominently. This is one of the code's strengths, as the Houston religion writer probably would agree.

Article V, which calls for impartiality, wisely suggests that opinion needs to be labeled as such when it slops off the editorial or Op-Ed pages. This article recognizes the need for occasional analysis pieces that draw upon a writer's background and educated views. Without such well-crafted stories, newspapers would be doing only half their job. They would be providing the facts, but not necessarily the truth. The code could be strengthened by adding a sentence that made it clear such articles were to be written by those with expertise in the field.

Fair play is a noble concept, and it is good that the code says a person should be given the earliest opportunity to respond to an accusation of wrongdoing. Even so, under the code, one could print innuendo and do it with a clear conscience so long as the accused had the right to say "No comment. Talk to my lawyer." This weakness in the code brings to mind the excesses of McCarthyism, when the press thought it had done its job when it got "no comments" from those McCarthy had smeared.

The ASNE code says journalists should respect the rights of people involved in the news. How much guidance, though, do those words give a reporter writing a story about a San Francisco AIDS hotel? How do you balance privacy vs. the public's need to know? This section of the code would be more useful if it had more details.

One section reminds reporters that confidentiality to news sources should not be given lightly. The code would be more useful if it gave examples of circumstances that would make confidentiality necessary—perhaps potential death of a source, loss of the source's job, or national security.

THE SIGMA DELTA CHI CODE

They defend their errors as if they were defending their inheritance.

—Edmund Burke

The Sigma Delta Chi code states that nothing of value should be accepted. Does that include a $5 lunch? Who decides what's valuable—the reporter, his or her editor, or the gift-giver?

The Sigma Delta Chi code warns against moonlighting and political activism—fine advice for the reporter and editor. But what of the spouse? Under this code or the ASNE guidelines, the newsperson would have trouble sorting out the problems of a spouse with antinuke sympathy or sympathy toward teachers.

Journalists should make constant efforts to assure that the public's business is conducted in public, according to the Sigma Delta Chi code. Is it kosher for a newspaper to go a step further and entrap public officials? The Chicago newspaper that set up a tavern and filmed inspectors taking pay-offs certainly discovered plenty about how the public's business is done. But was that method ethical? It would be hard to say under this code.

The Sigma Delta Chi code acknowledges the newsman's ethic of protecting confidential sources. This code would do well to make it clear that reporters shouldn't offer confidentiality if they are not willing to pay the price, including going to jail if they will not reveal the source.

Objectivity is a goal for those following the Sigma Delta Chi code. Objectivity, though, is being debated at length by editors. The *Washington Post*'s call for fairness, which will be described later in this review, seems more workable.

The Sigma Delta Chi code earns points for its uncompromising stand on accuracy, bias, partisanship, and analysis. Some questions crop up in the fair play section, though. Is it pandering to morbid curiosity when a newspaper writes about the AIDS hotels, or is it serving the public's need to know?

The Sigma Delta Chi code deserves praise for urging editors to correct mistakes and encourage the public to give its grievances. Harris and Gallup polls make it clear that the public thinks the press is arrogant. A little more accountability could help change that perception.

THE WASHINGTON POST CODE

> *We political journalists have access to the minds of many of our*
> *leading citizens. That is a rare privilege. It is also a form of power.*

—David Broder

The *Washington Post* code takes on the personality of the paper that created it: it's big and detailed.

The conflict of interest section makes clear what is or is not acceptable. If the reporter cannot figure it out, the code advises asking an executive editor. This is good; it makes it clear that monkey business will not be tolerated and that some editor somewhere is being paid to make such decisions. The same holds true for the guidelines for moonlighting, outside activities, and obscenity. The *Post* also does favor reporters by recognizing that relatives' involvement in causes can appear to compromise the paper's integrity. In Washington, a city where few activities aren't political, reporters need to think about integrity.

One of the *Post*'s strengths is its belief that reporters should remain in the audience. Another strength is its call for accuracy.

The Sigma Delta Chi and ASNE codes would be strengthened if they borrowed the *Post*'s section on sources. Readers deserve to know why sources don't want to be revealed, and the *Post* does the public a favor by demanding that its reporters request an on-the-record reason for restricting the source's identity.

The *Post* mentions something ignored in the other codes: plagiarism. Perhaps the other organizations figure it goes without saying that ethical reporters don't plagiarize. But if the students lie on resumes and if college presidents lift sections of another administrator's speech, plagiarism is at large in our society and the issue probably needs to be addressed.

The *Post* deserves credit for sidestepping the objectivity issue by demanding fairness. It deserves further recognition for bringing up subtle prejudices: pejorative words such as "refused" and "massive."

Opinion belongs on editorial and Op-Ed pages, under the *Post* guidelines. The paper allows in-depth reports, analysis, or commentary if the stories are labeled as such.

The *Washington Post* brings out the distinction between claims of community interest and actual interest in a topic. This is a strength, and one the other codes could copy. Usually, the issue is looked at backwards—a company or government has something to hide and the newspaper tries to flush it out. This part of the code is a reminder that newspapers are giving a picture of society as a whole. Omitting a newsworthy story or lumping in "schlock" is doing readers a disservice. Either act gives a false picture.

THE MOVIE CODE

> *Morality is the best of all devices for leading mankind by the nose.*
>
> —Friedrich Nietzsche

In contrast to the newspaper code, which is essentially a series of *positive* directions—what the newspaper *should do*—the motion picture code is essentially negative. It lays down a number of general and specific prohibitions.

The motion picture code has been almost exclusively negative. It has called for respect for "pure love" as exemplified by marriage and the home, and required that the moviemaker seek to curb the passions of his or her audience. It also called for respect for religion and national feelings. But the list of prohibitions was longer and more detailed. Designations such as "Chink," "Wop," and "Dago"; a depiction of nudity, sexual dances, and lustful love; profane and vulgar language (including "SOB," "louse," and "broad" as applied to a woman) have been prohibited.

By 1966, however, the Motion Picture Association of America (MPAA) became convinced that its code was almost useless. Flagrant violations had become common. The code was heavily revised, the MPAA announced, "to keep in closer harmony with the mores, the culture, the moral sense, and expectations of our society."

Replacing the strongly detailed provisions for production standards were the following:

> The basic dignity and value of human life shall be respected and upheld. Restraint shall be exercised in portraying the taking of life.

Evil, sin, crime and wrong-doing shall not be justified.

Special restraint shall be exercised in portraying criminal or antisocial activities in which minors participate [or] are involved.

Detailed and protracted acts of brutality, cruelty, physical violence, torture, and abuse shall not be presented.

Illicit sex relations shall not be justified. Intimate sex scenes violating common standards of decency shall not be portrayed. Restraint and care shall be exercised in presentations dealing with sexual aberrations.

Obscene speech, gestures, or movements shall not be presented. Undue profanity shall not be permitted.

Religion shall not be demeaned.

Words or symbols contemptuous of racial, religious, or national groups shall not be used so as to incite bigotry or hatred.

In 1968, the motion picture industry all but threw up its hands. The latest productions were ignoring even the relaxed standards set by the new codes, so industry leaders formalized a series of labels designed to guide parents toward suitable movies. Jack Valenti of the MPAA declared the idea a total success: 97 percent of those surveyed knew of the rating system and more than two-thirds considered it a useful guide for attending movies.

In 1984, the MPAA added PG-13, which means: "Parents are strongly cautioned to give special guidance for attendance of children under 13. Some material may be inappropriate for young children."

THE RADIO CODE

Radio, the great syllabic storm of the age.

−Edwin John Pratt

Although the courts decreed in 1983 that the National Association of Broadcasters' radio and television codes are illegal, many radio and television stations say they abide by the codes.

The radio code is both positive and negative. It states ideals of performance, but it also restricts content. Also, it represents a move from a pure code of ethics toward a code of ethics including a statement of trade practices.

The code regards radio as a medium of both enlightenment and entertainment. It combines features of both the newspaper code and the motion picture code in outlining ethical behavior. Unlike the ASNE code, it recognizes the commercial aspects of broadcasting and has an additional proviso for ethical conduct.

Ethical behavior consists of (1) promoting the democratic process by enlightening the public, (2) promoting accepted standards of public morality by presenting wholesome entertainment, and (3) maintaining a proper balance between enlighten-

JACK VALENTI

"Where's he from?" Johnson asked.

"Buffalo," Valenti said.

"Buffalo? Buffalo where?"

"Buffalo, New York."

"And you tell me he's the best? He can't be the best in the world and be from Buffalo!"

This exchange followed Jack Valenti's proclamation that he had found "the best eye doctor in the world" for President Lyndon Johnson. Valenti, currently the President of the Motion Picture Association of America, served as a special assistant to President Johnson from November 22, 1963, until mid-1966.

Because Valenti was a Johnson assistant, he was a Texan. Born in Houston in 1921, Valenti graduated from the University of Houston and received his M.B.A. from Harvard University. After serving as co-founder and executive vice president of Weekley & Valenti advertising agency in Houston for over twenty years, Valenti moved to Washington, D.C., to serve as Lyndon Johnson's speech writer and top assistant.

Known as "the nice guy in the White House," Valenti was considered friendly to all reporters. In a situation with an irate Dan Rather, Valenti served as mediator to the satisfaction of everyone involved. Unrecognized at a presidential press conference, Rather felt that his career as a CBS correspondent was being threatened, and he approached Valenti with his story. Valenti reassured Rather that Johnson liked him and that the White House was "for" him. He explained the President's "terrible eye problem" and his inability to spot Rather in the audience. At the next conference, Rather discovered that either his shape had become familiar or that the President's eyesight had displayed rapid improvement.

Since his position at the White House, Valenti has become the leader and spokesman for the American film production and distribution industry throughout the world. He is currently a member of the board of directors of TransWorld Airlines, the Kennedy Center, and the American Film Institute.

Valenti served as a B-25 pilot during World War II, flying in fifty-one combat missions with the Twelfth Air Force in Italty. He received many decorations, including the Distinguished Flying Cross.

A contributing writer to several publications, including the *New York Times,* the *Washington Post,* the *Los Angeles Times, Newsweek, Saturday Review,* and *Atlantic Monthly,* Valenti also wrote *The Bitter Taste of Glory* (nonfiction, 1971) and *A Very Human President* (1976) about his relationship with Lyndon Johnson. The "nice guy in the White House" is currently writing a novel about Washington, D.C., as well as a book on political power.

—Jennifer Koch

ment and entertainment, on the one hand, and contributions to the economic welfare, on the other, as well as high standards of advertising.

The code reflects trust in the self-righting process. Radio can expedite the process in such ways as presenting news from reliable sources, clearly distinguishing commentary from straight reporting, "willingness to expose its convictions to fair rebuttal," and ensuring equality of opportunity in alloting time for the presentation of public issues.

Broadcasters seem to doubt that radio is really self-righting. Reading the code, one suspects that they have reservations about human rationality, that they do not want discussion to be *too* controversial, and that they put narrower limits to it than do newspaper editors. The newspaper code positively and purposely states that the area of discussion should be large: "It is unquestionably right to discuss whatever is not explicitly forbidden by law." No such statement appears in the radio code. Instead, the radio code sets itself the difficult task of respecting "the rights and dignity of all people," which, if carried out thoroughly, would impose severe limitations on what can be discussed. Moreover, participation in the presentation of public issues should be "carefully reviewed with respect to the character and reputation of the group, campaign, or organization involved."

The public good for the broadcaster also includes a concern for public morals. Broadcasters should "observe both existing principles and developing concepts affecting our society." In news programs, they should not present "morbid, sensational, or alarming details." In entertainment—in children's programs especially—they should uphold accepted standards. Programs for children, the code notes, "should be based upon sound social concepts and should include positive sets of values which will allow children to become responsible adults. They should contribute to the healthy development of personality and character."

The broadcaster and the movie-maker will respect moral principles and institutions. He or she will not make crime attractive, will not encourage listeners to imitate criminals, and will not disparage law enforcement. He or she will respect what the motion picture code calls "pure love." He or she will, as the code says, "honor the sanctity of marriage and the home." All religion will be respected.

As for economic welfare, the broadcasters shall be judged by "high standards of performance," for they have a "responsibility to the public." They must keep advertising in proper proportion. The code suggests the maximum time to be used for advertising by a single sponsor at various periods. But the "quality and integration" of advertising are as important as its quantity. Broadcasters will make certain that advertising meets certain minimum standards.

THE TELEVISION CODE

No one reads any more—blame television. Families are breaking up—blame television. High culture is being despoiled—blame television. What a splendid all-purpose explanation televising has become!

—Anonymous

The television code is as heavily negative as the first versions of the motion picture code, which seems to have been a model for some sections of it. It also embodies a statement of good business practices.

The TV code stresses the duty of television to underscore the democratic process by public enlightenment. Responsible telecasters will offer a well balanced and adequate news presentation, which must be "factual, fair, and without bias." They will "seek out and develop with accountable individuals, groups, and organizations, programs relating to controversial public issues of import to his or her fellow citizens; and . . . give fair representation to opposing sides of issue which materially affect . . . a substantial segment of the public."

Overriding the telecaster's duty as enlightener, however, is his or her duty to have programs conform to the accepted beliefs and behavior of the majority. "Education via television," the code states, "may be taken to mean that process by which the individual is brought toward informed adjustment to his society."

Moreover, ethical telecasters will limit discussion to narrow bounds. They will make certain that the views presented are "responsible" ones, and they should weigh requests for discussion time "on the basis of their individual merits, and in the light of the contribution which the use requested would make to the public interest, and to a well-balanced program structure."

The television code links promoting the public good with promoting public morals. News and analysis must be given with concern for public morals. "At all times," says the code, "pictorial and verbal materials for both news and comment should conform to other sections of these standards, whether such sections are reasonably applicable."

The ethical telecaster has moral obligations similar to those of the moviemaker. The programs must respect law and order. The code recognizes that crime is a part of the world. Nonetheless, the ethical telecaster will not lead the young to believe that crime plays a greater part in life than it does. Criminality will be shown as "undesirable and unsympathetic," and will uphold law enforcement and stress the dignity of the law.

Telecasters will uphold respect for the sanctity of marriage. They will not depict divorce with levity or as a "solution for marital problems." They will not show illicit sex relations or sexual perversions.

The telecaster will try to keep in check the baser emotions of the viewers and to shield them from temptation. No scenes will be transmitted involving lascivious dances, indecorous costumes, excessive horror, or cruelty to animals. Drunkenness should never be presented as desirable. "Narcotic addition shall not be presented except as a destructive habit," the code holds. The code also forbids the advertising of hard liquor and requires that ads for beer and wine be "in the best of good taste."

"Broad religious precepts will be emphasized by the ethical telecaster." National feelings are to be respected by avoiding words derisive of any nationality or national derivation. Profanity of any sort will be forbidden.

The television code holds that advertising enables telecasters to make programs of enlightenment and entertainment available to viewers, but advertising must be kept in proper proportion. Almost half of the code deals with advertising, and this part amounts to a statement of good practices.

Ethical telecasters will try to make advertising carried by their stations conform to the standards of their programs of enlightenment and entertainment. Just as news is truthful and labeled as to source, so should advertising be free of misrepresentation and presented by firms of integrity. And as other programs should avoid offending the majority by profanity, indelicacy, and so on, so should advertising avoid being "objectionable to a substantial and responsible segment of the community."

SENSATION, CRIME, AND VIOLENCE

Most American television stations reproduce all night long what a
Roman could only have seen in the Coliseum during the reign of Nero.

—George Faludy

Most of the many codes hold that violence is never justified. The question is, then, how does television justify the enormous amount of violence, crime, and sensation it carries? And the answer seems to be that it makes an assumption of importance: That most of such material may be justified if the audience is informed that crime never pays, that evil-doing is punished, and that accepted social morés have a way of enforcing themselves.

This ethic is one of "have your cake and eat it too." For example, when some newspapers function more as entertainment media than as information channels and sensationalize news, their theory is that nothing destroys an evil as effectively as publicity. But is the desired result that everybody wallows in filth instead?

Consider the way power is treated. Attention to power is nothing unusual, and heroes since the beginning of story-telling have tended to be men of great power. In comic strips, crime dramas, and westerns, the leading characters have often had immense power and engaged in thrilling adventures.

Powerful villains are sometimes portrayed positively. For example, villains James Bond pursues are canny, strong, and daring. They are always captured and punished, but viewers may admire the character who has so much skill and makes fools of the police. George Orwell remarks on the tendency in America to tolerate crime, "even to admire the criminal so long as he is successful." It is this attitude, he wrote, "that has made it possible for crime to flourish upon so huge a scale. Books have been written about Al Capone that are hardly different in tone from the books written about Henry Ford, . . . Lord Northcliffe, and all the rest of the 'log cabin to White House' brigade." The codes permit villains to be portrayed positively as long as they are disposed of according to rule. But is it right?

In *Hollywood, The Dream Factory* (Little, Brown, 1950), Hortense Powdermaker wrote:

> The MPAA gave its seal of approval to a picture in which the two leading characters committed adultery and then murder, and, of course, were finally punished for all their sins. What the MPAA ignored were the implications of a sexy-looking, beautiful woman and a strong, handsome he-man, both popular stars, irresistibly drawn to each other, committing adultery, and finally murder. That they are punished at the end would not necessarily destroy the identification of the preceding sixty or eighty minutes.

Morally upright heroes may settle the problems of society as self-appointed enforcers of justice. These are Superman, Steve Roper, Wonder Woman, and all the successors of Robin Hood and Sherlock Holmes. All have charm and power, and all fall into one general pattern. Martha Wolfenstein describes it: "The hero, the self-appointed investigator and agent of justice, is able to set things right independently. The world, which is not effectively policed, does not need to be policed at all."

In *Movies: A Psychological Study* (Free Press, 1970), Wolfenstein paid her respects to another kind of falsity. It is in the false appearances, she wrote, that

> the forbidden wishes are realized which the hero and heroine so rarely carry into action. In a false appearance the heroine is promiscuous, the hero is a murderer, the young people carry on an illicit affair, two men share the favors of a woman. This device makes it possible for us to eat our cake and have it, since we can enjoy the suggested wish fulfillments without emphatic guilt; we know that the characters with whom we identify have not done anything.

It may be argued that there is a basic dishonesty in this whole area. In fiction, persons of great power can operate outside the accepted patterns of society, provided they do it for a good cause. Criminals may be shown as powerful, smart, attractive—as long as justice catches up with them in the end. All kinds of sexy and violent ideas may be written into scripts, provided we are told at the end that it is all a mistake; it didn't happen.

MORAL IN LITTLE THINGS

> *Getting an award from TV is like getting kissed by someone*
> *with bad breath.*
>
> —Mason Williams

The most fascinating of all these dishonesties is the way the codes enforce and the producers create shows that are moral in little things, but full of crime, cruelty, and violence. They observe the letter of the code but not its spirit. Does the code back-fire then? It is very difficult to demonstrate a causal relationship between the mass media and criminal behavior. Most research yields contradictory findings. Still, when audiences view or read popular fiction, their expectations are different from their expectations for the evening news or a street scene. For fiction, audiences suspend their critical faculties. They *feel* rather than *think* about what they receive and they *identify* with the characters.

People do accept some advice from the entertainment media, such as "help" from soap operas and similar sources. They also imitate characters with whom they identify. Some viewers are clearly more suggestible than others. A budding criminal may pick up tips on, say, how to burglarize a second story, strangle a victim, or avoid the police. What is not known is the extent of these effects.

After analyzing the results of twenty-three studies on televised violence, the U.S. Surgeon General reported in 1972:

> The overwhelming consensus and the unanimous scientific advisory commit-tees report indicates that televised violence, indeed, does have an adverse effect on certain members of our society. . . . The data on social phenomena such as television and violence and/or aggressive behavior will never be clear enough for all social scientists to agree on the formulation of a succinct state-ment of causality. But there comes a time when the data are sufficient to justify action. That time has come.*

By high school graduation, the average 17-year-old will have seen 350,000 commercials and 18,000 murders on television. Much of the sex and violence result from a weak imagination rather than artistic creativity. Many programs glorify brawling, frivolous militarism, and hyped-up, mindless violence. As the late Louis Kronenberger, professor at Brandeis, and *Time* critic for more than two decades, wrote:

> Without at all belittling TV's . . . serviceability to the many millions of people who use it as a food and not a drug, the glaring fact remains that TV has consistently imposed uncivilized elements on American life, or aggravated and intensified those it found there. It has helped destroy respect for privacy, it has helped foster a more rackety publicity. There has been nothing too elegant for it to coarsen, too artistic for it to vulgarize, too sacred for it to profane.†

---

*U.S. Senate Commerce Subcommittee, March 21, 1972 (Washington D.C.: U.S. Govern-ment Printing Office, 1972).

†Jay S. Harris, ed., *TV Guide: The First 25 Years* (New York: Random House, 1963), p. 43.

REALISM AND WRITING

A writer's problem does not change. He himself changes and the world he lives in changes, but his problem remains the same. It is always how to write truly and, having found out what is true, to project it in such a way that it becomes part of the experience of the person who reads it.

—Ernest Hemingway

If one is exposed to shows in which desired morés are demonstrated in an unreal and simple world, one will not learn desirable behavior for a much more complicated world.

When Wolcott Gibbs resigned as motion picture reviewer for the *New Yorker*, he characterized the world of Hollywood as

> an outstanding parody of life devoted to a society in which anything is physically and materially possible, including perfect happiness, to a race of people who operate intellectually on the level of the *New York Daily News*, morally on that of Dayton, Tennessee, and politically and economically in a total vacuum.

The enormous, undifferentiated television audience makes it difficult to deal with subtlety, and the need to produce a huge mass of material makes it difficult to create realistically complex characters. Instead, television promotes stereotypes. The Frenchman is likely to be excitable, to wear a beard, to gesticulate; Spaniards, Mexicans, Arabs, and Chinese are likely to be sinister. The Swede and the Dane are usually kindhearted but stupid. Right must triumph. Wrong must be punished. A character is always good or bad. It was impossible even to expatiate sin on the screen; the wrongdoer had to be carried to a sad end.

Hortense Powdermaker wrote:

> Only rarely does a movie-goer have the experience of seeing real human beings in a complicated world. Instead, he is treated to static characters not unlike the symbolic personifications of sin and virtue in medieval miracle plays. It is only the exceptional movie which portrays a human being, member of majority or minority group, with truthfulness or understanding. The reality of most movies usually consists only in the photography, the setting, the curve of a star's leg, the friendly or handsome looks of the hero and heroine, and other surface characteristics. Seldom is anyone concerned with the reality of emotions and with truthfulness of meaning.*

Wolfenstein analyzed several hundred films from several countries and con-

Hollywood, p. 72.

structed what she felt was the pattern of British, French, and American films. British films, she said, evoke the feeling that "danger lies in ourselves, especially in our impulses of destructiveness. . . . The essential plot is the conflict [that] the contending forces may win out." In French films, "human wishes are opposed by the nature of life itself. The main issue is not one of inner or outer conflicts in which we may win or lose, be virtuous or get penalized. It is a contest in which we all lose in the end, and the problem is to learn to accept it." As for American films, the major plot was like neither of the others:

> Winning is terribly important and always possible though it may be a tough fight. The conflict is not an internal one; it is not our scruples that stand in our way. The hazards are all external, but they are not rooted in the nature of life itself. They are the hazards of particular situations with which we find ourselves confronted. The hero is typically in a strange town where there are apt to be dangerous men and women of ambiguous character and where the forces of law and order are not to be relied on. If he sizes up the situation correctly, if he does not go off half-cocked but is still able to beat the other fellow to the punch, once he is sure who the enemy is, if he relies on no one but himself, if he demands sufficient evidence of virtue from the girl, he will emerge triumphant. He will defeat the dangerous men, get the girl, and show the authorities what's what.*

Films are deeply disappointing. We spend enough in money, for we are lavish with the cost of film, the cost of television, the cost of slick magazines—but not enough in emotion and insight. William E. Hocking wrote: "The most available emotion is the laugh, and the most external; it has become the habitual American sign of enjoyment, because it is cheapest in terms of sympathetic understanding. The moral emotions are most costly, the indignant response to injustice, pity toward misery, the expansion of one's being in the presence of an element of human greatness. Readers are not prepared to spend lavishly in these costly terms." And the mass media, Hocking continued, "must deal with entertainment, with the 'funnies,' with crime, catastrophe, and adventure, because these involve the common emotion of semi-physical 'reaction'; they make no heavy drafts on either thought or conscience or faith."†

Movie and TV critics have demanded little more than mechanical perfection and superior acting. Such practical criticism has turned Pauline Kael and others into modern superstars, but many critics have grown so enamored of "show business" that they have not insisted on creative realism. As a new breed of TV critics emerges perhaps they will expose triteness and sentimentality and demand realism.

Movies, p. 293.

†William E. Hocking, *Freedom of the Press: A Framework of Principle* (Chicago: University of Chicago Press, 1947), pp. 44–45.

MOVIES AND TV PROGRAMS

A movie written by the half-educated for the half-witted.

—John Ervine

Codes for the entertainment media seem to assume that audiences cannot be trusted with a realistic picture of life, the problems people face, and the way those problems are settled. The codes assume that the viewer cannot be trusted to distinguish good from evil, so they must see them a world in which human beings are either good or bad, and in which right always wins and wrong is always punished.

The codes presume that it is unsafe to portray many of the kinds of behavior that occur all around them in life. It is unsafe to let viewers see or hear anything that might arouse elemental emotions, or that might test their faith in the sanctity of marriage or the home, their religion, or in law or justice. They might fail the test. It is dangerous also to have them hear anything profane or vulgar. They might pick up bad habits.

The media seem to assume that by violence and sex they can attract an audience so defined, then cover up the sex and punish the violence in the show so that they will not see it, or at least will not find it in any way attractive.

There are many high-minded leaders in the media who have a more respectful view of their audiences. A few magazines do not seem to be edited with that kind of person in mind; Paul Schrader and Fred Wiseman produce films that are not made that way; *60 Minutes* is not prepared that way. But most entertainment films, crime dramas, serials, and variety shows on television, and much of the content of entertainment magazines, are written for such an audience.

If anyone asks whether that concept of humanity is adequate for today, we must answer that it is not. There are certainly children and fools among us, but in programming for them, are not the media selling us short?

Everything we have seen leads us to believe that most viewers could take a higher level of reality in stride, and that the danger would lie only with the more susceptible few—the children, the fools, and the disturbed. The description of a "bad" picture, program, or story, should refer to more than the morality portrayed in it. A definition has been developed by Josef Pieper in his provocative *Leisure: The Basis of Culture* (Random House, 1963). Pieper elevates human leisure as primary. His active and positive view makes leisure something festive, so that

> to hold a celebration means to affirm the basic meaningfulness of the universe and a sense of oneness with it, of inclusion within it. In celebrating, in holding festivals upon occasion, man experiences the world in an aspect other than the everyday one. The festival is the origin of leisure and the inward and ever-present meaning of leisure.

Thus, considering amusement as a mere escape from work leaves out something significant about human beings. Reversing the conceptual order—making playfulness and leisure rather than work the fountainhead of life—prevents us from trivializing entertainment and prods film producers and entertainment magazine writers to make human celebration pleasurable and meaningful. A world of artificial festival, meager ritual, and escapism starves man's creative spirit, and thereby makes work a drudgery.

A contrasting view of amusement is presented as the theme of a recent critique of the mass media by Neil Postman in his book *Amusing Ourselves to Death* (Penguin Books, 1986). As his title indicates, Postman is unhappy about the extent to which in today's television culture "all public discourse increasingly takes the form of entertainment." He says it is turning news and public affairs—in newspapers as well as in television—into show business and educating people to shun any information that is not presented in an entertaining fashion.

EXERCISES

1. Frank J. Prince, a prominent St. Louis businessman and the chief stockholder in the Universal Match Corporation, gave $500,000 to Washington University in St. Louis. The university planned to name a building after him. Assigned to do a background story on the benefactor, a *St. Louis Post-Dispatch* reporter discovered that the 71-year-old Prince had, as a young man, served three prison terms—totalling almost 10 years—for forgery, grand larceny, and issuing bad checks.

    Should the *Post-Dispatch* have reported this part of Prince's life? Did the paper's readers have a right to know about it? What would you do in similar circumstances?

2. John Mitchell, who is now a professor at Syracuse University, was once a public affairs reporter for the Lima, Ohio, newspaper. A local Congressman told the mayor of Lima that his city would receive a federal grant for which Lima had made an application. The mayor asked Mitchell to make up a quotation for the major, who said he was overjoyed at the news. Because Mitchell knew the major's vocabulary and speech pattern, Mitchell made up the quotation. Was Mitchell right about doing this?

CONFORMITY AND CONSCIENCE:
ABOUT PRESS COUNCILS AND OMBUDSMEN

If there is anything the nonconformist hates worse than a conformist it's another nonconformist who doesn't conform to the prevailing standards of nonconformity.

—Bill Vaughan

The race of men, while sheep in credulity, are wolves for conformity.

—Carl Van Doren

Conscience: A small, still voice that makes minority reports.

—Franklin P. Jones

In matters of conscience, the law of the majority has no place.

—Mohandas Gandhi

Every society honors its live conformists and its dead troublemakers.

—Mignon McLaughlin

The Anglo-Saxon conscience doesn't keep you from doing what you shouldn't; it just keeps you from enjoying it.

—Salvador de Madariaga

CHAPTER 14

Press Councils
and Ombudsmen

The press is an excellent servant, but a terrible master.
—James Fenimore Cooper

If the press is a watchdog, who shall watch the press? Because the press is free (relatively), the consensus is that the press will watch itself. Two main forms of self-watching have developed—press councils and ombudsmen. We shall examine both.

LOCAL PRESS COUNCILS

A good newspaper, I suppose, is a nation talking to itself.
—Arthur Miller

The idea of American press councils was probably first suggested in the 1930s by Chilton Bush, then head of the Stanford University Department of Communication. He believed that newspapers could strengthen themselves and their communities by working with citizen advisory groups. Bush promoted the idea among California publishers, at first in vain. Then, in 1950, William Townes, publisher of the *Santa Rosa Press Democrat*, decided to try it.

Townes chose the members of his "citizens advisory council" to represent community interests—labor, education, agriculture, city government, and business—and included a few outspoken critics of his policies. At the first meeting, Townes told council members that although he alone would decide publishing policies, he would welcome criticisms and suggestions. That meeting began hesitantly, but at subsequent meetings the members engaged in lively discussions. Townes spent most of his time listening. He did not even have to defend his paper against its harshest critic, a judge invited specifically because he was a well-known opponent of the *Press Democrat*; the other members were quick to challenge unfounded criticisms. Townes kept the council operating until he left Santa Rosa in 1951 and said that it helped him improve his paper. As *Editor & Publisher* commented in an editorial (July 28, 1951):

On the practical side, this particular newspaper reports that council meetings revealed several important stories that had not been covered. And council members felt free to visit the newspaper offices thereafter, something many of them might not have thought about previously.

This is an experiment in getting closer to the community which strikes us as valuable. The good points outweigh the bad, and if conducted properly and regularly can only result to the benefit of the paper.

Despite this endorsement, the press council idea languished for years. To be sure, Barry Bingham, president and editor of the two papers in Louisville, Kentucky, the *Courier-Journal* and the *Times*, publicly urged that local press councils be established. He subsequently appointed ombudsmen for his own papers. And local councils were tried here and there in the 1950s and 1960s, a typical effort being that of California publisher Ray Spangler, who regularly asked a few community leaders for advice on how his Redwood City *Tribune* could deal with the city's problems. But it was not until 1967 that the idea of press councils began to gain ground.

In that year, Ben Bagdikian became president of the Mellett Fund for a Free and Responsible Press. This small foundation had only $40,000 with which to carry out Lowell Mellett's wish—that his bequest be used to encourage responsible press performance without infringing First Amendment freedoms. Bagdikian suggested supporting university researchers in making press council experiments. The result was that six councils were established. Four were newspaper councils (one in California, one in Oregon, and two in Illinois). Another council was established in Seattle and still another in St. Louis, both involving broadcasters as well as publishers. The Seattle and St. Louis councils brought the newsmen together with spokesmen for the black community in each city.

There was little communication among those who established the first councils. The researchers adhered to the Mellett Fund guidelines, but they set up, operated, and evaluated their councils in different ways. Despite the absence of coordination and the differences in size among the cities involved (from Sparta, Illinois, with a population of 3500, to St. Louis, Missouri, with 750,000 people)—not to mention the differences between the general press councils and those devoted to the problems of Blacks—there were remarkable similarities. For at one time or other, most of the councils dealt with most of the central issues of mass communication in modern society.

For example, a continuing question in journalism is the stance of the editors or broadcasters. They may be "community-oriented" and seek consensus, perhaps even glossing over faults to promote what they consider to be the greater good. Or, they may be "journalist-oriented" and stress conflict, printing or broadcasting all the news, even though they may present to the community a view of itself that many citizens would prefer to ignore. At least a few of their editorials will injure some readers.

The typology is not really so neat, of course. The "journalist," however dedicated to disclosure, will publish much that the Chamber of Commerce approves.

The "community" person will at least on occasion print or broadcast news and editorials that reveal flaws. It may be, too, that most journalists shift between orientations, depending upon the issues, the personalities involved, and the circumstances.

The press councils met this basic question from a number of perspectives. They discussed community leadership: Is leading a basic function of the press? Should a newspaper carry on crusades? They discussed public relations: Should the press be the public relations organ of the community? They discussed culture: Should the press promote the arts?

The councils also grappled with a question that thoughtful journalists have been debating for years: Does freedom carry with it a demand that the press be responsible? If so, who judges responsible performance?

Questions that have sprung from recent events were also central to the discussions: Does the press make news in the process of covering it? Should the problems of minorities get special attention?

Because these discussions were practical rather than theoretical, at least in St. Louis, Sparta, and Redwood City, and because they involved laymen, there was a freshness that added significantly to the dialogue.

Two nine-member councils were established in Redwood City, California, and Bend, Oregon. The California council was a cross-section of the community, with members chosen by occupation. The Oregon Council was made up of leaders of Bend and its area, with some regard for differences in sex and occupation. The Bend council sought out known critics of the paper. The sessions in both cities were monthly dinner meetings lasting three to four hours. Redwood City *Tribune* publisher Ray Spangler and editor David Schutz attended regularly. *Bulletin* editor-owner Robert Chandler met regularly with the Bend council. On two occasions, *Bulletin* managing editor William Yates attended, and *Bulletin* reporter Dan Perry attended one meeting.

In Sparta, Illinois, the sixteen members represented a cross-section of the community. Twelve were active throughout the community. William Morgan, publisher of the *Sparta News-Plaindealer*, attended the monthly meetings regularly. The council decided—and Morgan agreed—that because Morgan was on a first-name basis with most of the members and his presence might inhibit criticism, he should attend only the second half of each meeting.

In Cairo, Illinois, fifteen residents agreed to serve on the council, and ten participated actively throughout the duration of the council. Martin Brown, who was then editor and general manager of the *Cairo Evening Citizen*, attended regularly except for the first three meetings, which were devoted to discussing the major theories underlying press functions and responsibilities.

Representatives of all the major news media of St. Louis participated. Concerned that the Black membership on the council should be broadly representative, the director asked Black individuals and organizations to list those who should be invited to serve. The lists were combined and the number pared to twelve. Later, two other Blacks were added.

When news of these local councils began to spread, new councils were established in several other cities across the United States. Most of them were in small cities and towns—the largest was statewide, the Minnesota Press Council—but the new councils seemed to open the idea to a national scope.

THE NATIONAL NEWS COUNCIL

> *Evil news flies faster than good.*
>
> —Thomas Kyd

What could provoke journalists' anger more than the establishment of a national press council? In December 1972, the Twentieth Century Fund, the widely respected New York foundation, announced that a consortium of foundations would finance a Council on Press Responsibility and Press Freedom (later, the National News Council) to investigate public complaints against major U.S. news organizations and to defend freedom of the press. Nine of the fourteen members of the Twentieth Century Fund Task Force, which unanimously recommended establishing the Council, were respected editors, publishers, and broadcasters. The Council could have no coercive power and no relationship to government. Still, acid reactions were entirely predictable. Two weeks after the announcement, an editor had collected enough savage editorials regarding the Council to paper the walls of his office.

A prominent place on one wall should have gone to a cartoon that appeared in the *New York Daily News*, titled "Endangering Freedom of the Press," which pictured a black glob labeled "Meddling Monitors" looming over a reporter. The accompanying editorial, "Who Needs Them?" was written with the charm that marks the *Daily News:*

> Having presumably solved mankind's other vexing problems, the Twentieth Century Fund has bowed graciously to the wishes of its own hand-picked panel and set up shop as guardian of the morals and ethics of the nation's news media. Foundation's pious words, "promote freedom of the press" by investigating public complaints of unfairness, error, bias, or prejudice and publishing their findings.
>
> The latter, we assume, will carry written guarantees that this panel of Paul Prys is itself 100 percent free of bias and prejudice.
>
> We don't care how much the Fund prates its virtuous intentions. This is a sneak attempt at press regulation, a bid for a role as unofficial news censor. . . .

The *Chicago Tribune* reflected in an editorial that trying to monitor the press without jeopardizing its freedom was "a little like trying to lasso a steer by mental telepathy." In Providence, Rhode Island, where editorial writers have no stockyards to lend their metaphors a comparable flavor, the *Journal* argued that "the rhetoric of high purpose in which the effort is being wrapped masks basic flaws." An NBC spokesman held that "the press already has too many people looking over its shoulder." A. M. Rosenthal, then managing editor of the *New York Times*, expressed the fear that the Council would endanger press freedom, focus undue attention on the shortcomings of the media, and become a loudspeaker for pressure groups "skilled in the methods of political propaganda."

A few media spokesmen did favor the Council. Barry Bingham of the *Louisville Courier-Journal*, who was a member, with Executive Editor Norman Isaacs, of the Twentieth Century Fund Task Force (later the National News Council chairman), had long urged newspapers to assess their performance. The *Courier-Journal* said of the national council, "Up to now, a citizen or group treated unfairly by a national news organization has been almost powerless to lodge an effective complaint. . . . If the unfair story originated with a wire service or a network, the ill-treated person's chances of getting to those really responsible are pretty slim." If the Council lives up to its mission, the *Courier-Journal* held, "it will perform an essential service for us all."

Robert Chandler, former president of the national journalism fraternity, the Society of Professional Journalists-Sigma Delta Chi, then a member of the Task Force, had benefited from a local advisory council for his Bend, Oregon, *Bulletin*. He remarked that he had become a missionary for press councils. The then-CBS News president, Richard Salant, who was also a member of the Task Force, said, "There hasn't been enough independent examination of what we do. Take it out of the hands of people who have an ax to grind—put it into the hands of systematic, independent investigators."

But there was no doubt that most of the news media opposed the Council. Almost simultaneously with the announcement of the new body, the American Society of Newspaper Editors (ASNE) completed a poll of 740 of its members. The 405 editors who returned questionnaires were opposed, three to one, to ASNE itself establishing a similar council. They were opposed, four to one, to a council established by any other organization.

For all its predictability, this hostile reaction was bewildering. Were the editors unaware of the decades of rapidly deteriorating esteem for the mass media? Did they not know that a 1966 Harris Poll gave the print media a confidence vote of only 29 percent, television a confidence vote of 25 percent, and advertising, 21 percent? Were they unaware that in November 1972, the same survey showed that the print media had only 18 percent confidence, television only 17 percent, and advertising only 12 percent? Some people, including many media spokesmen, rationalized that perhaps the mass media were only suffering from the general decline of confidence in all social institutions. But the Harris Poll surveyed attitudes towards 16 institutions, and only organized labor and advertising ranked lower than the print media and television.

Some tried to explain away public disaffection by arguing that, in troubled times, messengers are blamed for the messages they bring. But the media are not as innocent as the messengers of old. In gathering and reporting the news of the day, the media cuts it, splices it, condenses it, and shapes it, usually with laudable expertise, but sometimes erroneously.

The avenue open to anyone injured in this process was narrow and forbidding. They could protest, but seldom with real hope that their complaints would be heard and their grievances redressed. Editors were quite naturally skeptical of anyone who spoke in his or her own cause. They were often right in doubting that a particular complaint was justified. But when they were wrong, what then?

Even in the face of evidence that the media had lost credibility, editors opposed the coming of a council that could help them recover the public confidence on which their freedom depends. They should have pondered the British experience.

THE BRITISH PRESS COUNCIL

> *I am always in favor of the free press, but sometimes*
> *they say quite nasty things.*
>
> —Winston Churchill

The British Press Council was born as the result of a threat that surfaced in 1946. The House of Commons voted to appoint a Royal Commission to investigate the finances, control, management, and ownership of the press in order "to further the free expression of opinion through the press and the greatest practicable accuracy in the presentation of news."

Significantly, the motion was moved and seconded by two *journalist* members of the Commons, who feared that the growth of newspaper chains and the advent of big business into newspapers were inhibiting freedom of the press.

Journalism, the Commission decided, is a profession grafted to an industry, one that tries to reconcile the claims of society with the claims of commerce. The Commission recommended establishing a General Council of the Press to maintain standards of professional responsibility and integrity.

Various British press organizations discussed the council idea and approved it in general, but, as H. Philip Levy notes in his book *The Press Council* (St. Martin's Press, 1967), "The truth is that there was no real enthusiasm in press circles for a press council." In November 1952, a bill was introduced in the Commons to form the Press Council. This pushed the press into action, and, by February 1953, a joint committee of press organizations had agreed on a draft constitution. Although the Royal Commission had recommended that laymen be included, the council was made up entirely of twenty-five journalists—ten from the management level and fifteen from the editorial staffs. The Council was later reconstituted, reducing by five the number of professional members and taking in five lay members, including a lay chairman, Lord Devlin.

The complaints were varied. Some argued that if the newspapers had been open to ideas for universal peace, the two world wars never would have occurred;

others urged the Council to investigate incidents that were decades old. But many complaints were more immediate. A noted critic, for instance, complained that he had been invited by *The Daily Sketch* to write a series of reviews, but the first one had been twisted by the editors to give another view, though the critic's byline had remained on the article. The Press Council censured the *Sketch*—and it and other papers printed the Council's statement.

Others complained about the extravagant attention the newspapers gave to the Kinsey Report, a study of sex mores. The Council issued a widely publicized statement holding that "this Council, while defending the right of the Press in the contemporary world to deal in an adult manner with matters of sex, is deeply concerned by the unwholesome exploitation of sex by certain newspapers and periodicals."

The British Press Council praised newspapers for publicizing studies showing a relationship between tobacco and lung cancer and attacked them for individual and collective violations of good taste, as well as for emphasis on sex.

Any citizen may complain, but complaints are rejected if the aggrieved person has not first sought redress from the editor of the paper. The Council also will not consider a complaint if legal action is filed or threatened until proceedings have been concluded or abandoned.

An aggrieved person who fails to receive satisfaction from an editor must state his complaint in a letter to the Council and enclose copies of any correspondence with the editor, and a copy of the newspaper of the relevant date. He or she also is asked to give the names and addresses of any witnesses.

The Council informs the editor and invites his or her response. Then the Complaints Committee investigates, usually drawing its conclusions from written statements. On occasion, however, the parties concerned are asked to appear before the Council. A complete dossier on the matter is then prepared for each member of the Council and sent to him or her before the next meeting. Only the Council members attend the decision-making meeting. On a few occasions, the Council has reversed the recommendations of the Complaints Committee.

Finally, the Council releases a summary of the facts and its decision. Although the editor is held responsible for anything appearing in his or her paper, individual journalists are sometimes blamed as well. The Council issues two kinds of judgments when it finds a newspaper at fault: admonition, or, in serious cases, censure. In one three-year period, there were only two recorded cases in which offending newspapers failed to publish Council statements.

Sometimes the complaint is by one media organization against another. Here is a report on a Council ruling in such a case, published in *The Observer* on January 6, 1985:

> An allegation in "The Mail on Sunday" that a raid on a coal board transport depot was set up for a Canadian Broadcasting Corporation TV film crew was seriously unbalanced, the Press Council ruled today.
>
> It upheld a complaint by Mr. Cliff Lonsdale, CBS's head of radio and tele-

vision production for Europe, that the newspaper published inaccurate allegations of unethical conduct by a film crew.

The newspaper's managing editor, Mr. George Woodhouse, told the council the report was based on a Press Association story. The council said that from that story the paper used only the police version of events and not CBS's denial of filming.

TASK FORCE RECOMMENDATIONS

> *The farther backward you can look, the farther forward you are likely to see.*
>
> —Winston Churchill

When the Twentieth Century Fund convened its Task Force in 1970 to study the feasibility of a U.S. council, most of the members were doubtful that anything like the British model could work here. Because of the relatively small size of Great Britain, the London press is, in effect, the national press. The United States has no equivalent to a national press, but the Task Force decided nevertheless to establish a national council on the British model.

Unfortunately, too many media spokesmen echoed the point made by Elmer Lower, then president of ABC News: "At a time when newsmen are going to jail for practicing their craft, the appointment of yet another self-appointed monitoring organization is an unnecessary irony." The fact that newsmen were going to jail could be one reason for establishing the Council. A public that fears or distrusts the media does not protest when they are brought to heel—they applaud. Moreover, a council that calls the media into account could also speak forcefully *for* the media. When the American Society of Newspaper Editors speaks for freedom of the press, a wounded and skeptical public suspects self-interest. When a council that has demonstrated its concern for the public interest speaks for freedom of the press, its words were far more likely to be heeded.

Professor Donald E. Brown of Arizona State University reported in 1971 that the scoffing, disdain, and contempt that was so common among editors during the early years of the British Press Council has almost disappeared. "Antipathy has been replaced by respect and by a realization that the Council's accomplishments have considerably outweighed its shortcomings," Brown wrote.

A prime example is Hugh Cudlipp, who was long the editor of the *Daily Mirror*, a splashy tabloid. Cudlipp wrote a book in 1962 that carried eight references to the Council, all critical. Later, the chairman of the International Publishing Corporation, Cudlipp asserted that he and his huge company were "totally in favor of the Press Council." The hard-hitting *Daily Express* snapped in an editorial in 1949, "The proposal for a Press Council is the futile outcome of a phony agitation." But after the Council had been operating for several years, the *Express* held: "It is proper that the watchdogs should themselves have watchdogs."

One study showed that by 1967, 86 percent of the British editors favored the British Press Council. Citing the study, Brown wrote that his observations and interviews indicated that the percentage has increased since then.

OPERATIONS OF THE NATIONAL NEWS COUNCIL

> *I cannot give you the formula for success, but I can give you the formula for failure: Try to please everybody.*
>
> —Herbert Bayer Swope

When the National News Council began officially on August 1, 1973, the staff and the members had worked out a simple explanation of how to complain to the Council:

> Anyone—individual or organization—may bring a complaint to the National News Council concerning allegations of inaccuracy or unfairness by a national news organization.
>
> The procedure to follow is simple: Write to the news organization and send a copy of your letter or complaint to the Council.
>
> If you are not sure where to address your complaint at a news organization, send it directly to the Council. The Council then will forward it to the appropriate news executive.
>
> If your complaint concerns a printed news report, include a copy of the report, the name of the publication, and the date.
>
> If your complaint concerns a radio or television report, include the name of the station, the name of the network, the date and time of airing.
>
> In your letter, whether it concerns a printed report, include as specific information as possible as to why you are complaining.
>
> Complaints to the Council should be addressed to: The National News Council, One Lincoln Plaza, New York, N.Y. 10023.*

The Council's first members were: Rogert J. Traynor, Chairman, former Chief Justice of California; Robert McKay, Vice Chairman, Director of the Aspen Institute's Program on Justice, Society and the Individual; Loren Ghiglione, Editor and Publisher of the Southbridge, Massachusetts, *Evening News*; William A. Rusher, Treasurer, Publisher of *National Review*; William Brady, Jr., Chairman of W. H. Brady Company, Milwaukee, Wisconsin; Joan Ganz Cooney, President of Children's Television Workshop; Irving Dilliard, former Editorial Page Editor of the *St. Louis Post-Dispatch*; Edith Green, Congresswoman from Oregon; Dorothy Haight, President of the National Council for Negro Women; Mary (Molly) Ivins, Co-Editor of the *Texas Observer*; James Lawson, Jr., Pastor of a Los Angeles United Methodist Church; Ralph Otwell, Managing Editor of the *Chicago Sun-Times*; Ralph Renick,

---

*The National News Council, *In the Public Interest* (New York: The National News Council, Inc., 1975), p. 164.

Vice President and News Director of WTVJ, Miami; Sylvia Roberts, Baton Rouge, Louisiana, attorney; and R. Peter Straus, President of Straus Communications, which operates a radio station in New York City. This council had power to apply only *accuracy* and *fairness.*

These members were certainly impressive, and, to a limited extent, they probably noticed praise in stories and editorials from the *St. Louis Post-Dispatch,* the *Columbia Journalism Review,* the *Duke Law Journal,* the *Boston Globe,* the *Kansas City Star,* the *Bulletin of the American Society of Newspaper Editors,* the *Christian Science Monitor,* the *Wall Street Journal, TV Guide,* the *Des Moines Register,* and a number of other publications.

Though the publicity stretched across more than a year and a half, and Council members often ran into good friends who never heard of the National News Council; nonetheless, in the first two years of the Council, it received fifty-nine complaints and upheld five of them; all of the first seventeen complaints were held to be unwarranted, dismissed, or beyond the Council's purview.

The eighteenth complaint was made by Kenneth L. Rossman of Athens, Alabama. He wrote that when NBC News covered President Richard Nixon's February 18, 1974, visit to Huntsville, Alabama, to take part in "Honor America Day" observances there, NBC stated that local federal workers were given the day off by an act of Congress. Richard Wald, then the President of NBC News, countered that the error had already been called to their attention, but, as yet, there had not been a suitable occasion for a correction.

The Council responded to the complaint and to Wald's lame excuse with, "NBC News was in error in declaring that 'thousands of federal workers in the Huntsville area were given the day off to greet President Nixon. . .' when in fact they were off because of a federal holiday—Washington's Birthday." Although the complaint was filed on February 19, 1974, it was not until May 31, 1974, that NBC News confessed to its error.

Later, the Council decided to extend its boundaries to the total news flow in the United States. This was a significant step, as is shown by the Council's considering a dispute between a congressman and a local newspaper, the Camden, New Jersey, *Courier-Post.* The Council said that the *Courier-Post* made "a conscientious effort to set the record straight."

In judging other complaints, the Council made these judgments:

- Found that the *New York Times* used facts inappropriately to suggest that herbicides posed a health threat in Arkansas.
- Found that the Chicago *Sun-Times* did not disclose clearly enough a columnist's conflict of interest.
- Found that ABC News did not overplay the danger of contracting AIDS from a transfusion.
- Found that *Newsweek* did not set the record straight on a correction by merely publishing a letter to the editor.

- Criticized the *Washington Post* for publishing scientific material supplied by a critic of nuclear energy development without obtaining comment from opposing or neutral scientists.
- Declined to call a "heretical" medical columnist "irresponsible," but did say that news organizations should take precautions when using medical columns.

The *New York Times* continued to refuse to cooperate with the Council, but, in May 1983, the Council congratulated the paper for a significant step:

> A notable advance in print journalism is the institution by the *New York Times* of a feature called "Editor's note," which is to be run in the news index whenever the editors deem appropriate over and beyond the routine corrections which regularly appear there. Under this heading the *Times* will amplify or rectify what its editors consider significant lapses of fairness, balance, or perspective in news articles, even where specific factual inaccuracies are not involved.*

On April 13, 1984, eleven months after congratulating the *Times*, the Council died. It had helped many print and broadcast entities to "serve the public interest in preserving freedom of communication and advancing accurate and fair reporting of news" (words from the founders of the Council).

When the National News Council went out of existence, Elie Abel, vice chairman of the Council, blamed the press, saying, "They killed it over a ten-year period by ignoring it and denouncing it." He was particularly critical of the *New York Times*, a newspaper he had once worked for. Abel later explained the Council's demise at a meeting of the California Newspaper Editors. His remarks were later adapted into an article for the Fall 1984 issue of *feed/back:*

> It seems bizarre to be abandoning the idea of a voluntary council. Sooner rather than later, in one revised form or another, the National News Council will be reinvented. It may be a long wait, though. Let there be no mistake, however, about the reason the council died when it did. The *St. Paul Pioneer Press* called it "a significant self-inflicted loss by American Journalism." Hodding Carter, in the *Wall Street Journal*, wrote of "the conspiracy of silence that greeted its birth and smothered its life. . . ."

OMBUDSMEN

We need much more self-examination and a whole flock of ombudsmen. This is a very heady business, and we need a moral compass.

—James Atwater

To understand the role of a newspaper's in-house critic—the ombudsman—we must go back in history.

---

*National News Council, "Council commends *Times*, ABC, CBS," *The Quill*, May 1983, p. 31.

ELIE ABEL

After more than 40 years as a journalist and professor, Elie Abel has held so many titles that he must be bowed under their weight: Harry and Norman Chandler Professor of Communication at Stanford University; Godfrey Lowell Cabot Professor and Dean of Journalism at Columbia University; Washington and foreign correspondent of the *New York Times;* Diplomatic correspondent and chief of the London Bureau, NBC News; Chief of the Washington Bureau, the Detroit News. He has shared a Pulitzer Prize for international reporting, and so on. Abel, nonetheless, doesn't show the weight of the burdens he has carried. He is still teaching, still writing, still cheerful.

Why did Abel leave television to become a professor and dean? "I grew less and less enchanted with the show-business aspects of television news. The networks, I felt then and feel now, have all the money in the world but there is never enough taste or courage. Ratings are the paramount concern and news in many situations takes a back seat to cheap popular entertainment.

"TV's great strength is emotional impact. The viewer sits passively in front of the box and the visual images wash over him. But I wasn't satisfied the viewers were getting the kind of information that would help them to make decisions as citizens. I remember that a poll of American high school students, taken at a time when the Middle East dominated the headlines as well as the television news, identified Golda Meir as the President of Egypt."

Ironically, broadcasting has been the profession that won Abel the most awards: two Overseas Press Club Awards for best interpretation of foreign news in 1969 and for a documentary, Russia in the Mediterranean, in 1970; and the George Foster Peabody Award for radio news in 1970. For Abel, print is a close second: the Pulitzer Traveling Fellowship in 1942 after graduating with an M.A. from Columbia University, sharing a Pulitzer Prize in 1957 for coverage of Eastern Europe, including the Hungarian revolution.

Much of Abel's fame also has come from international reporting, but this should be no surprise. His parents were Russian Jews who immigrated to Canada; Elie was born in 1920 in Montreal. Abel remembers that: "My father was self-educated, but remarkably well educated. He learned a lot from books, newspapers, and listening to lectures; he loved to go to lectures. A lot of his interests rubbed off on me, like his interest in international relations. . . . [H]e would always bring books home for me to read."

His parents wanted Abel to become a dentist, but the books he read and a traveling experience made him think of journalism. "The idea of being a reporter was planted in my head, oh, when I was 12 or 13 . . . something like that. I was out in the country, hitchhiking with a young friend, and we were trying to get someone to pick us up when what seemed to me a very elegant tomato-colored convertible stopped. The man inside—he was very friendly—invited us to join him. It turned out that he was a reporter. And, as we drove along, he said that being a reporter was the greatest job in the world, something we ought to think about. So I guess I did."

As an undergraduate at McGill University, he worked on the college paper while completing a double major in English and economics. He went on from there to Columbia University for an M.S. degree in journalism before joining the Royal Canadian Air Force in World War II. He spent more than two years in the European theater.

After a brief postwar stint at the *Montreal Gazette*, Abel went back to Europe as a correspondent for the North American Newspaper Alliance. His assignments took him to the Nuremberg trials, Berlin, and Poland. He later worked as a rewrite man for the *Los Angeles Times* and as United Nations correspondent for the Overseas News Agency before joining the *New York Times* in 1949. Based in Detroit and then Washington, D.C., Abel also served the *Times* in Eastern Europe (based in Belgrade, Yugoslavia) and in India. After ten years he became Washington bureau chief of the *Detroit News.*

In 1961 he left newspapering for television, and, over the next nine years, worked as State Department correspondent, then London bureau chief, and finally as diplomatic correspondent of NBC News. When Columbia University in 1969 invited Abel to become Dean of its graduate school of journalism, he accepted for two personal reasons: his constant travel was beginning to affect his family life, and, having published one well-received book, he wanted to write more books. "It's impossible, I discovered, to do daily journalism and write books on the side. There is never enough time to do both."

Abel had written one good book while working at NBC News—*The Missile Crisis*, but, while a professor, he has written *Roots of Involvement, The U.S. in Asia, 1748-1971* (with Marvin Kalb); edited *What's News: The Media in American Society*; and written his best book, published in 1975, *Special Envoy to Churchill and Stalin, 1941-46* (with W. Averell Harriman).*

Writing a review of the Harriman-Abel book, Peter Mayer wrote: "A fascinating, honest account of diplomacy in the highest places! There is no person interested in military-political history to whom this book cannot be enthusiastically recommended."

An unsigned review in the *New Yorker:* "A collaboration between the noted public figure and the noted dean of Columbia's School of Journalism. . . . Harriman's recollections remain vivid indeed—a reader can still laugh over a funny ride with deGaulle in a plane too small for a pair of very long-legged passengers."

Abel, now working on a book about leaks in government, is a highly expressive man, one who seems to look forward to his writing and teaching tasks each day. He is also a devoted grandfather. His daughter, Suzanne, is an archaeologist, and his son, Mark, is an editor at the *San Francisco Chronicle.*

---

*Elie Abel, *The Missile Crisis* (New York: Lippincott, 1966); *Roots of Involvement, The U.S. in Asia, 1784-1971,* with Marvin Kalb (New York: W. W. Norton, 1971); ed., *What's News: The Media in American Society* (San Francisco: Institute for Contemporary Studies, 1981); *Special Envoy to Churchill and Stalin, 1941-46,* with W. Averell Harriman (New York: Random House, 1975).

Decades ago, as long as publishers of newspapers showed respect for a few laws, they could do whatever they liked with their newspapers. If they opposed the Democratic candidate for President, they could eliminate the candidate's name from the paper. If publishers hated golf, they could instruct their sports editors to forget that the game exists. If the publishers thought readers would be offended by photos revealing the sex of naked animals, they could have their art departments use airbrushes appropriately. The Democrats, the golfers, and the artists on their staffs could rebel, readers protest, rival papers thrive as a result, but the publishers' decisions were paramount.

At one time, more newspapers and magazines served more specific publics. If the papers had a relatively slender circulation, the editors nevertheless spoke directly to a self-selected audience and could usually count on its loyalty. The editors' views might be opposed and their plants attacked, but most readers opposed to the editors' views subscribed to papers that squared with their own prejudices.

As newspapers and magazines became larger and fewer and editors had to corral mass audiences, separate voices grew to be few in the "free marketplace of ideas."

The only business specifically protected by the Constitution, the press was given its broad measure of freedom precisely so that citizens could have the information needed to participate fully in democracy. "A people who mean to be their own governors," James Madison wrote, "will arm themselves with the power knowledge gives. A popular government without popular information is but a prologue to a farce, a tragedy, or perhaps both." But, as government became larger and more distant, the press also became much more of a business, and almost equally distant. At the turn of the twentieth century, Lincoln Steffens, a keen analyst of American institutions, reported that newspaper executives talking shop at a convention had spoken of their properties as factories and likened editorial management to that of department stores. "Journalism today is a business," Steffens wrote, "with a little of the awe of discovery."

Later critics—Will Irwin, Upton Sinclair, George Seldes—made clear exactly how business-like many newspapers had become. Writer A. J. Liebling described the press thus:

> It is the weak slat under the bed of democracy. It is an anomaly that information, the one thing most necessary to our survival as choosers of our own way, should be a commodity subject to the same rules as chewing gum, while armament, a secondary instrument of liberty, is a government concern. A man is not free if he cannot see where he is going, even if he has a gun to help him get there.*

Some editors and broadcasters began to realize years ago that the distance between journalist and reader had become too vast for effective two-way communi-

---

*A. J. Liebling, *The Most of A. J. Liebling* (New York: Simon and Schuster, 1963) p. 135.

cation. A few editors enlarged their letters-to-the-editor space and started "Action Line" columns to encourage readers to participate. Some radio and television stations began to program call-in and talk shows to give listeners and viewers a chance to speak.

But many critics view these as only token measures. Indeed, some suspect not just this newspaper or that editor, this station or that newscaster, but *all* the "media."

Those arguing minority causes are especially apt to emphasize their lack of access to the media. Professor Jerome Barron of George Washington University supported this viewpoint. He argued that the free press guarantee of the First Amendment was meant to assure that every voice should be heard, but, actually, only the media proprietors have prevented some voices from being heard by denying access, so the First Amendment must be reinterpreted.

Clifton Daniel, then associate editor of the *New York Times*, pointed out that in one recent year the *Times* received 37,719 letters to the editor—and that if all eighteen million words in those letters had been printed (and every letter writer probably thought he or she had a right of access), they would have filled 135 complete issues of the paper. Nonetheless, the freedom of print media to use their columns as they wish is a source of deep bitterness among many readers.

THE INSIDER'S CRITICISM

> *A gift, an intuition, a matter of tact and flair; it cannot be taught or demonstrated—it is an art.*
>
> —Henry F. Amiel

Perhaps the chief reason news executives are no longer belligerently defensive against criticism is that some of their employees are among their most vehement critics. At one time, reporters who were themselves privately critical reacted to outside attacks like a herd of angry animals—rumps together, horns out. Some still react that way. But few outsiders can match the acid insights of some journalists who are now quite outspoken. Almost any news medium of size and pretensions to excellence harbors fierce critics, and, perhaps, an incipient revolt among its younger, brighter reporters. This is much more than the traditional grousing of the tyro who thinks that the old-timers are naturally old-fashioned. It means that older journalists, who believe that their present efforts are sufficient unto the need of the hour, don't know what time it is.

Ben Bagdikian, one of the older men who sympathize with most aspirations of the young reporters, has written: "Trying to be a first-rate reporter on the average American newspaper is like trying to play Bach's *St. Matthew's Passion* on a ukulele: the instrument is too crude for the work, for the audience, and for the performer." This wraps up in a sentence a major fault of American journalism, which is so devoted to the isolated fact that it ignores the necessity for interpretation: for clarifying, explaining, and placing facts in a meaningful context.

At the time the *Louisville Courier-Journal & Times* appointed the first ombudsman in 1967, not only did the newspapers face criticisms from the public and from young reporters, but television was encroaching on advertising. Soon, a few newspapers, including the *Washington Post*, had ombudsmen. By mid-1985, 35 of the 1,688 daily newspapers in the United States had ombudsmen, although most of them were called "readers' representatives," a term considered more meaningful to the readers. Now the idea still lives, but it obviously has a long way to go to gain wide acceptance. The readers' representatives have established an Organization of News Ombudsmen to promote that acceptance.

We present this description of an ideal ombudsman with thanks to Richard P. Cunningham, once a *Minneapolis Tribune* ombudsman:

The job of ombudsmen differs from newspaper to newspaper. But the elements that make good ombudsmen are quite clear: They include job definition, mandate, and the characteristics of the ombudsman.

1. The definition must make it plain that the ombudsman is not a media critic. The ombudsman must have access to space in the newspaper where he or she can disagree with the editors. Moreover, the purpose of that space should give the ombudsman impact because he or she can criticize the newspaper. The ombudsman's job description also must make clear that the ombudsman is the representative of the reader and the community.

2. The mandate must allow the ombudsman to ask embarrassing questions and to get clear answers whenever the questions arise after, not before, publication of a story.

3. The personal attributes of the ombudsman are a factor in whether his or her function will be effective. He or she must be a person of seniority and professional depth.

Ombudsmen must know that they are primarily the representatives of the reader and the community. They represent their newspapers only to the extent that they can explain their functions and their limitations to readers. Ombudsmen must have an informed understanding of just how lonely it may be to take a reader's, a staff member's, or their own complaints and pursue them with vigor.

Ombudsmen must be fair. They must not try to defeat or to diminish their newspapers or editors when they pursue an issue. They must see that questions, criticisms, or suspicions are presented to the news organizations at their highest level and are given respectful answers. If they do not agree with answers, ombudsmen ought to say so internally and in their column space.

The ombudsman's goal must be to facilitate constructive dialogue. On one side of the dialogue is the newspaper. On the other side are the people who depend upon the newspaper for fair and accurate reporting.

THE WASHINGTON POST'S OMBUDSMAN

Nobody ever told me you have to be suspicious of 105 percent of everything that everybody tells you.

—Dan Dorfman

The best-known case in which an ombudsman was a principal figure came at the *Washington Post.*

Early in April 1981, Janet Cooke was awarded a Pulitzer Prize for her feature writing about an 8-year-old boy, "Jimmy," who supposedly had been injected with heroin while Cooke was present. Two days after the award to Cooke, the editors of the *Washington Post* returned the prize to Columbia University.

What had happened? Cooke later became known to all American journalists, not because she had won a Pulitzer Prize, but because she had fabricated her prize-winning story—as well as much of her own background. Hours after the Pulitzer Prizes were awarded, Vassar College and the Associated Press called the *Washington Post* about the discrepancies in Cooke's biography, released when the prizes were announced. Her biography said that Cooke had been graduated magna cum laude from Vassar, studied at the Sorbonne in Paris, and earned a master's degree from the University of Toledo. Vassar and the University of Toledo confirmed that Cooke attended Vassar for one year, graduated without honors from the University of Toledo, and had no master's degree. Executive Editor Benjamin Bradlee also tested Cooke in French and found that she was not fluent.

The conclusion came when the editors questioned Cooke for hours about "Jimmy." Although she had published her story without last names—because Cooke claimed that the names were confidential—she at last confessed that "Jimmy" did not exist. Cooke then resigned.

Executive Editor Ben Bradlee invited Bill Green, the *Post*'s ombudsman, who had worked there for only a month, to examine and report in the *Post* on the "Jimmy's World" hoax. Green began collecting information at 10 a.m. on Wednesday, April 15, a few hours after reporter Janet Cooke had confessed. He began writing at 8 a.m. on Friday and wrote for more than 24 hours, ending with 18,000 words.

Green said he had three goals in reporting:

It should be as comprehensive as possible; it should be fair; and it should get the hell published. The *Post*'s handling of "Jimmy's World," or "Janet's World" was inexcusable. But I don't know any parallel for any industry having done what the *Post* did. . . . They gave me absolute liberty to explore it any way I wanted and published it without changing it. It was the second-longest story the *Post* has ever published.

Bradlee and *Post* publisher Donald Graham sent out word that "full disclosure" should be the staff's attitude. Green said that none of his questions went unanswered, although David Maraniss, deputy metropolitan editor, guarded off-the-record conversations with Cooke.

Milton Coleman, city editor, said, "There is some hope that the inviolability of the ombudsman position is increased by the part Bill played. Nobody else could have done what he did with the same credibility."

CASEY'S ADVICE

> *When a man comes to me for advice, I find out the kind of advice*
> *he wants, and I give it to him.*
>
> —Josh Billings

Some lessons learned by the ombudsmen were summed up by Donald "Casey" Jones, who was the ombudsman for the *Kansas City Star and Times*. Here is what he said, in part:

> I do not believe that as a profession we're "unfair, arrogant, slanted, irresponsible, and dishonest." I don't believe that. But a lot of our readers do. As the ombudsman two years for the *Kansas City Star and Times*, I have listened to an average of 25 complaints a day, answered dozens of letters, questions from Rotarians, groups, etc.
>
> The reading public does not trust us. Last month, the University of Chicago released a survey of how much confidence Americans place in each of 25 institutions. Only 13.9 percent trusted the leadership of the American press. Papers ranked ninth in their survey, just below banks. . . .
>
> Publishers will be pleased to hear it doesn't take money. It does take conviction and commitment. Any paper can do it. Any editor can spark it. And, with luck, the American reading public will be ready to give us back a higher credibility rating. Maybe higher even than banks.*

EXERCISES

1. If you were a member of a press council for your school's newspaper, what would you criticize about the paper?
2. If you were an ombudsman for your school's newspaper, what would you most likely defend about the paper?
3. Your college radio station needs guidance from other students. Write a paper, of 500 words, as to whether you favor a press council of students or having one intelligent student act as ombudsman.

*Donald "Casey" Jones, "Editors chastised and cheered at 'mass paranoia' session," *APME News*, January 1984, p. 8.

Appendix A

American Society of Newspaper Editors
Statement of Principles*

PREAMBLE

The First Amendment, protecting freedom of expression from abridgment by any law, guarantees to the people through their press a constitutional right, and thereby places on newspaper people a particular responsibility.

Thus journalism demands of its practitioners not only industry and knowledge but also the pursuit of a standard of integrity proportionate to the journalist's singular obligation.

To this end the American Society of Newspaper Editors sets forth this Statement of Principles as a standard encouraging the highest ethical and professional performance.

ARTICLE I—Responsibility

The primary purpose of gathering and distributing news and opinion is to serve the general welfare by informing the people and enabling them to make judgments on the issues of the time. Newspapermen and women who abuse the power of their professional role for selfish motives or unworthy purposes are faithless to that public trust.

The American press was made free not just to inform or just to serve as a forum for debate but also to bring an independent scrutiny

---

*Adopted by the ASNE board of directors, October 23, 1975; this code supplants the "Canons of Journalism" first adopted unanimously in 1923.

to bear on the forces of power in the society, including the conduct of official power at all levels of government.

ARTICLE II—Freedom of the Press

Freedom of the press belongs to the people. It must be defended against encroachment or assault from any quarter, public or private.

Journalists must be constantly alert to see that the public's business is conducted in public. They must be vigilant against all who would exploit the press for selfish purposes.

ARTICLE III—Independence

Journalists must avoid impropriety and the appearance of impropriety as well as any conflict of interest or the appearance of conflict. They should neither accept anything nor pursue any activity that might compromise or seem to compromise their integrity.

ARTICLE IV—Truth and Accuracy

Good faith with the reader is the foundation of good journalism. Every effort must be made to assure that the news content is accurate, free from bias and in context, and that all sides are presented fairly. Editorials, analytical articles and commentary should be held to the same standards of accuracy with respect to facts as news reports.

Significant errors of fact, as well as errors of omission, should be corrected promptly and prominently.

ARTICLE V—Impartiality

To be impartial does not require the press to be unquestioning or to refrain from editorial expression. Sound practice, however, demands a clear distinction for the reader between news reports and opinion. Articles that contain opinion or personal interpretation should be clearly identified.

ARTICLE VI—Fair Play

Journalists should respect the rights of people involved in the news, observe the common standards of decency and stand accountable to the public for the fairness and accuracy of their news reports.

Persons publicly accused should be given the earliest opportunity to respond.

Pledges of confidentiality to news sources must be honored at all costs, and therefore should not be given lightly. Unless there is clear and pressing need to maintain confidences, sources of information should be identified.

These principles are intended to preserve, protect and strengthen the bond of trust and respect between American journalists and the American people, a bond that is essential to sustain the grant of freedom entrusted to both by the nation's founders.

Society of Professional Journalists, Sigma Delta Chi, Code of Ethics*

The Society of Professional Journalists, Sigma Delta Chi, believes the duty of journalists is to serve the truth.

We believe the agencies of mass communication are carriers of public discussion and information, acting on their Constitutional mandate and freedom to learn and report the facts.

We believe in public enlightenment as the forerunner of justice, and in our Constitutional role to seek the truth as part of the public's right to know the truth.

We believe those responsibilities carry obligations that require journalists to perform with intelligence, objectivity, accuracy, and fairness.

To these ends, we declare acceptance of the standards of practice here set forth.

RESPONSIBILITY
The public's right to know of events of public importance and interest is the overriding mission of the mass media. The purpose of distributing news and enlightened opinion is to serve the general welfare. Journalists who use their professional status as representatives of the public for selfish or other unworthy motives violate a high trust.

---

* Adopted by the 1973 annual convention of Sigma Delta Chi.

FREEDOM OF THE PRESS

Freedom of the press is to be guarded as an inalienable right of people in a free society. It carries with it the freedom and the responsibility to discuss, question, and challenge actions and utterances of our government and of our public and private institutions. Journalists uphold the right to speak unpopular opinions and the privilege to agree with the majority.

ETHICS

Journalists must be free of obligation to any interest other than the public's right to know the truth.

1. Gifts, favors, free travel, special treatment, or privileges can compromise the integrity of journalists and their employers. Nothing of value should be accepted.
2. Secondary employment, political involvement, holding public office, and service in community organizations should be avoided if it compromises the integrity of journalists and their employers. Journalists and their employers should conduct their personal lives in a manner which protects them from conflict of interest, real or apparent. Their responsibilities to the public are paramount. That is the nature of their profession.
3. So-called news communications from private sources should not be published or broadcast without substantiation of their claims to news value.
4. Journalists will seek news that serves the public interest, despite the obstacles. They will make constant efforts to assure that the public's business is conducted in public and that public records are open to public inspection.
5. Journalists acknowledge the newsman's ethic of protecting confidential sources of information.
6. Plagiarism is dishonest and unacceptable.

ACCURACY AND OBJECTIVITY

Good faith with the public is the foundation of all worthy journalism.

1. Truth is our ultimate goal.
2. Objectivity in reporting the news is another goal, which serves as the mark of an experienced professional. It is a standard of per-

formance toward which we strive. We honor those who achieve it.

3. There is no excuse for inaccuracies or lack of thoroughness.
4. Newspaper headlines should be fully warranted by the contents of the articles they accompany. Photographs and telecasts should give an accurate picture of an event and not highlight a minor incident out of context.
5. Sound practice makes clear distinction between news reports and expressions of opinion. News reports should be free of opinion or bias and represent all sides of an issue.
6. Partisanship in editorial comment which knowingly departs from the truth violates the spirit of American journalism.
7. Journalists recognize their responsibility for offering informed analysis, comment, and editorial opinion on public events and issues. They accept the obligation to present such material by individuals whose competence, experience, and judgment qualify them for it.
8. Special articles or presentations devoted to advocacy or the writer's own conclusions and interpretations should be labeled as such.

FAIR PLAY

Journalists at all times will show respect for the dignity, privacy, rights, and well-being of people encountered in the course of gathering and presenting the news.

1. The news media should not communicate unofficial charges affecting reputation or moral character without giving the accused a chance to reply.
2. The news media must guard against invading a person's right to privacy.
3. The media should not pander to morbid curiosity about details of vice and crime.
4. It is the duty of news media to make prompt and complete correction of their errors.
5. Journalists should be accountable to the public for their reports and the public should be encouraged to voice its grievances against the media. Open dialogue with our readers, viewers, and listeners should be fostered.

PLEDGE

Journalists should actively censure and try to prevent violations of these standards, and they should encourage their observance by all newspeople. Adherence to this code of ethics is intended to preserve the bond of mutual trust and respect between American journalists and the American people.

WASHINGTON POST Standards and Ethics*

The *Washington Post* is pledged to an aggressive, responsible and fair pursuit of the truth without fear of any special interest, and with favor to none.

Washington Post reporters and editors are pledged to approach every assignment with the fairness of open minds and without prior judgment. The search for opposing views must be routine. Comment from persons accused or challenged in stories must be included. The motives of those who press their views upon us must routinely be examined and it must be recognized that these motives can be noble and ignoble, obvious and ulterior.

We fully recognize that the power we have inherited as the monopoly morning newspaper in the capital of the free world carries with it special responsibilities:

1. To listen to the voiceless.
2. To avoid any and all acts of arrogance.
3. To face the public with politeness and candor.

CONFLICT OF INTEREST

This newspaper is pledged to avoid conflict of interest or the appearance of conflict of interest, wherever or whenever possible. In particular:

1. We pay our own way.
2. We accept no gifts from news sources. Exceptions are minimal

---

* Issued November 1977 by the executive editor.

(tickets to cultural events to be reviewed) or obvious (invitations to meals). Occasionally, other exceptions might qualify. If in doubt, consult the executive editor or the managing editor or his deputy.

3. We work for no one except the *Washington Post* without permission from supervisors, which will be granted in the rarest of circumstances.

4. We free-lance for no one without permission from department heads. Permission will be granted only if the *Post* has no interest in the story, and only if it is to appear in a medium that does not compete with the *Washington Post*.

5. Many outside activities and jobs are incompatible with the proper performance of work on an independent newspaper. Connections with government are perhaps the most objectionable.

6. We avoid any practice that interferes with our ability to report and present the news with independence.

7. We make every reasonable effort to be free of obligation to news sources and to special interests.

8. We avoid active involvement in causes of any kind—politics, community affairs, social action, demonstrations—that could compromise, or seem to compromise, our ability to report and edit with fairness. Relatives cannot fairly be subject to *Post* rules, but it should be recognized that their involvement in causes can at least appear to compromise our integrity.

THE REPORTER'S ROLE

Although it has become increasingly difficult for this newspaper and for the press generally to do so since Watergate, reporters should make every effort to remain in the audience, to stay off the stage, to report history, not to make history.

ERRORS

This newspaper is pledged to minimize errors and to correct them when they occur. Accuracy is our goal; candor is our defense.

ATTRIBUTION OF SOURCES

This newspaper is pledged to disclose the source of all information unless disclosure would endanger the source's security. When we agree to protect a source's identity, that identity will not be made known to anyone outside the *Post*.

Before any information is accepted without full attribution, reporters must make every reasonable effort to get it on the record. If that is not possible, reporters should consider seeking the information elsewhere. If that in turn is not possible, reporters should request an on-the-record reason for restricting the source's identity and should include the reason in the story.

In any case, some kind of identification is almost always possible—by department or by position, for example—and should be reported.

PLAGIARISM

Attribution of material from other newspapers and other media must be total. Plagiarism is one of journalism's unforgivable sins.

FAIRNESS

Reporters and editors of the *Post* are committed to fairness. While arguments about objectivity are endless, the concept of fairness is something that editors and reporters can easily understand and pursue.

Fairness results from a few simple practices:

1. No story is fair if it omits facts of major importance or significance. So fairness includes completeness.
2. No story is fair if it includes essentially irrelevant information at the expense of significant facts. So fairness includes relevance.
3. No story is fair if it consciously or unconsciously misleads or even deceives the reader. So fairness includes honesty—leveling with the reader.
4. No story is fair if reporters hide their biases or emotions behind such subtly pejorative words as "refused," "despite," "admit," and "massive." So fairness requires straightforwardness ahead of flashiness.

Reporters and editors should routinely ask themselves at the end of every story: "Have I been as fair as I can be?"

OPINION

On this newspaper, the separation of news columns from the Editorial pages and the Op-Ed pages is solemn and complete. This separation is intended to serve the reader, who is entitled to the facts in the news columns and to opinions on the Editorial and Op-Ed pages. But nothing in this separation of function and powers is intended to eliminate from the news columns honest, in-depth reporting, or analysis, or commentary, when such departures from strictly factual reporting are plainly labeled.

THE NATIONAL AND COMMUNITY INTEREST

The *Washington Post* is vitally concerned with the national interest and with the community interest. We believe these interests are best served by the widest possible dissemination of information. The claim of national interest by a federal official does not automatically equate with the national interest. The claim of community interest by a local official does not automatically equate with the community interest.

TASTE

The *Washington Post* as a newspaper respects taste and decency, understanding that society's concepts of taste and decency are constantly changing. A word offensive to the last generation can be part of the next generation's common vocabulary. But we shall avoid prurience. We shall avoid profanities and obscenities unless their use is so essential to a story of significance that its meaning is lost without them. In no case shall obscenities be used without the approval of the executive editor or the managing editor or his deputy.

THE *POST'S* PRINCIPLES

After Eugene Meyer bought the *Washington Post* in 1933 and began the family ownership which continues today, he published "These Principles":

> The first mission of a newspaper is to tell the truth as nearly as the truth may be ascertained.
>
> The newspaper shall tell *all* the truth, so far as it can learn it, concerning the important affairs of America and the world.
>
> As a disseminator of the news, the paper shall observe the decencies that are obligatory upon a private gentleman.
>
> What it prints shall be fit reading for the young as well as for the old.
>
> The newspaper's duty is to its readers and to the public at

large, and not to the private interests of its owner.

In the pursuit of truth, the newspaper shall be prepared to make sacrifice of its material fortunes if such course be necessary for the public good.

The newspaper shall not be the ally of any special interest, but shall be fair and free and wholesome in its outlook on public affairs and public men.

"These Principles" are reendorsed herewith.

Appendix B

The Movie Rating System 1978*
Motion Picture Association of America

THE PURPOSE OF THE RATING SYSTEM

From the outset the purpose of the rating system was to provide *advance information to enable parents* to make judgments on movies they wanted their children to see or not to see. Basic to the program was and is the *responsibility of the parent to make the decision.*

The Rating Board does not rate for quality or the lack of it. That role is left to the movie critic and the audience. We would have destroyed the rating program in its infancy if we had become arbiters of how "good" or how "bad" creatively a movie was.

The only objective of the ratings is to advise the parent in advance so he may determine the possible suitability or unsuitability of viewing by his children. But, to repeat, the rating would not even make a final judgment on that; except for the X rating, the parent's decision remained the key to children's attendance.

Inherent in the rating system is the fact that to those 17 and over, and/or married without children, the ratings have little if any meaning.

Among the Rating Board's criteria are: theme, language, nudity and sex, and violence, and part of the rating comes from the assessment of how each of these elements is treated in each individual film.

There is no special emphasis on any of the elements. All are consid-

---

* First adopted 1974; revised annually.

ered and all are examined before a rating is given.

Contrary to popular but uninformed notions, violence has from the outset been a key factor in ratings. (Many violent films would have been given X ratings, but most of the directors chose, on their own, to revise the extremely violent sequences in order to receive an R rating.)

HOW THE RATINGS ARE ARRIVED AT

The ratings are decided by a Rating Board located in Hollywood. It is a full-time Board, composed of seven persons, headed by a chairman. There are no special qualifications for Board membership, except one must love movies, must possess an intelligent maturity of judgment, and have the capacity to put himself or herself in the role of most parents and view a film as most parents might—parents trying to decide whether their younger children ought to see a specific film.

No one is forced to submit a film to the Board for rating, but some 99% of the producers creating entertaining, seriously intended, responsible films (*not* hard core pornography) do in fact submit their films for ratings. Most makers of pornographic movies do not submit their films but instead, within the rules of the rating system, self-apply an X rating and go to market. The other symbols, G, PG, and R, are registered with the U.S. Patent and Trademark Office as Certification marks of the MPAA and cannot be used on the film in advertising by any company which has not officially submitted its film and received a rating. They may *not* be self-applied.

NATO estimates that about 85% of the exhibitors in the nation participate in the rating program and enforce its admission restrictions.

The Board views each film and after group discussion votes on the rating. Each Board member completes a rating form spelling out his or her reason for the rating in each of several categories of concern, and then gives the film an overall rating based on the category assessments.

The rating is decided by majority vote.

The producer of a film has a right under the rules to inquire as to the "why" of the rating. The producer also has the right, based on the reasons for his rating, to edit his film if he chooses to try for a less severe rating. The re-edited film is brought back to the Rating Board, and the process of rating goes forward again.

ADVERTISING CODE AND TRAILER POLICY

Film advertising is also part of the film industry's self-regulatory mechanism.

All advertising for rated motion pictures must be submitted to the Advertising Code Administration for approval prior to release of the film to the public. This includes, but is not limited to, print ads, radio and TV spots, pressbooks, and theatrical trailers.

Trailers are an important aspect of the program. Trailers are either designated G, which means they may be shown with all feature films, or R, which limits their use to feature films rated R or X. There will be in G-designated trailers no scenes that caused the feature to be rated PG, R, or X.

Each trailer carries two tags. The front tag indicates the designation of the trailer. The second tag at the end of the trailer indicates the rating of the film being advertised.

APPEAL OF RATINGS

Should a producer for any reason be displeased with his film's rating he could appeal the decision to the Rating Appeals Board, which sits as the final arbiter of ratings.

The Appeals Board comprises 22 members, men and women from MPAA, NATO, and IFIDA.

They gather as a quasi-judicial body to view the film and hear the appeal. After the screening, the producer whose film is being appealed explains why he believes the rating was wrongly decided. The chairman of the Rating Board states the reason for the film's rating. Both the producer and the Rating Board representative have an opportunity for rebuttal. In addition, the producer, if he desires, may submit a written presentation to the Board prior to the oral hearing.

After Appeals Board members question the two opposing representatives they are excused from the room. The Board discusses the appeal and then takes a secret ballot. It requires a two-thirds vote of those present to overturn a Rating Board decision.

By this method of appeal, controversial decisions of the Rating Board can be examined and any rating deemed a mistake set right.

The decision of the Appeals Board is final and cannot be appealed, although the Appeals Board has the authority to grant a rehearing on the request of the producer.

WHAT THE RATINGS MEAN

Essentially the ratings mean the following:

*G: "General Audiences—*All ages admitted."

This is a film which contains nothing in theme, language, nudity and sex, or violence which would, in the view of the Rating Board, be offensive to parents whose younger children view the film. The G rating is *not* a "certificate of approval," nor does it signify a children's film. Some profoundly significant films are rated G (for example, "A Man For All Seasons").

Some snippets of language may go beyond polite conversation but they are common everyday expressions. No words with sexual connotations are present in G-rated films. The violence is at a minimum. Nudity and sex scenes are not present.

PG: "Parental Guidance Suggested; some material may not be suitable for children." This is a film which clearly needs to be examined or inquired about by parents before they let their younger children attend. The label PG plainly states that parents *may* consider some material unsuitable for their children, but the parent must make this decision.

Parents are warned against sending their children, unseen without inquiry, to PG-rated movies.

There may be profanity in these films, but the harsher sexually derived word will vault a film into the R category. There may be violence but it is not deemed so strong that everyone under 17 need be restricted unless accompanied by a parent. Nor is there cumulative horror or violence that may take a film into the R category.

There is no explicit sex on the screen, although there may be some indication of sensuality. Brief nudity may appear in PG-rated films, but anything beyond that puts the film into R.

The PG rating, suggesting parental guidance, is thus an alert for special examination of a film by parents before deciding on its viewing by their children.

PG-13: Parents are strongly cautioned to give special guidance for children under 13. Some material may be inappropriate for young children.

Obviously the line is difficult to draw and the PG-rated film is the category most susceptible to criticism. In our plural society it is not easy to make subjective judgments for more than 215 million persons without some disagreement. So long as the parent knows he must exercise his parental responsibility, the PG rating serves as a meaningful guide and as a warning.

R: "Restricted, under 17s require accompanying parent or guardian."

This is an adult film in some of its aspects and treatment so far as language, violence, or nudity, sexuality or other content is concerned. The parent is advised in advance the film contains adult material and he takes his children with him with this advisory clearly in mind.

The language may be rough, the violence may be hard, and while explicit sex is not to be found in R-rated films, nudity and love-making may be involved.

Therefore, the R rating is strong in its advance advisory to parents as to the adult content of the film.

X: "No one under 17 admitted." This is patently an adult film and no children are allowed to attend. It should be noted, however, that X does *not* necessarily mean obscene or pornographic in terms of sex or violence. Serious films by lauded and skilled filmmakers may be rated X. The Rating Board does not attempt to mark films as obscene or pornographic; that is for the courts to decide legally. The reason for not admitting children to X-rated films can relate to the accumulation of brutal or sexually connected language, or of explicit sex or excessive and sadistic violence.

HOW THE CRITERIA ARE CONSTRUCTED

To oversee the Rating Board, the film industry has set up a Policy Review Committee consisting of officials of MPAA, NATO, and IFIDA. These men and women gather quarterly to monitor past ratings, to set guidelines for the Rating Board to follow, and to make certain that the Rating Board carries them out reasonably and appropriately.

Because the rating program is a self-regulatory apparatus of the film industry, it is important that no single element of the industry take on the authority of a "czar" beyond any discipline or self-restraint.

Appendix C

The Radio Code*
National Association of Broadcasters

PREAMBLE

In 1937 a major segment of U.S. commercial radio broadcasters first adopted industry-wide standards of practice. The purpose of such standards then, as now, is to establish guideposts and professional tenets for performance in the areas of programming and advertising content.

Admittedly, such standards for broadcasting can never be final or complete, because broadcasting is a creative art, always seeking new ways to achieve maximum appeal and service. Therefore, its standards are subject to periodic revision to reasonably reflect changing attitudes in our society.

In 1945 after two years devoted to reviewing and revising the 1937 document, new standards were promulgated. Further revisions were made in subsequent years when deemed necessary. The objectives behind them have been to assure that advertising messages be presented in an honest, responsible and tasteful manner and that broadcasters, in their programming, tailor their content to meet the needs and expectations of that particular audience to which their programming is directed.

The growth of broadcasting as a medium of entertainment, education and information has been made possible by its commercial underpinning. This aspect of commercial broadcasting as it has developed

---

* Twenty-First Edition, June 1978.

in the United States has enabled the industry to grow as a free medium in the tradition of American enterprise. The extent of this freedom is underscored by those laws which prohibit censorship of broadcast material. Rather, those who own the nation's radio broadcasting stations operate them—pursuant to this self-adopted Radio Code—in recognition of the needs of the American people and the reasonable self-interests of broadcasters and broadcast advertisers.

THE RADIO BROADCASTER'S CREED

We Believe:

That Radio Broadcasting in the United States of America is a living symbol of democracy; a significant and necessary instrument for maintaining freedom of expression, as established by the First Amendment to the Constitution of the United States;

That its contributions to the arts, to science, to education, to commerce, and therefore to the public welfare have the potential of influencing the common good achievements of our society as a whole;

That it is our obligation to serve the people in such manner as to reflect credit upon our profession and to encourage aspiration toward a better estate for our audiences. This entails making available to them through all phases of the broadcasting art such programming as will convey the traditional strivings of the U.S. towards goals beneficial to the populace;

That we should make full and ingenious use of the many sources of knowledge, talents and skills and exercise critical and discerning judgment concerning all broadcasting operations to the end that we may, intelligently and sympathetically:

Observe both existing principles and developing concepts affecting our society;

Respect and advance the rights and the dignity of all people;

Enrich the daily life of the people through the factual reporting and analysis of news, and through programming of education, entertainment, and information;

Provide for the fair discussion of matters of public concern; engage in works directed toward the common good; and volunteer our aid and comfort in times of stress and emergency;

Contribute to the economic welfare of all by expanding the channels of trade, by encouraging the development and conservation of natural resources, and by bringing together the buyer and seller through the broadcasting of information pertaining to goods and services.

Toward the achievement of these purposes we agree to observe the following:

I. PROGRAM STANDARDS

A. NEWS

Radio is unique in its capacity to reach the largest number of people first with reports on current events. This competitive advantage bespeaks caution—being first is not as important as being accurate. The Radio Code standards relating to the treatment of news and public events are, because of constitutional considerations, intended to be exhortatory. The standards set forth hereunder encourage high standards of professionalism in broadcast journalism. They are not to be interpreted as turning over to others the broadcaster's responsibility as to judgments necessary in news and public events programming.

1. *News Sources.* Those responsible for news on radio should exercise constant professional care in the selection of sources—on the premise that the integrity of the news and the consequent good reputation of radio as a dominant well-balanced news medium depend largely upon the reliability of such sources.

2. *News Reporting.* News reporting should be factual, fair and without bias. Good taste should prevail in the selection and handling of news. Morbid, sensational, or alarming details not essential to factual reporting should be avoided. News should be broadcast in such a manner as to avoid creation of panic and unnecessary alarm. Broadcasters should be diligent in their supervision of content, format, and presentation of news broadcasts. Equal diligence should be exercised in selection of editors and reporters who direct news gathering and dissemination, since the station's performance in this vital informational field depends largely upon them.

3. *Commentaries and Analyses.* Special obligations devolve upon those who analyse and/or comment upon news developments, and management should be satisfied completely that the task is to be per-

formed in the best interest of the listening public. Programs of news analysis and commentary should be clearly identified as such, distinguishing them from straight news reporting.

4. *Editorializing.* Broadcasts in which stations express their own opinions about issues of general public interest should be clearly identified as editorials.

5. *Coverage of News and Public Events.* In the coverage of news and public events broadcasters should exercise their judgments consonant with the accepted standards of ethical journalism and should provide accurate, informed and adequate coverage.

6. *Placement of Advertising.* Broadcasters should exercise particular discrimination in the acceptance, placement and presentation of advertising in news programs so that such advertising is clearly distinguishable from the news content.

B. Controversial Public Issues

1. Radio provides a valuable forum for the expression of responsible views on public issues of a controversial nature. Controversial public issues of importance to fellow citizens should give fair representation to opposing sides of issues.

2. Requests by individuals, groups or organizations for time to discuss their views on controversial public issues should be considered on the basis of their individual merits, and in the light of the contributions which the use requested would make to the public interest.

3. Discussion of controversial public issues should not be presented in a manner which would create the impression that the program is other than one dealing with a public issue.

C. Community Responsibility

1. Broadcasters and their staffs occupy a position of responsibility in the community and should conscientiously endeavor to be acquainted with its needs and characteristics to best serve the welfare of its citizens.

2. Requests for time for the placement of public service announcements or programs should be carefully reviewed with respect to the character and reputation of the group, campaign or organization in-

volved, the public interest content of the message, and the manner of its presentation.

D. POLITICAL BROADCASTS

1. Political broadcasts, or the dramatization of political issues designed to influence voters, shall be properly identified as such.

2. Political broadcasts should not be presented in a manner which would mislead listeners to believe that they are of any other character. (Reference: Communications Act of 1934, as amended, Secs. 315 and 317, and FCC Rules and Regulations, Secs. 3.654, 3.657, 3.663, as discussed in NAB's "Political Broadcast Catechism & The Fairness Doctrine.")

3. Because of the unique character of political broadcasts and the necessity to retain broad freedoms of policy void of restrictive interference, it is incumbent upon all political candidates and all political parties to observe the canons of good taste and political ethics, keeping in mind the intimacy of broadcasting in the American home.

E. ADVANCEMENT OF EDUCATION AND CULTURE

1. Because radio is an integral part of American life, there is inherent in radio broadcasting a continuing opportunity to enrich the experience of living through the advancement of education and culture.

2. Radio broadcasters, in augmenting the educational and cultural influences of the home, schools, religious institutions and institutions of higher education and other entities should:

(a) be thoroughly conversant with the educational and cultural needs and aspirations of the community served;

(b) develop programming consonant with the station's particular target audience.

F. RELIGION AND RELIGIOUS PROGRAMMING

1. Religious programming shall be presented by responsible individuals, groups or organizations.

2. Radio broadcasting reaches audiences of all creeds simultane-

ously. Therefore, both the advocates of broad or ecumenical religious precepts, and the exponents of specific doctrines, are urged to present their positions in a manner conducive to listener enlightenment on the role of religion in society.

G. Responsibility Toward Children

Broadcasters have a special responsibility to children. Programming which might reasonably be expected to hold the attention of children should be presented with due regard for its effect on children.

1. Programming should be based upon sound social concepts and should include positive sets of values which will allow children to become responsible adults, capable of coping with the challenges of maturity.

2. Programming should convey a reasonable range of the realities which exist in the world to help children make the transition to adulthood.

3. Programming should contribute to the healthy development of personality and character.

4. Programming should afford opportunities for cultural growth as well as for wholesome entertainment.

5. Programming should be consistent with integrity of realistic production, but should avoid material of extreme nature which might create undesirable emotional reaction in children.

6. Programming should avoid appeals urging children to purchase the product specifically for the purpose of keeping the program on the air or which, for any reason, encourage children to enter inappropriate places.

7. Programming should present such subjects as violence and sex without undue emphasis and only as required by plot development or character delineation.

Violence, physical or psychological, should only be projected in responsibly handled contexts, not used to excess or exploitatively. Programs involving violence should present the consequences of it to its victims and perpetrators.

The depiction of conflict, and of material reflective of sexual considerations, when presented in programs designed primarily for children, should be handled with sensitivity.

8. The treatment of criminal activities should always convey their social and human effects.

H. Dramatic Programming

1. In the design of dramatic programs it is in the interest of radio as a vital medium to encourage those that are innovative, reflect a high degree of creative skill, deal with significant moral and social issues and present challenging concepts and other subject matter that relate to the world in which the listener lives.

2. Radio programming should not only reflect the influence of the established institutions that shape our values and culture, but also expose the dynamics of social change which bear upon our lives.

3. To achieve these goals, radio broadcasters should be conversant with the general and specific needs, interests and aspirations of all the segments of the communities they serve.

4. Radio should reflect realistically the experience of living, in both its pleasant and tragic aspects, if it is to serve the listener honestly. Nevertheless, it holds a concurrent obligation to provide programming which will encourage positive adjustments to life.

In selecting program subjects and themes, great care must be exercised to be sure that treatment and presentation are made in good faith and not for the purpose of sensationalism or to shock or exploit the audience or appeal to prurient interests or morbid curiosity.

5. In determining the acceptability of any dramatic program, especially those containing elements of crime, mystery, or horror, consideration should be given to the possible effect on all members of the listening audience.

In addition, without sacrificing integrity of presentation, dramatic programs on radio shall avoid:

(a) the presentation of techniques of crime in such detail as to be instructional or invite imitation;

(b) presentation of the details of violence involving the excessive, the gratuitous and the instructional;

(c) sound effects calculated to mislead, shock, or unduly alarm the listener;

(d) portrayals of law enforcement in a manner which does not contribute to its proper role in our society.

I. GENERAL

1. The intimacy and confidence placed in radio demand of the broadcaster, the networks and other program sources that they be vigilant in protecting the audience from deceptive broadcast practices.

2. Sound effects and expressions characteristically associated with news broadcasts (such as "bulletin," "flash," "we interrupt this program to bring you," etc.) shall be reserved for announcement of news, and the use of any deceptive techniques in connection with fictional events and non-news programming shall not be employed.

3. The broadcasters shall be constantly alert to prevent inclusion of elements within programming dictated by factors other than the requirements of the programming itself. The acceptance of cash payments or other considerations in return for including the choice and identification of prizes, the selection of music and other creative programming elements and inclusion of any identification of commercial products or services, trade names or advertising slogans within the programming are prohibited unless consideration for such inclusion is revealed to the listeners in accordance with Sections 317 and 508 of the Communications Act.

4. Special precautions should be taken to avoid demeaning or ridiculing members of the audience who suffer from physical or mental afflictions or deformities.

5. The broadcast of gambling sequences deemed necessary to the development of plot or as appropriate background is acceptable only when presented with discretion and in moderation, and in a manner which would not excite interest in, or foster, betting nor be instructional in nature.

6. Quiz and similar programming that is presented as a contest of knowledge, information, skill or luck must, in fact, be a genuine contest and the results must not be controlled by collusion with or between contestants, or by any other action which will favor one contestant against any other.

7. Contests may not constitute a lottery.

8. Listener contests should not mislead as to the nature or value of prizes, likelihood of winning, nor encourage thoughtless or unsafe acts.

9. No programming shall be presented in a manner which through artifice or simulation would mislead the audience as to any material fact. Each broadcaster must exercise reasonable judgment to determine whether a particular method of presentation would constitute a material deception, or would be accepted by the audience as normal theatrical illusion.

10. Legal, medical and other professional advice will be permitted only in conformity with law and recognized ethical and professional standards.

11. Narcotic addiction shall not be presented except as a destructive habit. The use of illegal drugs or the abuse of legal drugs shall not be encouraged or be presented as desirable or socially acceptable.

12. Material pertaining to fortune-telling, occultism, astrology, phrenology, palm-reading, numerology, mind-reading, character-reading, or subjects of a like nature, is unacceptable if it encourages people to regard such fields as providing commonly accepted appraisals of life.

13. Representations of liquor and smoking shall be de-emphasized. When represented, they should be consistent with plot and character development.

14. Obscene, indecent or profane matter, as proscribed by law, is unacceptable.

15. Special sensitivity is necessary in the use of material relating to sex, race, color, age, creed, religious functionaries or rites, or national or ethnic derivation.

16. The presentation of marriage, the family and similarly important human relationships, and material with sexual connotations, should not be treated exploitatively or irresponsibly, but with sensitivity.

17. Broadcasts of actual sporting events at which on-the-scene betting is permitted by law should be presented in a manner in keeping with federal, state and local laws, and should concentrate on the subject as a public sporting event.

18. Detailed exposition of hypnosis or material capable of having an hypnotic effect on listeners is forbidden.

19. Any technique whereby an attempt is made to convey information to the listener by transmitting messages below the threshold of normal awareness is not permitted.

20. The commonly accepted standards of humane animal treatment should be adhered to as applicable in programming.

21. Broadcasters are responsible for making good faith determinations on the acceptability of lyrics under applicable Radio Code standards.

22. Guests on discussion/interview programs and members of the public who participate in phone-in programs shall be treated with due respect by the program host/hostess.

Interview/discussion programs, including telephone participation programs, should be governed by accepted standards of ethical journalism. Any agreement substantively limiting areas of discussion/questions should be announced at the outset of the program.

23. The standards of this Code covering programming content are also understood to include, wherever applicable, the standards contained in the advertising section of the Code.

24. To assure that broadcasters have the freedom to program fully and responsibly, none of the provisions of this Code should be construed as preventing or impeding broadcasts of the broad range of material necessary to help broadcasters fulfill their obligations to operate in the public interest.

II. ADVERTISING STANDARDS

Advertising is the principal source of revenue of the free, competitive American system of radio broadcasting. It makes possible the presentation to all American people of the finest programs of entertainment, education, and information.

Since the great strength of American radio broadcasting derives from the public respect for and the public approval of its programs, it must be the purpose of each broadcaster to establish and maintain high standards of performance, not only in the selection and production of all programs, but also in the presentation of advertising.

This Code establishes basic standards for all radio broadcasting. The principles of acceptability and good taste within the Program Standards section govern the presentation of advertising where applicable. In addition, the Code establishes in this section special standards which apply to radio advertising.

A. General Advertising Standards

1. Commercial radio broadcasters make their facilities available for the advertising of products and services and accept commercial presentations for such advertising. However, they shall, in recognition of their responsibility to the public, refuse the facilities of their stations to an advertiser where they have good reason to doubt the integrity of the advertiser, the truth of the advertising representations, or the compliance of the advertiser with the spirit and purpose of all applicable legal requirements.

2. In consideration of the customs and attitudes of the communities served, each radio broadcaster should refuse his/her facilities to the advertisement of products and services, or the use of advertising scripts, which the station has good reason to believe would be objectionable to a substantial and responsible segment of the community. These standards should be applied with judgment and flexibility, taking into consideration the characteristics of the medium, its home and family audience, and the form and content of the particular presentation.

B. Presentation of Advertising

1. The advancing techniques of the broadcast art have shown that the quality and proper integration of advertising copy are just as important as measurement in time. The measure of a station's service to its audience is determined by its overall performance.

2. The final measurement of any commercial broadcast service is quality. To this, every broadcaster shall dedicate his/her best effort.

3. Great care shall be exercised by the broadcaster to prevent the presentation of false, misleading or deceptive advertising. While it is entirely appropriate to present a product in a favorable light and atmosphere, the presentation must not, by copy or demonstration, involve a material deception as to the characteristics or performance of a product.

4. The broadcaster and the advertiser should exercise special caution with the content and presentation of commercials placed in or near programs designed for children. Exploitation of children should

be avoided. Commercials directed to children should in no way mislead as to the product's performance and usefulness. Appeals involving matters of health which should be determined by physicians should be avoided.

5. Reference to the results of research, surveys or tests relating to the product to be advertised shall not be presented in a manner so as to create an impression of fact beyond that established by the study. Surveys, tests or other research results upon which claims are based must be conducted under recognized research techniques and standards.

C. ACCEPTABILITY OF ADVERTISERS AND PRODUCTS

In general, because radio broadcasting is designed for the home and the entire family, the following principles shall govern the business classifications:

1. The advertising of hard liquor shall not be accepted.

2. The advertising of beer and wines is acceptable when presented in the best of good taste and discretion.

3. The advertising of fortune-telling, occultism, astrology, phrenology, palm-reading, numerology, mind-reading, character-reading, or subjects of a like nature, is not acceptable.

4. Because the advertising of all products and services of a personal nature raises special problems, such advertising, when accepted, should be treated with emphasis on ethics and the canons of good taste, and presented in a restrained and inoffensive manner.

5. The advertising of tip sheets and other publications seeking to advertise for the purpose of giving odds or promoting betting is unacceptable.

The lawful advertising of government organizations which conduct legalized lotteries and the advertising of private or governmental organizations which conduct legalized betting on sporting contests are acceptable provided such advertising does not unduly exhort the public to bet.

6. An advertiser who markets more than one product shall not be permitted to use advertising copy devoted to an acceptable product for purposes of publicizing the brand name or other identification of a product which is not acceptable.

7. Care should be taken to avoid presentation of "bait-switch" advertising whereby goods or services which the advertiser has no intention of selling are offered merely to lure the customer into purchasing higher-priced substitutes.

8. Advertising should offer a product or service on its positive merits and refrain from discrediting, disparaging or unfairly attacking competitors, competing products, other industries, professions or institutions.

Any identification or comparison of a competitive product or service, by name, or other means, should be confined to specific facts rather than generalized statements or conclusions, unless such statements or conclusions are not derogatory in nature.

9. Advertising testimonials should be genuine, and reflect an honest appraisal of personal experience.

10. Advertising by institutions or enterprises offering instruction with exaggerated claims for opportunities awaiting those who enroll, is unacceptable.

11. The advertising of firearms/ammunition is acceptable provided it promotes the product only as sporting equipment and conforms to recognized standards of safety as well as all applicable laws and regulations. Advertisements of firearms/ammunition by mail order are unacceptable.

D. ADVERTISING OF MEDICAL PRODUCTS

Because advertising for over-the-counter products involving health considerations is of intimate and far-reaching importance to the consumer, the following principles should apply to such advertising:

1. When dramatized advertising material involves statements by doctors, dentists, nurses or other professional people, the material should be presented by members of such profession reciting actual experience, or it should be made apparent from the presentation itself that the portrayal is dramatized.

2. Because of the personal nature of the advertising of medical products, the indiscriminate use of such words as "safe," "without risk," "harmless," or other terms of similar meaning, either direct or implied, should not be expressed in the advertising of medical products.

3. Advertising material which offensively describes or dramatizes distress or morbid situations involving ailments is not acceptable.

E. TIME STANDARDS FOR ADVERTISING COPY

1. As a general rule, up to 18 minutes of advertising time within any clock hour are acceptable. However, for good cause and when in the public interest, broadcasters may depart from this standard in order to fulfill their responsibilities to the communities they serve.

2. Any reference to another's products or services under any trade name, or language sufficiently descriptive to identify it, shall, except for normal guest identification, be considered as advertising copy.

3. For the purpose of determining advertising limitations, such program types as "classified," "swap shop," "shopping guides," and "farm auction" programs, etc., shall be regarded as containing one and one-half minutes of advertising for each five-minute segment.

F. CONTESTS

1. Contests shall be conducted with fairness to all entrants, and shall comply with all pertinent laws and regulations.

2. All contest details, including rules, eligibility requirements, opening and termination dates, should be clearly and completely announced or easily accessible to the listening public; and the winners' names should be released as soon as possible after the close of the contest.

3. When advertising is accepted which requests contestants to submit items of product identification or other evidence of purchase of products, reasonable facsimiles thereof should be made acceptable. However, when the award is based upon skill and not upon chance, evidence of purchase may be required.

4. All copy pertaining to any contest (except that which is required by law) associated with the exploitation or sale of the sponsor's product or service, and all references to prizes or gifts offered in such connection should be considered a part of and included in the total time limitations heretofore provided. *(See Time Standards for Advertising Copy.)*

G. PREMIUMS AND OFFERS

1. The broadcaster should require that full details of proposed offers be submitted for investigation and approval before the first announcement of the offer is made to the public.

2. A final date for the termination of an offer should be announced as far in advance as possible.

3. If a consideration is required, the advertiser should agree to honor complaints indicating dissatisfaction with the premium by returning the consideration.

4. There should be no misleading descriptions or comparisons of any premiums or gifts which will distort or enlarge their value in the minds of the listeners.

Appendix D

The Television Code*
National Association of Broadcasters

PREAMBLE

BROADCASTERS' RESPONSIBILITIES

Television is seen and heard in nearly every American home. These homes include children and adults of all ages, embrace all races and all varieties of philosophic or religious conviction and reach those of every educational background. Television broadcasters must take this pluralistic audience into account in programming their stations. They are obligated to bring their positive responsibility for professionalism and reasoned judgment to bear upon all those involved in the development, production and selection of programs.

ADVERTISERS' RESPONSIBILITIES

The free, competitive American system of broadcasting which offers programs of entertainment, news, general information, education and culture is supported and made possible by revenues from advertising. While television broadcasters are responsible for the programming and advertising on their stations, the advertisers who use televisior to convey their commercial messages also have a responsibility to the viewing audience. Their advertising messages should be presented in an honest, responsible and tasteful manner. Advertisers should also

---

* Twentieth Edition, June 1978.

support the endeavors of broadcasters to offer a diversity of programs that meet the needs and expectations of the total viewing audience.

VIEWERS' RESPONSIBILITIES

The viewer also has a responsibility to help broadcasters serve the public. All viewers should make their criticisms and positive suggestions about programming and advertising known to the broadcast licensee. Parents particularly should oversee the viewing habits of their children, encouraging them to watch programs that will enrich their experience and broaden their intellectual horizons.

PROGRAM STANDARDS

I. PRINCIPLES GOVERNING PROGRAM CONTENT

General goals. It is in the interest of television as a vital medium to encourage programs that are innovative, reflect a high degree of creative skill, deal with significant moral and social issues and present challenging concepts and other subject matter that relate to the world in which the viewer lives.

Television programs should not only reflect the influence of the established institutions that shape our values and culture, but also expose the dynamics of social change which bear upon our lives.

Responsibly exercised artistic freedom. To achieve these goals, television broadcasters should be conversant with the general and specific needs, interests and aspirations of all the segments of the communities they serve. They should affirmatively seek out responsible representatives of all parts of their communities so that they may structure a broad range of programs that will inform, enlighten, and entertain the total audience.

Broadcasters should also develop programs directed toward advancing the cultural and educational aspects of their communities.

To assure that broadcasters have the freedom to program fully and responsibly, none of the provisions of this Code should be construed as preventing or impeding broadcast of the broad range of material necessary to help broadcasters fulfill their obligations to operate in the public interest.

The challenge to the broadcaster is to determine how suitably to present the complexities of human behavior. For television, this requires exceptional awareness of considerations peculiar to the medium.

Accordingly, in selecting program subjects and themes, great care must be exercised to be sure that treatment and presentation are made in good faith and not for the purpose of sensationalism or to shock or exploit the audience or appeal to prurient interests or morbid curiosity.

Family viewing considerations. Additionally, entertainment programming inappropriate for viewing by a general family audience should not be broadcast during the first hour of network entertainment programming in prime time and in the immediately preceding hour. In the occasional case when an entertainment program in this time period is deemed to be inappropriate for such an audience, advisories should be used to alert viewers. Advisories should also be used when programs in later prime time periods contain material that might be disturbing to significant segments of the audience.

These advisories should be presented in audio and video form at the beginning of the program and when deemed appropriate at a later point in the program. Advisories should also be used responsibly in promotional material in advance of the program. When using an advisory, the broadcaster should attempt to notify publishers of television program listings.

Special care should be taken with respect to the content and treatment of audience advisories so that they do not disserve their intended purpose by containing material that is promotional, sensational, or exploitative. Promotional announcements for programs that include advisories should be scheduled on a basis consistent with the purpose of the advisory.

The scheduling provisions of Section I (Principles Governing Program Content) shall not apply to programs under contract to a station as of April 8, 1975, all episodes of which were then in existence, if such station is unable, despite reasonable good faith efforts, to edit such programs to make them appropriate for family viewing or to reschedule them so as not to occupy family viewing periods. This exception shall in no event apply after September 1, 1977. Any such programs excepted from scheduling provisions shall, of course, bear the required advisory notices. *(Interpretation No. 5)*

II. Responsibility Toward Children

Broadcasters have a special responsibility to children. Programs designed primarily for children should take into account the range of interests and needs of children from instructional and cultural material to a wide variety of entertainment material. In their totality, programs should contribute to the sound, balanced development of children to help them achieve a sense of the world at large and informed adjustments to their society.

In the course of a child's development, numerous social factors and forces, including television, affect the ability of the child to make the transition to adult society.

The child's training and experience during the formative years should include positive sets of values which will allow the child to become a responsible adult, capable of coping with the challenges of maturity.

Children should also be exposed, at the appropriate times, to a reasonable range of the realities which exist in the world sufficient to help them make the transition to adulthood.

Because children are allowed to watch programs designed primarily for adults, broadcasters should take this practice into account in the presentation of material in such programs when children may constitute a substantial segment of the audience.

All the standards set forth in this section apply to both program and commercial material designed and intended for viewing by children.

III. Community Responsibility

1. Television broadcasters and their staffs occupy positions of unique responsibility in their communities and should conscientiously endeavor to be acquainted fully with the community's needs and characteristics in order better to serve the welfare of its citizens.

2. Requests for time for the placement of public service announcements or programs should be carefully reviewed with respect to the character and reputation of the group, campaign or organization involved, the public interest content of the message, and the manner of its presentation.

IV. Special Program Standards

1. Violence; conflict.

A. Violence, physical or psychological, may only be projected in responsibly handled contexts, not used exploitatively. Programs involving violence should present the consequences of it to its victims and perpetrators.

Presentation of the details of violence should avoid the excessive, the gratuitous and the instructional.

The use of violence for its own sake and the detailed dwelling upon brutality or physical agony, by sight or by sound, are not permissible.

B. **Conflict and children.** The depiction of conflict, when presented in programs designed primarily for children, should be handled with sensitivity.

2. Anti-social behavior; crime. The treatment of criminal activities should always convey their social and human effects.

The presentation of techniques of crime in such detail as to be instructional or invite imitation shall be avoided.

3. Self-destructive behavior: drugs; gambling; alcohol.

A. Narcotic addiction shall not be presented except as a destructive habit. The use of illegal drugs or the abuse of legal drugs shall not be encouraged or shown as socially acceptable.

B. The use of gambling devices or scenes necessary to the development of plot or as appropriate background is acceptable only when presented with discretion and in moderation, and in a manner which would not excite interest in, or foster, betting nor be instructional in nature.

C. The use of liquor and the depiction of smoking in program content shall be deemphasized. When shown, they should be consistent with plot and character development.

4. Sports programs. Telecasts of actual sports programs at which on-the-scene betting is permitted by law shall be presented in a manner in keeping with federal, state and local laws, and should concentrate on the subject as a public sporting event.

5. Mental/physical disadvantages. Special precautions must be taken to avoid demeaning or ridiculing members of the audience who suffer from physical or mental afflictions or deformities.

6. Human relationships; sex; costume. The presentation of marriage, the family and similarly important human relationships, and material with sexual connotations, shall not be treated exploitatively or irresponsibly, but with sensitivity. Costuming and movements of all performers shall be handled in a similar fashion.

7. Pluralism; minorities. Special sensitivity is necessary in the use of material relating to sex, race, color, age, creed, religious functionaries or rites, or national or ethnic derivation.

8. Obscenity; profanity. Subscribers shall not broadcast any material which they determine to be obscene, profane or indecent.

Above and beyond the requirements of law, broadcasters must consider the family atmosphere in which many of their programs are viewed.

There shall be no graphic portrayal of sexual acts by sight or sound. The portrayal of implied sexual acts must be essential to the plot and presented in a responsible and tasteful manner.

Subscribers are obligated to bring positive responsibility and reasoned judgment to bear upon all those involved in the development, production, and selection of programs.

9. Hypnosis. The creation of a state of hypnosis by act or detailed demonstration on camera is prohibited, and hypnosis as a form of "parlor game" antics to create humorous situations within a comedy setting is forbidden.

10. Superstition; pseudo-sciences. Program material pertaining to fortune-telling, occultism, astrology, phrenology, palm-reading, numerology, mind-reading, character-reading, and the like is unacceptable if it encourages people to regard such fields as providing commonly accepted appraisals of life.

11. Professional advice/diagnosis/treatment. Professional advice, diagnosis and treatment will be presented in conformity with law and recognized professional standards.

12. Subliminal perception. Any technique whereby an attempt is made to convey information to the viewer by transmitting messages below the threshold of normal awareness is not permitted.

13. Animals. The use of animals, consistent with plot and character delineation, shall be in conformity with accepted standards of humane treatment.

14. Game programs; contests.

A. Quiz and similar programs that are presented as contests of knowledge, information, skill or luck must, in fact, be genuine contests; and the results must not be controlled by collusion with or between contestants, or by any other action which will favor one contestant against any other.

B. Contests may not constitute a lottery.

15. Prizes: credits, acknowledgements. The broadcaster shall be constantly alert to prevent inclusion of elements within a program dictated by factors other than the requirements of the program itself. The acceptance of cash payments or other considerations in return for including scenic properties, the choice and identification of prizes, the selection of music and other creative program elements and inclusion of any identification of commercial products or services, their trade names or advertising slogan within the program are prohibited except in accordance with Sections 317 and 508 of the Communications Act.

16. Misrepresentation; deception.

A. No program shall be presented in a manner which through artifice or simulation would mislead the audience as to any material fact. Each broadcaster must exercise reasonable judgment to determine whether a particular method of presentation would constitute a material deception, or would be accepted by the audience as normal theatrical illusion.

B. A television broadcaster should not present fictional events or other non-news material as authentic news telecasts or announcements, nor permit dramatizations in any program which would give the false impression that the dramatized material constitutes news.

17. Applicability of Code standards. The standards of this Code covering program content are also understood to include, wherever applicable, the standards contained in the advertising section of the Code.

V. TREATMENT OF NEWS AND PUBLIC EVENTS

General.

Television Code standards relating to the treatment of news and public events are, because of constitutional considerations, intended to be exhortatory. The standards set forth hereunder encourage high standards of professionalism in broadcast journalism. They are not to be interpreted as turning over to others the broadcaster's responsibility as to judgments necessary in news and public events programming.

News.

1. A television station's news schedule should be adequate and well-balanced.

2. News reporting should be factual, fair and without bias.

3. A television broadcaster should exercise particular discrimination in the acceptance, placement and presentation of advertising in news programs so that such advertising should be clearly distinguishable from the news content.

4. At all times, pictorial and verbal material for both news and comment should conform to other sections of these standards, wherever such sections are reasonably applicable.

5. Good taste should prevail in the selection and handling of news:

Morbid, sensational or alarming details, not essential to the factual report, especially in connection with stories of crime or sex, should be avoided. News should be telecast in such a manner as to avoid panic and unnecessary alarm.

6. Commentary and analysis should be clearly identified as such.

7. Pictorial material should be chosen with care and not presented in a misleading manner.

8. All news interview programs should be governed by accepted standards of ethical journalism, under which the interviewer selects the questions to be asked. Where there is advance agreement materially restricting an important or newsworthy area of questioning, the interviewer will state on the program that such limitation has been agreed upon. Such disclosure should be made if the person being interviewed requires that questions be submitted in advance or participates in editing a recording of the interview prior to its use on the air.

9. A television broadcaster should exercise due care in the supervision of content, format, and presentation of newscasts originated by his/her station, and in the selection of newscasters, commentators, and analysts.

Public Events.

1. A television broadcaster has an affirmative responsibility at all times to be informed of public events, and to provide coverage consonant with the ends of an informed and enlightened citizenry.

2. The treatment of such events by a television broadcaster should provide adequate and informed coverage.

VI. Controversial Public Issues

1. Television provides a valuable forum for the expression of responsible views on public issues of a controversial nature. The television broadcaster should seek out and develop with accountable individuals, groups and organizations, programs relating to controversial public issues of import to his/her fellow citizens; and to give fair representation to opposing sides of issues which materially affect the life or welfare of a substantial segment of the public.

2. Requests by individuals, groups or organizations for time to discuss their views on controversial public issues should be considered on the basis of their individual merits, and in the light of the contribution which the use requested would make to the public interest, and to a well-balanced program structure.

3. Programs devoted to the discussion of controversial public issues should be identified as such. They should not be presented in a manner which would mislead listeners or viewers to believe that the program is purely of an entertainment, news, or other character.

4. Broadcasts in which stations express their own opinions about issues of general public interest should be clearly identified as editorials. They should be unmistakably identified as statements of station opinion and should be appropriately distinguished from news and other program material.

VII. Political Telecasts

1. Political telecasts should be clearly identified as such. They should not be presented by a television broadcaster in a manner which would mislead listeners or viewers to believe that the program is of any other character. (Ref.: Communications Act of 1934, as amended. Secs.

315 and 317, and FCC Rules and Regulations, Secs. 3.654, 3.657, 3.663, as discussed in NAB's "Political Broadcast Catechism & The Fairness Doctrine.")

VIII. Religious Programs

1. It is the responsibility of a television broadcaster to make available to the community appropriate opportunity for religious presentations.

2. Programs reach audiences of all creeds simultaneously. Therefore, both the advocates of broad or ecumenical religious precepts, and the exponents of specific doctrines, are urged to present their positions in a manner conducive to viewer enlightenment on the role of religion in society.

3. In the allocation of time for telecasts of religious programs, the television station should use its best efforts to apportion such time fairly among responsible individuals, groups and organizations.

ADVERTISING STANDARDS

IX. Presentation of Advertising

1. Applicability of Code Standards.

A. This Code establishes basic standards for all television broadcasting. The principles of acceptability and good taste within the Program Standards section govern the presentation of advertising where applicable. In addition, the Code establishes in this section special standards which apply to television advertising.

B. Commercial television broadcasters make their facilities available for the advertising of products and services and accept commercial presentations for such advertising. However, television broadcasters should, in recognition of their responsibility to the public, refuse the facilities of their stations to an advertiser where they have good reason to doubt the integrity of the advertiser, the truth of the advertising representations, or the compliance of the advertiser with the spirit and purpose of all applicable legal requirements.

C. Since advertising by television is a dynamic technique, a television broadcaster should keep under surveillance new advertising devices so that the spirit and purpose of these standards are fulfilled.

2. Sponsor identification. Identification of sponsorship must be made in all sponsored programs in accordance with the requirements of the Communications Act of 1934, as amended, and the Rules and Regulations of the Federal Communications Commission.

3. Safety considerations. Representations which disregard normal safety precautions shall be avoided.

Children shall not be represented, except under proper adult supervision, as being in contact with or demonstrating a product recognized as potentially dangerous to them.

4. Audience sensibilities: general.

A. In consideration of the customs and attitudes of the communities served, each television broadcaster should refuse his/her facilities to the advertisement of products and services, or the use of advertising scripts, which the station has good reason to believe would be objectionable to a substantial and responsible segment of the community. These standards should be applied with judgment and flexibility, taking into consideration the characteristics of the medium, its home and family audience, and the form and content of the particular presentation.

B. Advertising messages should be presented with courtesy and good taste; disturbing or annoying material should be avoided; every effort should be made to keep the advertising message in harmony with the content and general tone of the program in which it appears.

5. Audience perceptions of clutter. A multiple product announcement is one in which two or more products or services are presented within the framework of a single announcement. A multiple product announcement shall not be scheduled in a unit of time less than 60 seconds, except where integrated so as to appear to the viewer as a single message. A multiple product announcement shall be considered integrated and counted as a single announcement if:

—the products or services are related and interwoven within the framework of the announcement (related products or services shall be defined as those having a common character, purpose and use); and

—the voice(s), setting, background and continuity are used consistently throughout so as to appear to the viewer as a single message. Multiple product announcements of 60 seconds in length or longer not meeting this definition of integration shall be counted as two or more announcements under this section of the Code. This provision shall not apply to retail or service establishments.

6. Audience sensibilities; children.

A. The broadcaster and the advertiser should exercise special caution with the content and presentation of television commercials placed in or near programs designed for children. Exploitation of children should be avoided. Commercials directed to children should in no way mislead as to the product's performance and usefulness.

B. Commercials, whether live, film or tape, within programs initially designed primarily for children under 12 years of age shall be clearly separated from program material by an appropriate device.

C. Trade name identification or other merchandising practices involving the gratuitous naming of products is discouraged in programs designed primarily for children.

D. Appeals involving matters of health which should be determined by physicians should not be directed primarily to children.

E. No children's program personality or cartoon character shall be utilized to deliver commercial messages within or adjacent to the programs in which such a personality or cartoon character regularly appears. This provision shall also apply to lead-ins to commercials when such lead-ins contain sell copy or imply endorsement of the product by program personalities or cartoon characters.

Restricted or unacceptable categories:

7. Alcoholic beverages.

A. The advertising of hard liquor (distilled spirits) is not acceptable.

B. The advertising of beer and wines is acceptable only when presented in the best of good taste and discretion, and is acceptable only subject to federal and local laws.

This requires that commercials involving beer and wine avoid any representation of on-camera drinking. *(Interpretation No. 4)*

8. Vocational training. Advertising by institutions or enterprises which in their offers of instruction imply promises of employment or make exaggerated claims for the opportunities awaiting those who enroll for courses is generally unacceptable.

9. Ammunition; firearms; fireworks. The advertising of firearms/ ammunition is acceptable provided it promotes the product only as sporting equipment and conforms to recognized standards of safety as well as all applicable laws and regulations. Advertisements of firearms/ammunition by mail order are unacceptable. The advertising of fireworks is unacceptable.

10. Astrology, etc. The advertising of fortune-telling, occultism, astrology, phrenology, palm-reading, numerology, mind-reading, character-reading or subjects of a like nature is not permitted.

11. Personal products. Because all products of a personal nature create special problems, acceptability of such products should be determined with especial emphasis on ethics and the canons of good taste. Such advertising of personal products as is accepted must be presented in a restrained and obviously inoffensive manner.

12. Betting/gambling. The advertising of tip sheets and other publications seeking to advertise for the purpose of giving odds or promoting betting is unacceptable.

The lawful advertising of government organizations which conduct legalized lotteries and the advertising of private or governmental organizations which conduct legalized betting on sporting contests are acceptable provided such advertising does not unduly exhort the public to bet.

Restricted or unacceptable advertising techniques:

13. Indirect advertising. An advertiser who markets more than one product should not be permitted to use advertising copy devoted to an acceptable product for purposes of publicizing the brand name or other identification of a product which is not acceptable.

14. Bait and switch. "Bait-switch" advertising, whereby goods or services which the advertiser has no intention of selling are offered merely to lure the customer into purchasing higher-priced substitutes, is not acceptable.

15. Pitch techniques. The "pitchman" technique of advertising on television is inconsistent with good broadcast practice and generally damages the reputation of the industry and the advertising profession.

Sponsored program-length segments consisting substantially of continuous demonstrations or sales presentation, violate not only the time standards established in the Code but the broad philosophy of improvement implicit in the voluntary Code operation and are not acceptable. *(Interpretation No. 1)*

16. Testimonials. Personal endorsements (testimonials) shall be genuine and reflect personal experience. They shall contain no statement that cannot be supported if presented in the advertiser's own words.

17. Policy regarding religious time sales. A charge for television time to churches and religious bodies is not recommended.

X. Claims: General

1. False, misleading or deceptive advertising. The role and capability of television to market sponsors' products are well recognized. In turn, this fact dictates that great care be exercised by the broadcaster to prevent the presentation of false, misleading or deceptive advertising. While it is entirely appropriate to present a product in a favorable light and atmosphere, the presentation must not, by copy or demonstration, involve a material deception as to the characteristics, performance or appearance of the product.

Broadcast advertisers are responsible for making available, at the request of the Code Authority, documentation adequate to support the validity and truthfulness of claims, demonstrations and testimonials contained in their commercial messages.

2. Use of research, surveys or tests. Reference to the results of bona fide research, surveys or tests relating to the product to be advertised shall not be presented in a manner so as to create an impression of fact beyond that established by the work that has been conducted.

3. Fictitious exploitations. Appeals to help fictitious characters in television programs by purchasing the advertiser's product or service or sending for a premium should not be permitted, and such fictitious characters should not be introduced into the advertising message for such purposes.

4. Competitive references. Advertising should offer a product or service on its positive merits and refrain from discrediting, disparaging or unfairly attacking competitors, competing products, other industries, professions or institutions.

5. Placement of advertising messages. A sponsor's advertising messages should be confined within the framework of the sponsor's program structure. A television broadcaster should avoid the use of commercial announcements which are divorced from the program either by preceding the introduction of the program (as in the case of so-called "cowcatcher" announcements) or by following the apparent sign-off of the program (as in the case of so-called trailer or "hitchhike" announcements). To this end, the program itself should be announced and clearly identified, both audio and video, before the sponsor's advertising material is first used, and should be signed off, both audio and video, after the sponsor's advertising material is last used.

XI. ADVERTISING OF MEDICAL PRODUCTS/SERVICES

1. The advertising of medical products presents considerations of intimate and far-reaching importance to consumers because of the direct bearing on their health.

2. Because of the personal nature of the advertising of medical products, claims that a product will effect a cure and the indiscriminate use of such words as "safe," "without risk," "harmless," or terms of similar meaning should not be accepted in the advertising of medical products on television stations.

3. A television broadcaster should not accept advertising material which in his/her opinion offensively describes or dramatizes distress or morbid situations involving ailments, by spoken word, sound or visual effects.

4. Commercials for services or over-the-counter products involving health considerations are of intimate and far-reaching importance to the consumer. The following principles should apply to such advertising:

A. Physicians, dentists or nurses or actors representing physicians, dentists or nurses, shall not be employed directly or by implication. These restrictions also apply to persons professionally engaged in medical services (e.g., physical therapists, pharmacists, dental assistants, nurses' aides).

B. Visual representations of laboratory settings may be employed, provided they bear a direct relationship to bona fide research which has been conducted for the product or service. *(See Television Code X-2)* In such cases, laboratory technicians shall be identified as such and shall not be employed as spokespersons or in any other way speak on behalf of the product.

C. Institutional announcements not intended to sell a specific product or service to the consumer and public service announcements by non-profit organizations may be presented by accredited physicians, dentists or nurses, subject to approval by the broadcaster. An accredited professional is one who has met required qualifications and has been licensed in his/her resident state.

XII. CONTESTS

1. Contests shall be conducted with fairness to all entrants, and shall comply with all pertinent laws and regulations. Care should be taken to avoid the concurrent use of the three elements which together constitute a lottery—prize, chance and consideration.

2. All contest details, including rules, eligibility requirements, opening and termination dates should be clearly and completely announced and/or shown, or easily accessible to the viewing public, and the winners' names should be released and prizes awarded as soon as possible after the close of the contest.

3. When advertising is accepted which requests contestants to submit items of product identification or other evidence of purchase of products, reasonable facsimiles thereof should be made acceptable unless the award is based upon skill and not upon chance.

4. All copy pertaining to any contest (except that which is required by law) associated with the exploitation or sale of the sponsor's product or service, and all references to prizes or gifts offered in such connection should be considered a part of and included in the total time allowances as herein provided. *(See Television Code XIV)*

XIII. PREMIUMS AND OFFERS

1. Full details of proposed offers should be required by the television broadcaster for investigation and approved before the first announcement of the offer is made to the public.

2. A final date for the termination of an offer should be announced as far in advance as possible.

3. Before accepting for telecast offers involving a monetary consideration, a television broadcaster should be satisfied as to the integrity of the advertiser and the advertiser's willingness to honor complaints, indicating dissatisfaction with the premium by returning the monetary consideration.

4. There should be no misleading descriptions or visual representa-

tions of any premiums or gifts which would distort or enlarge their value in the minds of the viewers.

5. Assurances should be obtained from the advertiser that premiums offered are not harmful to person or property.

6. Premiums should not be approved which appeal to superstition on the basis of "luck-bearing" powers or otherwise.

XIV. Time Standards for Network-Affiliated Stations

In order that the time for non-program material and its placement shall best serve the viewer, the following standards are set forth in accordance with sound television practice:

1. Non-Program Material Definition. Non-program material, in both prime and all other time, includes billboards, commercials and promotional announcements.

Non-program material also includes:

A. In programs of 90 minutes in length or less, credits in excess of 30 seconds per program, except in feature films, shall be counted against the allowable time for non-program material. In no event should credits exceed 40 seconds in such programs.

The 40 second limitation on credits shall not apply, however, in any situation governed by a contract entered into before October 1, 1971.

B. In programs longer than 90 minutes, credits in excess of 50 seconds per program, except in feature films, shall be counted against the allowable time for non-program material. In no event should credits exceed 60 seconds in such programs.

Public service announcements and promotional announcements for the same program are excluded from this definition.

2. Allowable time for non-program material.

A. In prime time on network affiliated stations, non-program material shall not exceed nine minutes 30 seconds in any 60-minute period.

Prime time is a continuous period of not less than three consecutive hours per broadcast day as designated by the station between the hours of 6:00 PM and midnight.

B. In all other time, non-program material shall not exceed 16 minutes in any 60-minute period.

C. **Children's programming time.** Defined as those hours other than prime time in which programs initially designed primarily for children under 12 years of age are scheduled.

Within this time period on Saturday and Sunday, non-program material shall not exceed nine minutes 30 seconds in any 60-minute period.

Within this time period on Monday through Friday, non-program material shall not exceed 12 minutes in any 60-minute period.

3. Program interruptions.

A. Definition: A program interruption is any occurrence of non-program material within the main body of the program.

B. In prime time, the number of program interruptions shall not exceed two within any 30-minute program, or four within any 60-minute program.

Programs longer than 60 minutes shall be prorated at two interruptions per half-hour.

The number of interruptions in 60-minute variety shows shall not exceed five.

C. In all other time, the number of interruptions shall not exceed four within any 30-minute program period.

D. In children's weekend programming time, as above defined in 2C., the number of program interruptions shall not exceed two within any 30-minute program or four within any 60-minute program.

E. In both prime time and all other time, the following interruption standard shall apply within programs of 15 minutes or less in length:

> 5-minute program—1 interruption;
> 10-minute program—2 interruptions;
> 15-minute program—2 interruptions.

F. News, weather, sports and special events programs are exempt from the interruption standard because of the nature of such programs.

4. Consecutive announcements. No more than four non-program material announcements shall be scheduled consecutively within programs, and no more than three non-program material announcements shall be scheduled consecutively during station breaks. The consecutive non-program material limitation shall not apply to a single sponsor who wishes to further reduce the number of interruptions in the program.

5. Prize and donor identification. Reasonable and limited identification of prizes and donors' names where the presentation of contest awards or prizes is a necessary part of program content shall not be included as non-program material as defined above.

Aural and/or visual prize identification of up to 10 seconds duration may be deemed "reasonable and limited." Where such identification is longer than 10 seconds, the entire announcement or visual presentation will be charged against the total commercial time for the program period. *(Interpretation No. 3)*

6. Shopping guides/service formats. Programs presenting women's/men's service features, shopping guides, fashion shows, demonstrations and similar material provide a special service to the public in which certain material normally classified as non-program is an informative and necessary part of the program content. Because of this, the time standards may be waived by the Code Authority to a reasonable extent on a case-by-case basis.

7. Product or service references. Gratuitous references in a program to a non-sponsor's product or service should be avoided except for normal guest identification.

8. Film promotion. The presentation of commentary or film excerpts from current theatrical releases in some instances may constitute commercial material under the Time Standards for Non-Program Material. Specifically, for example, when such presentation, directly or by inference, urges viewers to attend, it shall be counted against the commercial allowance for the program of which it is a part. *(Interpretation No. 2)*

9. Trade name identification. Stationary backdrops or properties in television presentations showing the sponsor's name or product, the name of the sponsor's product, trade-mark or slogan should be used only incidentally and should not obtrude on program interest or entertainment.

XV. TIME STANDARDS FOR INDEPENDENT STATIONS

1. Non-program elements shall be considered as all-inclusive, with the exception of required credits, legally required station identifica-

tions, and "bumpers." Promotion spots and public service announcements, as well as commercials, are to be considered non-program elements.

2. The allowed time for non-program elements, as defined above, shall not exceed seven minutes in a 30-minute period or multiples thereof in prime time (prime time is defined as any three contiguous hours between 6:00 PM and midnight, local time), or eight minutes in a 30-minute period or multiples thereof during all other times.

3. Where a station does not carry a commercial in a station break between programs, the number of program interruptions shall not exceed four within any 30-minute program, or seven within any 60-minute program, or 10 within any 90-minute program, or 13 in any 120-minute program. Stations which do carry commercials in station breaks between programs shall limit the number of program interruptions to three within any 30-minute program, or six within any 60-minute program, or nine within any 90-minute program, or 12 in any 120-minute program. News, weather, sports, and special events are exempted because of format.

4. Not more than four non-program material announcements, as defined above, shall be scheduled consecutively. An exception may be made only in the case of a program 60 minutes or more in length, when no more than seven non-program elements may be scheduled consecutively by stations who wish to reduce the number of program interruptions.

5. The conditions of paragraphs three and four shall not apply to live sports programs where the program format dictates and limits the number of program interruptions.

(For children's time standards on independent stations see provisions XIV-2C, 3D under Time Standards for Network-Affiliated Stations.)

Appendix E

Declaration of Principles*
Public Relations Society of America

Members of the Public Relations Society of America base their professional principles on the fundamental value and dignity of the individual, holding that the free exercise of human rights, especially freedom of speech, freedom of assembly and freedom of the press, is essential to the practice of public relations.

In serving the interests of clients and employers, we dedicate ourselves to the goals of better communication, understanding and cooperation among the diverse individuals, groups and institutions of society.

We pledge:

To conduct ourselves professionally, with truth, accuracy, fairness and responsibility to the public;

To improve our individual competence and advance the knowledge and proficiency of the profession through continuing research and education;

And to adhere to the articles of the Code of Professional Standards for the Practice of Public Relations as adopted by the governing Assembly of the Society.

---

* This Code, adopted by the PRSA Assembly, replaces a similar Code of Professional Standards for the Practice of Public Relations previously in force since 1954 and strengthened by revisions in 1959, 1963 and 1977.

Code of Professional Standards for the Practice of Public Relations

These articles have been adopted by the Public Relations Society of America to promote and maintain high standards of public service and ethical conduct among its members.

1. A member shall deal fairly with clients or employers, past and present, with fellow practitioners and the general public.
2. A member shall conduct his or her professional life in accord with the public interest.
3. A member shall adhere to truth and accuracy and to generally accepted standards of good taste.
4. A member shall not represent conflicting or competing interests without the express consent of those involved, given after a full disclosure of the facts; nor place himself or herself in a position where the member's interest is or may be in conflict with a duty to a client, or others, without a full disclosure of such interests to all involved.
5. A member shall safeguard the confidences of both present and former clients or employers and shall not accept retainers or employment which may involve the disclosure or use of these confidences to the disadvantage or prejudice of such clients or employers.
6. A member shall not engage in any practice which tends to corrupt the integrity of channels of communication or the processes of government.
7. A member shall not intentionally communicate false or misleading information and is obligated to use care to avoid communication of false or misleading information.
8. A member shall be prepared to identify publicly the name of the client or employer on whose behalf any public communication is made.
9. A member shall not make use of any individual or organization purporting to serve or represent an announced cause, or purporting to be independent or unbiased, but actually serving an undis-

closed special or private interest of a member, client or employer.

10. A member shall not intentionally injure the professional reputation or practice of another practitioner. However, if a member has evidence that another member has been guilty of unethical, illegal or unfair practices, including those in violation of this Code, the member shall present the information promptly to the proper authorities of the Society for action in accordance with the procedure set forth in Article XIII of the Bylaws.

11. A member called as a witness in a proceeding for the enforcement of this Code shall be bound to appear, unless excused for sufficient reason by the Judicial Panel.

12. A member, in performing services for a client or employer, shall not accept fees, commissions or any other valuable consideration from anyone other than the client or employer in connection with those services without the express consent of the client or employer, given after a full disclosure of the facts.

13. A member shall not guarantee the achievement of specified results beyond the member's direct control.

14. A member shall, as soon as possible, sever relations with any organization or individual if such relationship requires conduct contrary to the articles of this Code.

Official Interpretations of the Code of Professional Standards for the Practice of Public Relations

Interpretation of Code Paragraph 2 which reads, "A member shall conduct his or her professional life in accord with the public interest."

The public interest is here defined primarily as comprising respect for and enforcement of the rights guaranteed by the Constitution of the United States of America.

Interpretation of Code Paragraph 5 which reads, "A member shall safeguard the confidences of both present and former clients or employers and shall not accept retainers or employment which may involve the disclosure or use of these confidences to the disadvantage or prejudice of such clients or employers."

This article does not prohibit a member who has knowledge of client or employee activities which are illegal from making such disclosures to the proper authorities as he or she believes are legally required.

Interpretation of Code Paragraph 6 which reads, "A member shall not engage in any practice which tends to corrupt the integrity of channels of communication or the processes of government."

1. Practices prohibited by this paragraph are those which tend to place representatives of media or government under an obligation to the member, or the member's employer or client, which is in conflict with their obligations to media or government, such as:

   a. the giving of gifts of more than nominal value;
   b. any form of payment or compensation to a member of the media in order to obtain preferential or guaranteed news or editorial coverage in the medium;
   c. any retainer or fee to a media employee or use of such employee if retained by a client or employer, where the circumstances are not fully disclosed to and accepted by the media employer;
   d. providing trips for media representatives which are unrelated to legitimate news interest;
   e. the use by a member of an investment or loan or advertising commitment made by the member, or the member's client or employer, to obtain preferential or guaranteed coverage in the medium.

2. This Code paragraph does not prohibit hosting media or government representatives at meals, cocktails, or news functions or special events which are occasions for the exchange of news information or views, or the furtherance of understanding which is part of the public relations function. Nor does it prohibit the bona fide press event or tour when media or government representatives are given an opportunity for on-the-spot viewing of a newsworthy product, process or event in which the media or

government representatives have a legitimate interest. What is customary or reasonable hospitality has to be a matter of particular judgement in specific situations. In all of these cases, however, it is or should be understood that no preferential treatment or guarantees are expected or implied and that complete independence always is left to the media or government representative.

3. This paragraph does not prohibit the reasonable giving or lending of sample products or services to media representatives who have a legitimate interest in the products or services.

Interpretation of Code Paragraph 13 which reads, "A member shall not guarantee the achievement of specified results beyond the member's direct control."

> This Code paragraph, in effect, prohibits misleading a client or employer as to what professional public relations can accomplish. It does not prohibit guarantees of quality or service. But it does prohibit guaranteeing specific results which, by their very nature, cannot be guaranteed because they are not subject to the member's control. As an example, a guarantee that a news release will appear specifically in a particular publication would be prohibited. This paragraph should not be interpreted as prohibiting contingent fees.

An Official Interpretation of the PRSA Code of Professional Standards as it Applies to Political Public Relations

PREAMBLE

In the practice of political public relations, a PRSA member must have professional capabilities to offer an employer or client quite apart from any political relationships of value, and members may serve their employer or client without necessarily having attributed to them the character, reputation or beliefs of those they serve. It is understood that members may choose to serve only those interests with whose political philosophy they are personally comfortable.

DEFINITION

"Political Public Relations" is defined as those areas of public relations which relate to:

a. the counseling of political organizations, committees, candidates or potential candidates for public office; and groups constituted for the purpose of influencing the vote on any ballot issue:

b. the counseling of holders of public office;

c. the management, or direction, of a political campaign for or against a candidate for political office; or for or against a ballot issue to be determined by voter approval or rejection;

d. the practice of public relations on behalf of a client or an employer in connection with that client's or employer's relationships with any candidates or holders of public office with the purpose of influencing legislation or government regulation or treatment of a client or employer, regardless of whether the PRSA member is a recognized lobbyist;

e. the counseling of government bodies, or segments thereof, either domestic or foreign.

PRECEPTS

1. It is the responsibility of PRSA members practicing political public relations, as defined above, to be conversant with the various statutes, local, state, and federal, governing such activities and to adhere to them strictly. This includes, but is not limited to, the various local, state and federal laws, court decisions and official interpretations governing lobbying, political contributions, disclosure, elections, libel, slander and the like. In carrying out this responsibility, members shall seek appropriate counseling whenever necessary.

2. It is also the responsibility of members to abide by PRSA's Code of Professional Standards.

3. Members shall represent clients or employers in good faith, and while partisan advocacy on behalf of a candidate or public issue may be expected, members shall act in accord with the public interest and adhere to truth and accuracy and to generally accepted standards of good taste.

4. Members shall not issue descriptive material or any advertising or publicity information or participate in the preparation or use

thereof which is not signed by responsible persons or is false, misleading or unlabeled as to its source, and are obligated to use care to avoid dissemination of any such material.

5. Members have an obligation to clients to disclose what remuneration beyond their fees they expect to receive as a result of their relationship, such as commissions for media advertising, printing and the like, and should not accept such extra payment without their clients' consent.

6. Members shall not improperly use their positions to encourage additional future employment or compensation. It is understood that successful campaign directors or managers, because of the performance of their duties and the working relationship that develops, may well continue to assist and counsel, for pay, the successful candidate.

7. Members shall voluntarily disclose to employers or clients the identity of other employers or clients with whom they are currently associated and whose interests might be affected favorably or unfavorably by their political representation.

8. Members shall respect the confidentiality of information pertaining to employers or clients even after the relationships cease, avoiding future associations wherein insider information is sought that would give a desired advantage over a member's previous clients.

9. In avoiding practices which might tend to corrupt the processes of government, members shall not make undisclosed gifts of cash or other valuable considerations which are designed to influence specific decisions of voters, legislators or public officials on public matters. A business lunch or dinner, or other comparable expenditure made in the course of communicating a point of view or public position, would not constitute such a violation. Nor, for example, would a plant visit designed and financed to provide useful background information to an interested legislator or candidate.

10. Nothing herein should be construed as prohibiting members from making legal, properly disclosed contributions to the candidates, party or referenda issues of their choice.

11. Members shall not, through the use of information known to be false or misleading, conveyed directly or through a third party, intentionally injure the public reputation of an opposing interest.

Appendix F

Standards of Practice of the American Association of Advertising Agencies*

We hold that a responsibility of advertising agencies is to be a constructive force in business.

We further hold that, to discharge this responsibility, advertising agencies must recognize an obligation, not only to their clients, but to the public, the media they employ, and to each other.

We finally hold that the responsibility will best be discharged if all agencies observe a common set of standards of practice.

To this end, the American Association of Advertising Agencies has adopted the following Standards of Practice as being in the best interests of the public, the advertisers, the media owners, and the agencies themselves.

These standards are voluntary. They are intended to serve as a guide to the kind of agency conduct which experience has shown to be wise, foresighted, and constructive.

It is recognized that advertising is a business and as such must operate within the framework of competition. It is further recognized that keen and vigorous competition, honestly conducted, is necessary to the growth and health of American business generally, of which advertising is a part.

However, *unfair* competitive practices in the advertising agency business lead to financial waste, dilution of service, diversion of man-

---

* First adopted October 16, 1924—most recently revised April 28, 1962. Copyright 1962, American Association of Advertising Agencies, Inc.

power, and loss of prestige. Unfair practices tend to weaken public confidence both in advertisements and in the institution of advertising.

1. CREATIVE CODE

We the members of the American Association of Advertising Agencies, in addition to supporting and obeying the laws and legal regulations pertaining to advertising, undertake to extend and broaden the application of high ethical standards. Specifically, we will not knowingly produce advertising which contains:

a. False or misleading statements or exaggerations, visual or verbal.
b. Testimonials which do not reflect the real choice of a competent witness.
c. Price claims which are misleading.
d. Comparisons which unfairly disparage a competitive product or service.
e. Claims insufficiently supported, or which distort the true meaning or practicable application of statements made by professional or scientific authority.
f. Statements, suggestions or pictures offensive to public decency.

We recognize that there are areas which are subject to honestly different interpretations and judgment. Taste is subjective and may even vary from time to time as well as from individual to individual. Frequency of seeing or hearing advertising messages will necessarily vary greatly from person to person.

However, we agree not to recommend to an advertiser and to discourage the use of advertising which is in poor or questionable taste or which is deliberately irritating through content, presentation or excessive repetition.

Clear and willful violations of this Code shall be referred to the Board of Directors of the American Association of Advertising Agencies for appropriate action, including possible annulment of membership as provided by Article IV, Section 5, of the Constitution and By-Laws.

2. CONTRACTS

a. The advertising agency should where feasible enter into written contracts with media in placing advertising. When entered into, the agency should conform to its agreements with media. Failure to do so may result in loss of standing or litigation, either on the contract or for violations of the Clayton or Federal Trade Commission Acts.
b. The advertising agency should not knowingly fail to fulfill all lawful contractual commitments with media.

3. OFFERING CREDIT EXTENSION

It is unsound and uneconomic to offer extension of credit or banking service as an inducement in solicitation.

4. UNFAIR TACTICS

The advertising agency should compete on merit and not by depreciating a competitor or his work directly or inferentially, or by circulating harmful rumors about him, or by making unwarranted claims of scientific skill in judging or prejudging advertising copy, or by seeking to obtain an account by hiring a key employee away from the agency in charge in violation of the agency's employment agreements.

These Standards of Practice of the American Association of Advertising Agencies come from the belief that sound practice is good business. Confidence and respect are indispensable to success in a business embracing the many intangibles of agency service and involving relationships so dependent upon good faith. These standards are based on a broad experience of what has been found to be the best advertising practice.

Appendix G

National Press Photographers Association, Inc.
Code of Ethics

The National Press Photographers Association, a professional society dedicated to the advancement of photojournalism, acknowledges concern and respect for the public's natural-law right to freedom in searching for the truth and the right to be informed truthfully and completely about public events and the world in which we live.

We believe that no report can be complete if it is not possible to enhance and clarify the meaning of words. We believe that pictures, whether used to depict news events as they actually happen, illustrate news that has happened or to help explain anything of public interest, are an indispensable means of keeping people accurately informed; that they help all people, young and old, to better understand any subject in the public domain.

Believing the foregoing we recognize and acknowledge that photojournalists should at all times maintain the highest standards of ethical conduct in serving the public interest. To that end the National Press Photographers Associations sets forth the following Code of Ethics which is subscribed to by all of its members:

1. The practice of photojournalism, both as a science and art, is worthy of the very best thought and effort of those who enter into it as a profession.
2. Photojournalism affords an opportunity to serve the public that is equalled by few other vocations and all members of the profession

should strive by example and influence to maintain high standards of ethical conduct free of mercenary considerations of any kind.

3. It is the individual responsibility of every photojournalist at all times to strive for pictures that report truthfully, honestly and objectively.

4. Business promotion in its many forms is essential, but untrue statements of any nature are not worthy of a professional photojournalist and we severely condemn any such practice.

5. It is our duty to encourage and assist all members of our profession, individually and collectively, so that the quality of photojournalism may constantly be raised to higher standards.

6. It is the duty of every photojournalist to work to preserve all freedom-of-the-press rights recognized by law and to work to protect and expand freedom-of-access to all sources of news and visual information.

7. Our standards of business dealings, ambitions and relations shall have in them a note of sympathy for our common humanity and shall always require us to take into consideration our highest duties as members of society. In every situation in our business life, in every responsibility that comes before us, our chief thought shall be to fulfill that responsibility and discharge that duty so that when each of us is finished we shall have endeavored to lift the level of human ideals and achievement higher than we found it.

8. No Code of Ethics can prejudge every situation, thus common sense and good judgement are required in applying ethical principles.

Index